CAPTAIN AMERICA

THE DEATH OF
CAPTAIN
AMERICA
THE MAN WHO BOUGHT AMERICA

WRITER: Ed Brubaker

Penciler, Issues #37-38 & #40-42:
Steve Epting with Luke Ross (Issue #42)
Inkers, #37-38 & #40-42:
Steve Epting, Mike Perkins, Rick Magyar
& Fabio Laguna
Artist, Issue #39: Roberto De La Torre
Colorist: Frank D'Armata
Letterer: VC's Joe Caramagna

Cover Art: Steve Epting
Associate Editors:
Molly Lazer & Jeanine Schaefer
Editor: Tom Brevoort

New Captain America costume
design by Alex Ross
Captain America created by
Joe Simon & Jack Kirby

Collection Editor: Jennifer Grünwald
Editorial Assistant: Alex Starbuck
Assistant Editors: Cory Levine & John Denning
Editor, Special Projects: Mark D. Beazley
Senior Editor, Special Projects: Jeff Youngquist
Senior Vice President of Sales: David Gabriel

Production: Jerron Quality Color
& Jerry Kalinowski
Vice President of Creative: Tom Marvelli

Editor in Chief: Joe Quesada
Publisher: Dan Buckley

Previously:

The Red Skull, with the help of megalomaniacal psychiatrist Dr. Faustus, manipulated Sharon Carter, former Agent 13 of S.H.I.E.L.D., into taking the life of Steve Rogers, the man who was Captain America. Now pregnant with Steve Rogers' baby, Sharon is held prisoner, both physically and mentally, by her enemies.

Cap's former partner James "Bucky" Barnes has agreed to don the mantle of Captain America and go after the Red Skull. However, Aleksander Lukin, the ex-Soviet General whose mind the Red Skull has secretly been sharing, faked his death in a plane crash. Meanwhile, Lukas's Kronas Corporation is making moves that rock the American economy and the Red Skull has set up his own politician to further his political agenda.

And, while looking around in the Red Skull's base, Sharon Carter has stumbled upon a figure that looks very much like the deceased Steve Rogers...

CAPTAIN AMERICA: THE DEATH OF CAPTAIN AMERICA VOL. 3 — THE MAN WHO BOUGHT AMERICA. Contains material originally published in magazine form as CAPTAIN AMERICA #37-42. First printing 2008. Hardcover ISBN# 978-0-7851-2970-7. Softcover ISBN# 978-0-7851-2971-4. Published by MARVEL PUBLISHING, INC., a subsidiary of MARVEL ENTERTAINMENT, INC. OFFICE OF PUBLICATION: 417 5th Avenue, New York, NY 10016. Copyright © 2008 Marvel Characters, Inc. All rights reserved. Hardcover: $19.99 per copy in the U.S. and $21.00 in Canada (GST #R127032852). Softcover: $14.99 per copy in the U.S. and $15.75 in Canada (GST #R127032852). Canadian Agreement #40668537. All characters featured in this issue and the distinctive names and likenesses thereof, and all related indicia are trademarks of Marvel Characters, Inc. No similarity between any of the names, characters, persons, and/or institutions in this magazine with those of any living or dead person or institution is intended, and any such similarity which may exist is purely coincidental. Printed in the U.S.A. ALAN FINE, CEO Marvel Toys & Publishing Divisions and CMO Marvel Characters, Inc.; DAVID GABRIEL, SVP of Publishing Sales & Circulation; DAVID BOGART, SVP of Business Affairs & Talent Management; MICHAEL PASCIULLO, VP of Merchandising & Communications; JIM O'KEEFE, VP of Operations & Logistics; DAN CARR, Executive Director of Publishing Technology; JUSTIN F. GABRIE, Director of Editorial Operations; SUSAN CRESPI, Editorial Operations Manager; OMAR OTIEKU, Production Manager; STAN LEE, Chairman Emeritus. For information regarding advertising in Marvel Comics or on Marvel.com, please contact Mitch Dane, Advertising Director, at mdane@marvel.com. For Marvel subscription inquiries, please call 800-217-9158.

10 9 8 7 6 5 4 3 2 1

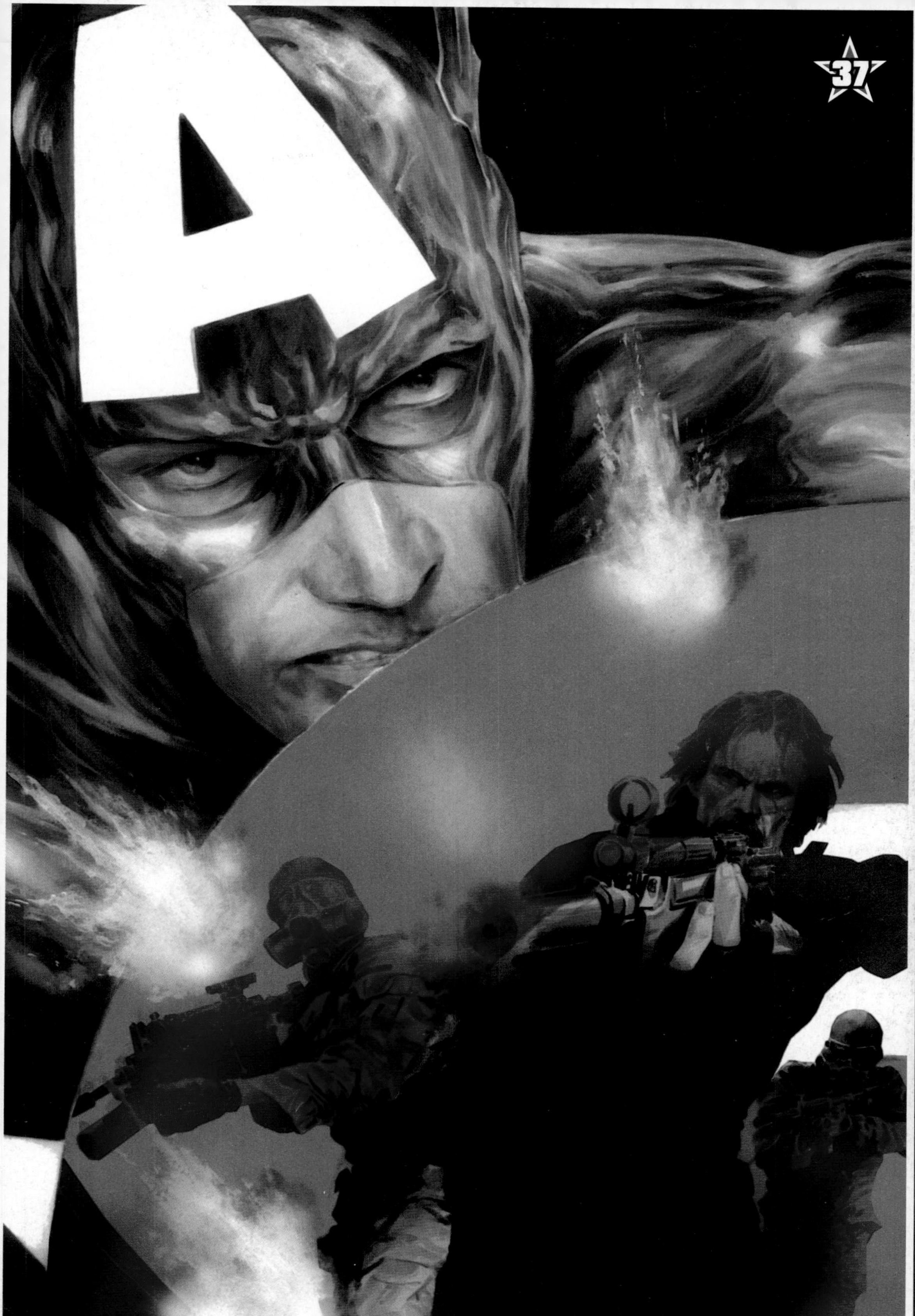
37

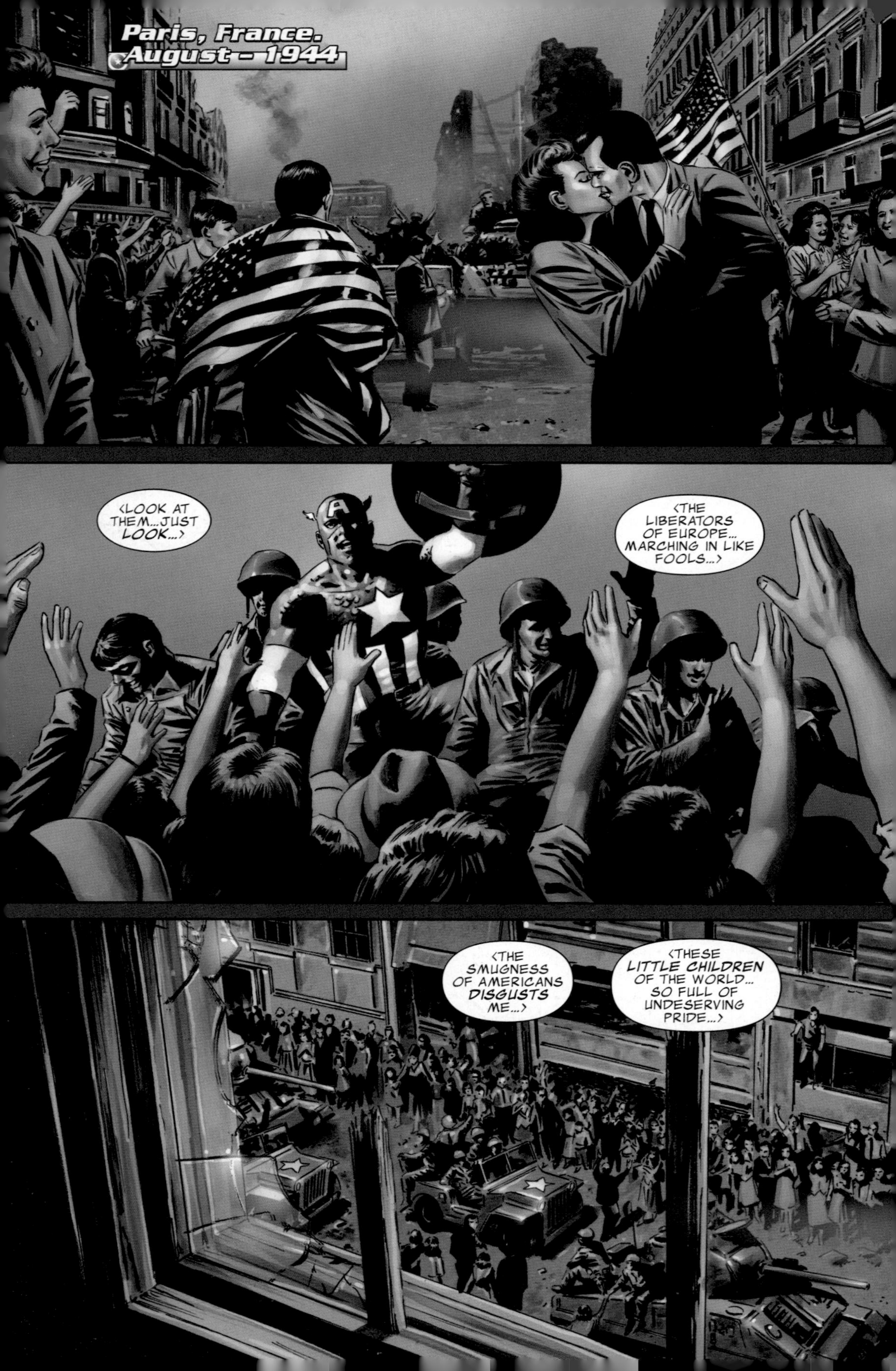
Paris, France.
August – 1944
<LOOK AT THEM...JUST LOOK...>
<THE LIBERATORS OF EUROPE... MARCHING IN LIKE FOOLS...>
<THE SMUGNESS OF AMERICANS DISGUSTS ME...>
<THESE LITTLE CHILDREN OF THE WORLD... SO FULL OF UNDESERVING PRIDE...>

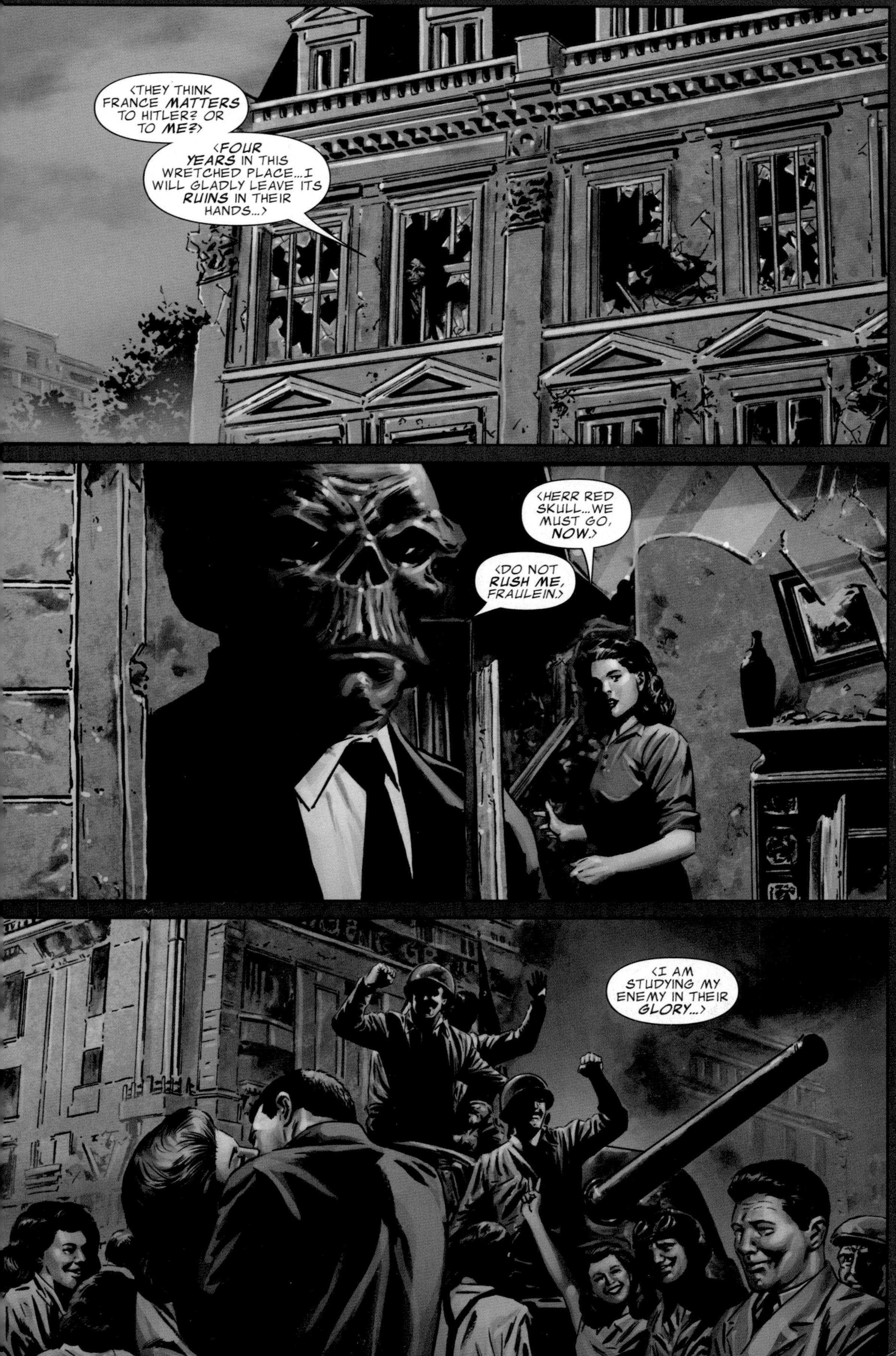

<THEY THINK FRANCE MATTERS TO HITLER? OR TO ME?>
<FOUR YEARS IN THIS WRETCHED PLACE...I WILL GLADLY LEAVE ITS RUINS IN THEIR HANDS...>
<HERR RED SKULL...WE MUST GO, NOW.>
<DO NOT RUSH ME, FRAULEIN.>
<I AM STUDYING MY ENEMY IN THEIR GLORY...>

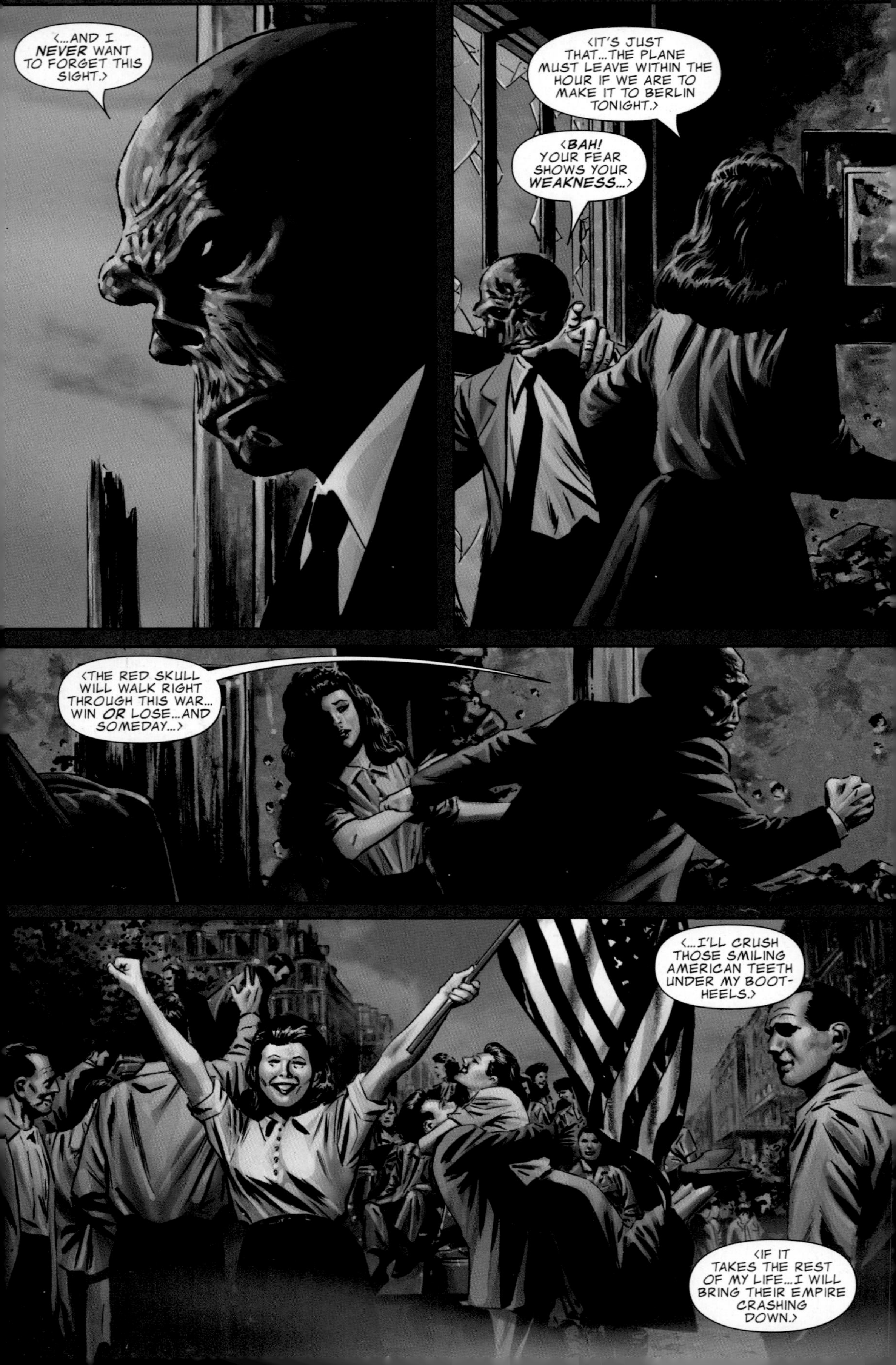
<...AND I NEVER WANT TO FORGET THIS SIGHT.>
<IT'S JUST THAT...THE PLANE MUST LEAVE WITHIN THE HOUR IF WE ARE TO MAKE IT TO BERLIN TONIGHT.>
<BAH! YOUR FEAR SHOWS YOUR WEAKNESS...>
<THE RED SKULL WILL WALK RIGHT THROUGH THIS WAR... WIN OR LOSE...AND SOMEDAY...>
<...I'LL CRUSH THOSE SMILING AMERICAN TEETH UNDER MY BOOT-HEELS.>
<IF IT TAKES THE REST OF MY LIFE...I WILL BRING THEIR EMPIRE CRASHING DOWN.>

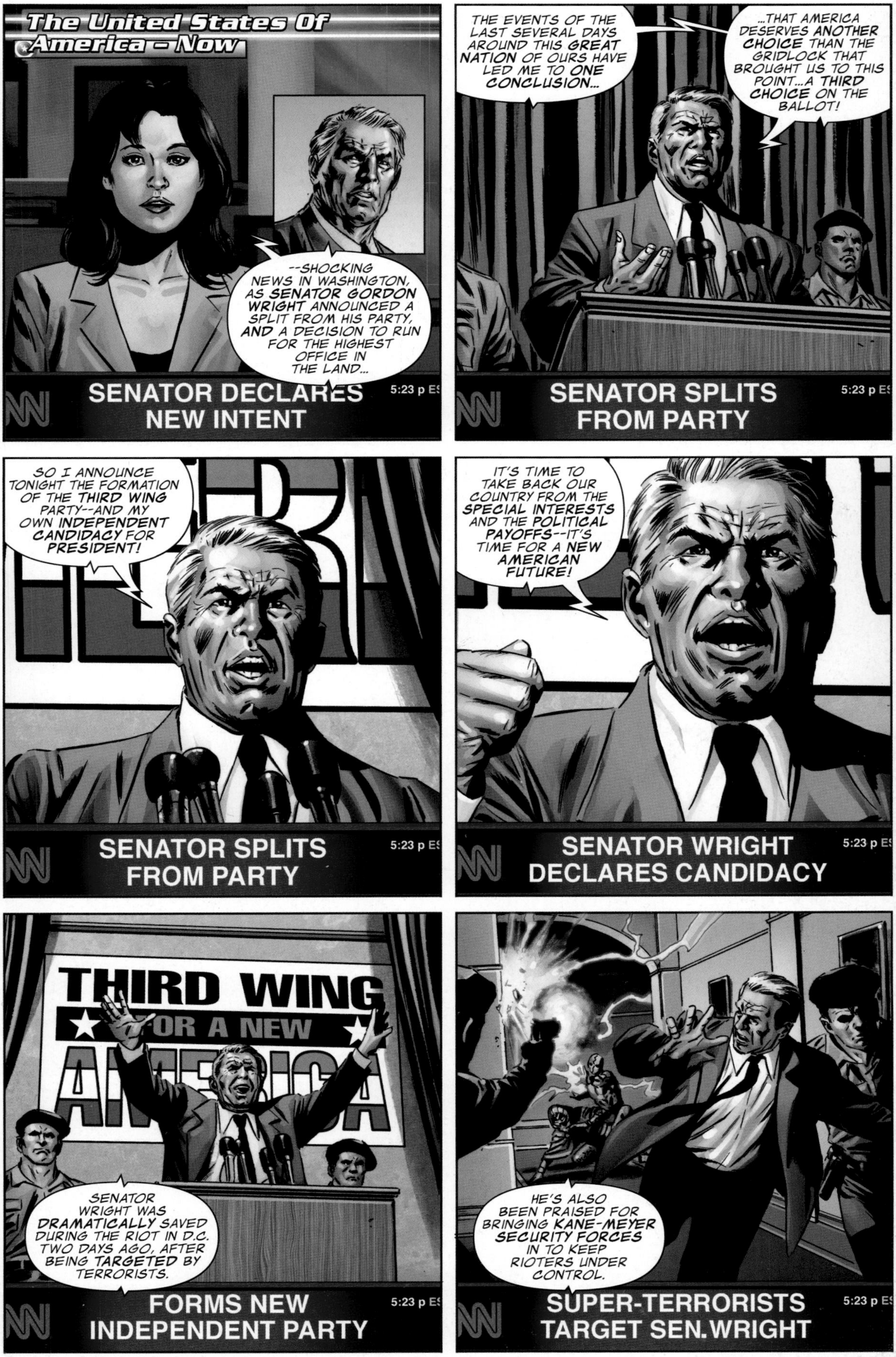
The United States Of America – Now
--SHOCKING NEWS IN WASHINGTON, AS SENATOR GORDON WRIGHT ANNOUNCED A SPLIT FROM HIS PARTY, AND A DECISION TO RUN FOR THE HIGHEST OFFICE IN THE LAND...
SENATOR DECLARES NEW INTENT
5:23 p ES
THE EVENTS OF THE LAST SEVERAL DAYS AROUND THIS GREAT NATION OF OURS HAVE LED ME TO ONE CONCLUSION...
...THAT AMERICA DESERVES ANOTHER CHOICE THAN THE GRIDLOCK THAT BROUGHT US TO THIS POINT...A THIRD CHOICE ON THE BALLOT!
SENATOR SPLITS FROM PARTY
5:23 p ES
SO I ANNOUNCE TONIGHT THE FORMATION OF THE THIRD WING PARTY--AND MY OWN INDEPENDENT CANDIDACY FOR PRESIDENT!
SENATOR SPLITS FROM PARTY
5:23 p ES
IT'S TIME TO TAKE BACK OUR COUNTRY FROM THE SPECIAL INTERESTS AND THE POLITICAL PAYOFFS--IT'S TIME FOR A NEW AMERICAN FUTURE!
SENATOR WRIGHT DECLARES CANDIDACY
5:23 p ES
THIRD WING
FOR A NEW
AMERICA
SENATOR WRIGHT WAS DRAMATICALLY SAVED DURING THE RIOT IN D.C. TWO DAYS AGO, AFTER BEING TARGETED BY TERRORISTS.
FORMS NEW INDEPENDENT PARTY
5:23 p ES
HE'S ALSO BEEN PRAISED FOR BRINGING KANE-MEYER SECURITY FORCES IN TO KEEP RIOTERS UNDER CONTROL.
SUPER-TERRORISTS TARGET SEN. WRIGHT
5:23 p ES

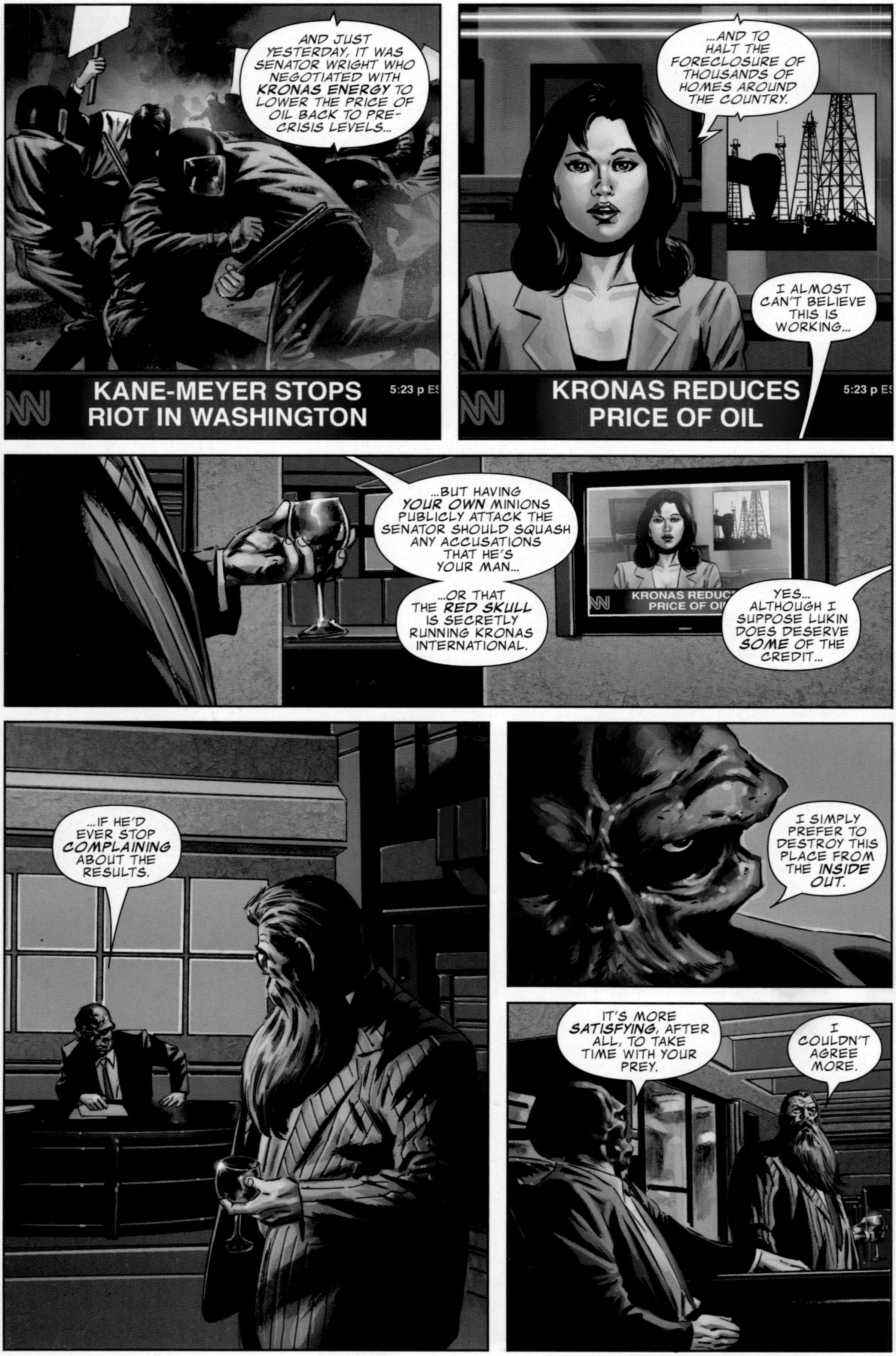
AND JUST YESTERDAY, IT WAS SENATOR WRIGHT WHO NEGOTIATED WITH KRONAS ENERGY TO LOWER THE PRICE OF OIL BACK TO PRE-CRISIS LEVELS...
KANE-MEYER STOPS RIOT IN WASHINGTON
5:23 p ES
...AND TO HALT THE FORECLOSURE OF THOUSANDS OF HOMES AROUND THE COUNTRY.
I ALMOST CAN'T BELIEVE THIS IS WORKING...
KRONAS REDUCES PRICE OF OIL
5:23 p ES
...BUT HAVING YOUR OWN MINIONS PUBLICLY ATTACK THE SENATOR SHOULD SQUASH ANY ACCUSATIONS THAT HE'S YOUR MAN...
...OR THAT THE RED SKULL IS SECRETLY RUNNING KRONAS INTERNATIONAL.
KRONAS REDUC PRICE OF OI
YES... ALTHOUGH I SUPPOSE LUKIN DOES DESERVE SOME OF THE CREDIT...
...IF HE'D EVER STOP COMPLAINING ABOUT THE RESULTS.
I SIMPLY PREFER TO DESTROY THIS PLACE FROM THE INSIDE OUT.
IT'S MORE SATISFYING, AFTER ALL, TO TAKE TIME WITH YOUR PREY.
I COULDN'T AGREE MORE.

NOW OUR MAN CAN RUN AS THE *OUTSIDER* WHO *SAVED* HIS COUNTRY FROM RUIN...

AND SLOWLY, HE'LL SHOW THEM THAT A *POLICE STATE* IS THE ONLY ANSWER TO THE CHAOS OF DEMOCRACY.

SOON *KANE-MEYER* SECURITIES WILL BE PROTECTING *EVERY CITY* IN THIS NATION...

MY HAND WILL WRAP AROUND THE THROAT OF THE WHOLE UNITED STATES.

YOU MEAN, *OUR HAND,* I BELIEVE.

DON'T YOU HAVE SOMETHING *ELSE* TO DO, FAUSTUS?

A WOMAN CARRYING A *BABY* THAT SHE KEPT *SECRET* FROM YOU, PERHAPS?

AGENT 13 WILL *KEEP...*I THOUGHT YOU WANTED TO DISCUSS OUR *NEW* PATIENT.

OR IS ZOLA STILL FIGURING OUT HOW TO *AWAKEN* HIM?

NO, EVERYTHING IS ON SCHEDULE.

HE'LL BE CONSCIOUS SOON, AND THEN IT WON'T JUST BE THIS *STRIPLING* WEARING THE FLAG.

IS THERE A NEW CAPTAIN AMERICA?

THERE WILL BE MORE THAN *ONE* CAPTAIN AMERICA FOR THIS COUNTRY TO DEAL WITH...

IS THERE A NEW CAPTAIN AMERICA

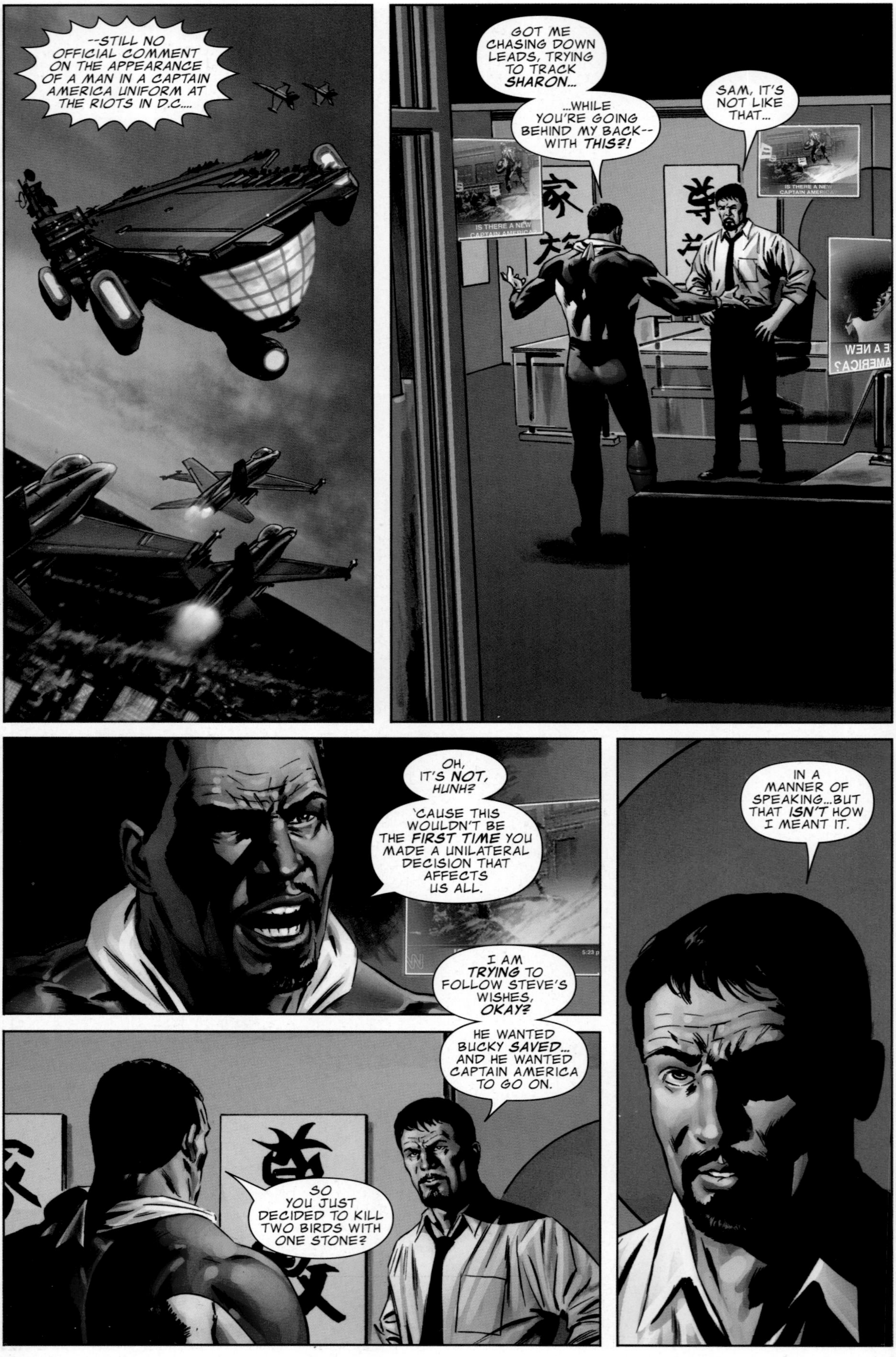
--STILL NO OFFICIAL COMMENT ON THE APPEARANCE OF A MAN IN A CAPTAIN AMERICA UNIFORM AT THE RIOTS IN D.C....
GOT ME CHASING DOWN LEADS, TRYING TO TRACK SHARON...
...WHILE YOU'RE GOING BEHIND MY BACK-- WITH THIS?!
SAM, IT'S NOT LIKE THAT...
IS THERE A NEW CAPTAIN AMERICA?
OH, IT'S NOT, HUNH?
'CAUSE THIS WOULDN'T BE THE FIRST TIME YOU MADE A UNILATERAL DECISION THAT AFFECTS US ALL.
IN A MANNER OF SPEAKING...BUT THAT ISN'T HOW I MEANT IT.
I AM TRYING TO FOLLOW STEVE'S WISHES, OKAY?
HE WANTED BUCKY SAVED... AND HE WANTED CAPTAIN AMERICA TO GO ON.
SO YOU JUST DECIDED TO KILL TWO BIRDS WITH ONE STONE?

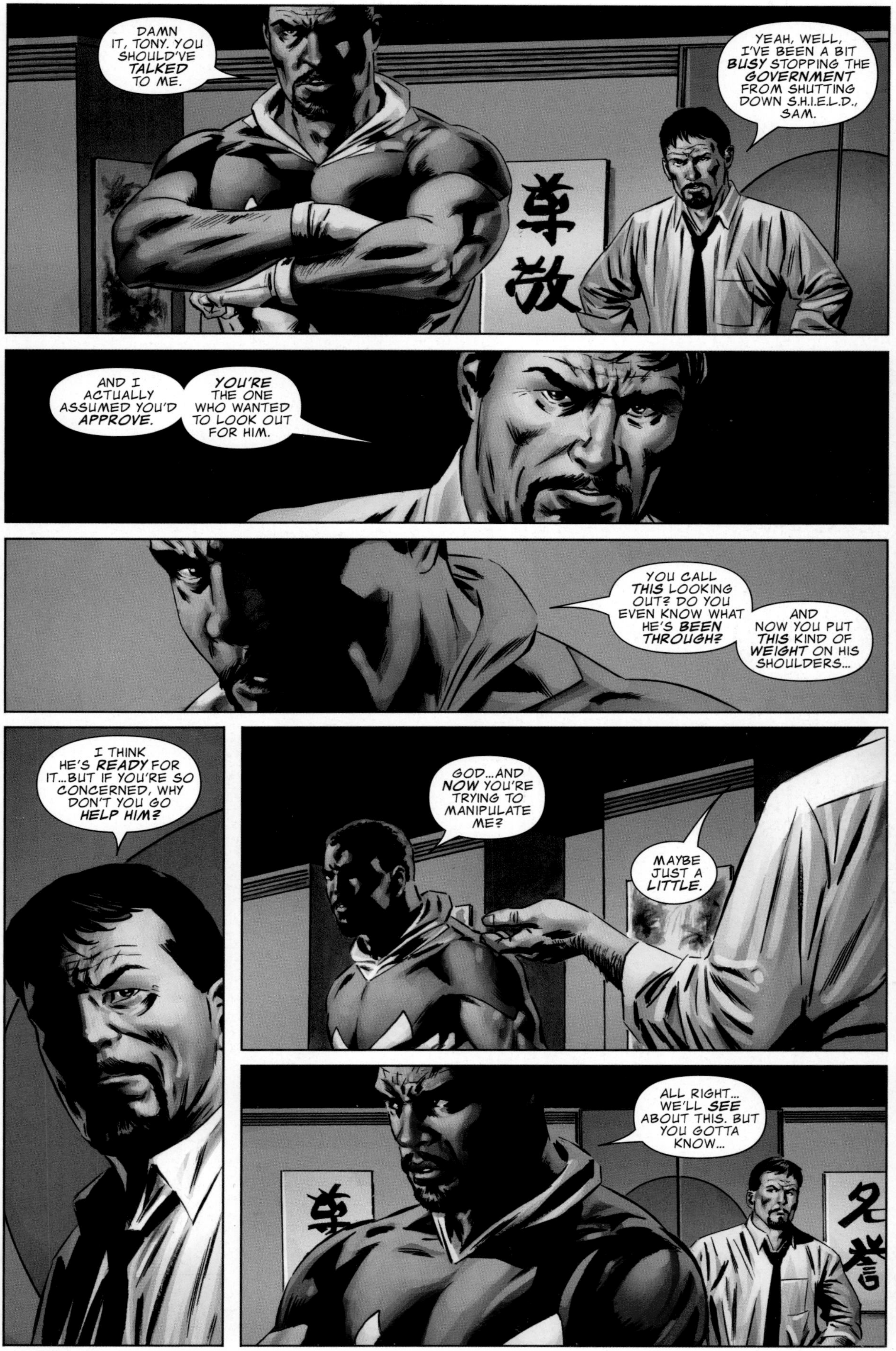
DAMN IT, TONY. YOU SHOULD'VE TALKED TO ME.
YEAH, WELL, I'VE BEEN A BIT BUSY STOPPING THE GOVERNMENT FROM SHUTTING DOWN S.H.I.E.L.D., SAM.
AND I ACTUALLY ASSUMED YOU'D APPROVE.
YOU'RE THE ONE WHO WANTED TO LOOK OUT FOR HIM.
YOU CALL THIS LOOKING OUT? DO YOU EVEN KNOW WHAT HE'S BEEN THROUGH?
AND NOW YOU PUT THIS KIND OF WEIGHT ON HIS SHOULDERS...
I THINK HE'S READY FOR IT...BUT IF YOU'RE SO CONCERNED, WHY DON'T YOU GO HELP HIM?
GOD...AND NOW YOU'RE TRYING TO MANIPULATE ME?
MAYBE JUST A LITTLE.
ALL RIGHT... WE'LL SEE ABOUT THIS. BUT YOU GOTTA KNOW...

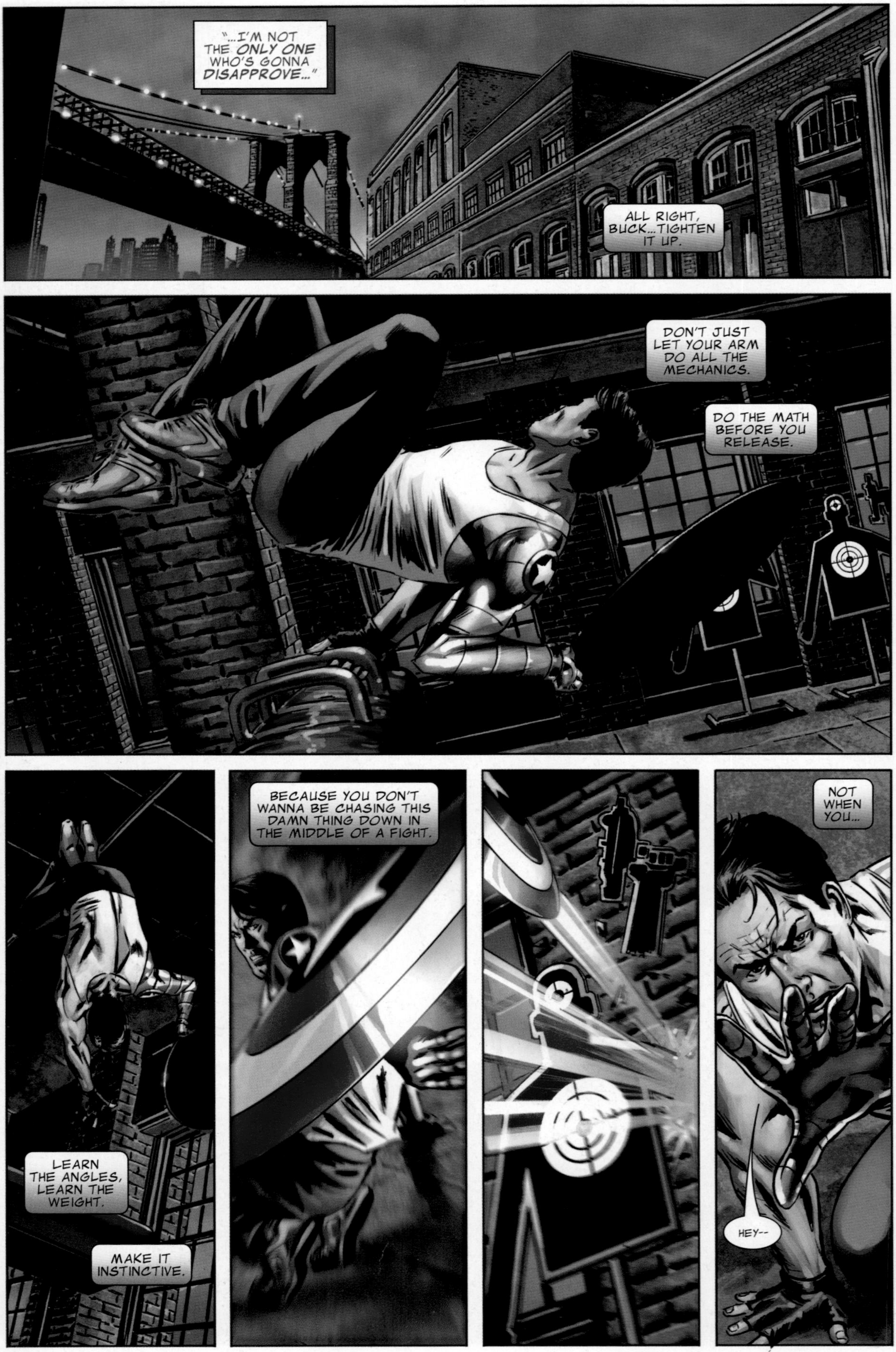
"...I'M NOT THE ONLY ONE WHO'S GONNA DISAPPROVE..."
ALL RIGHT, BUCK...TIGHTEN IT UP.
DON'T JUST LET YOUR ARM DO ALL THE MECHANICS.
DO THE MATH BEFORE YOU RELEASE.
LEARN THE ANGLES, LEARN THE WEIGHT.
MAKE IT INSTINCTIVE.
BECAUSE YOU DON'T WANNA BE CHASING THIS DAMN THING DOWN IN THE MIDDLE OF A FIGHT.
NOT WHEN YOU...
HEY--

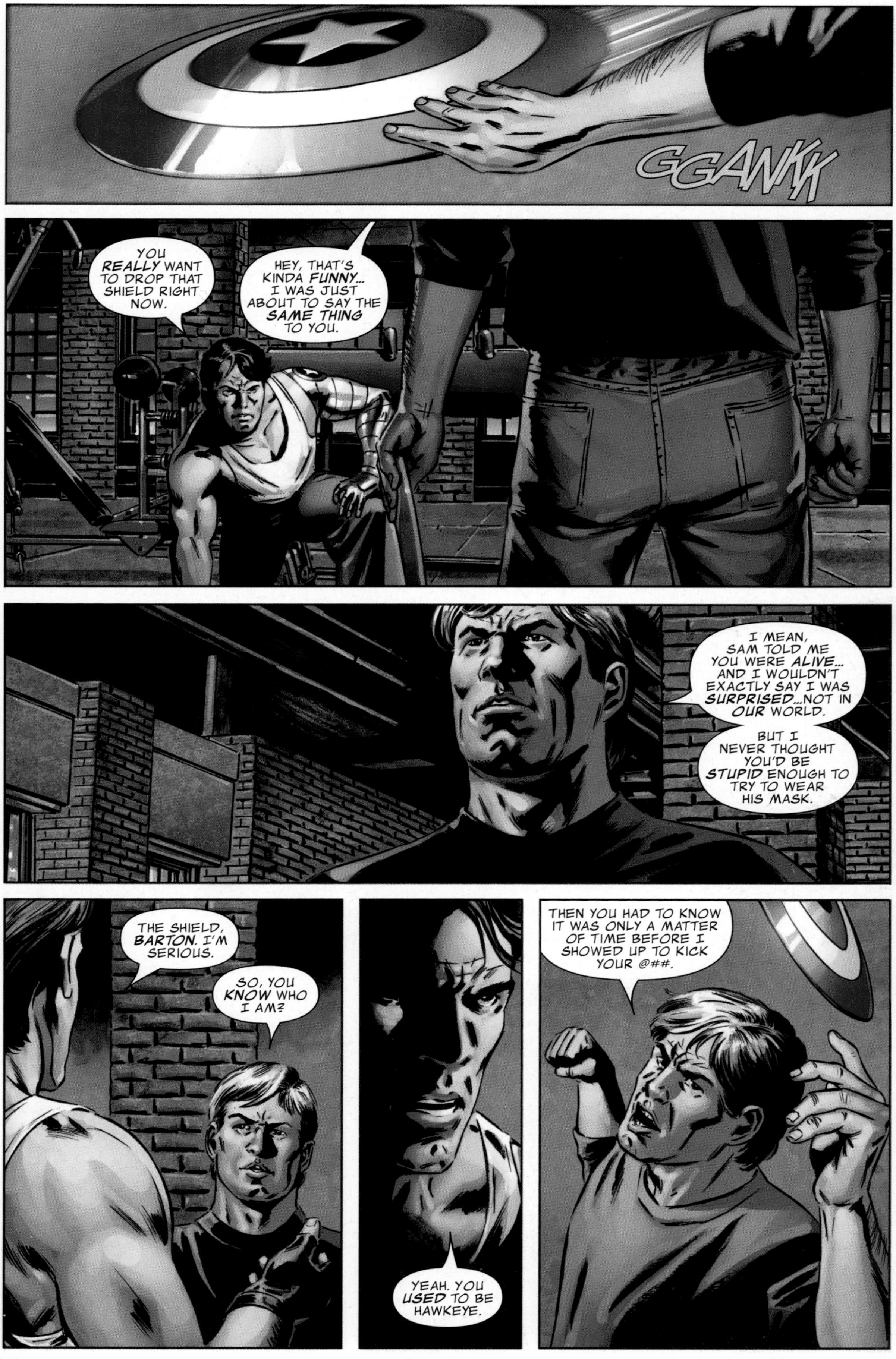
GGANKK
YOU REALLY WANT TO DROP THAT SHIELD RIGHT NOW.
HEY, THAT'S KINDA FUNNY... I WAS JUST ABOUT TO SAY THE SAME THING TO YOU.
I MEAN, SAM TOLD ME YOU WERE ALIVE... AND I WOULDN'T EXACTLY SAY I WAS SURPRISED...NOT IN OUR WORLD.
BUT I NEVER THOUGHT YOU'D BE STUPID ENOUGH TO TRY TO WEAR HIS MASK.
THE SHIELD, BARTON. I'M SERIOUS.
SO, YOU KNOW WHO I AM?
YEAH. YOU USED TO BE HAWKEYE.
THEN YOU HAD TO KNOW IT WAS ONLY A MATTER OF TIME BEFORE I SHOWED UP TO KICK YOUR @##.

ACTUALLY, IT DIDN'T EVEN *CROSS* MY MIND.

WHERE *I'M* FROM, THE GOOD GUYS FOUGHT ON THE *SAME* SIDE...

THEY DIDN'T JUST START *THROWING PUNCHES* AT EACH OTHER.

SMATT

HUNH...

YEAH, HE TAUGHT *ME* THAT MOVE, TOO.

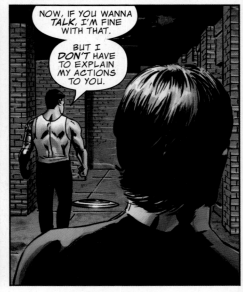

NOW, IF YOU WANNA *TALK,* I'M FINE WITH THAT.

BUT I *DON'T* HAVE TO EXPLAIN MY ACTIONS TO YOU.

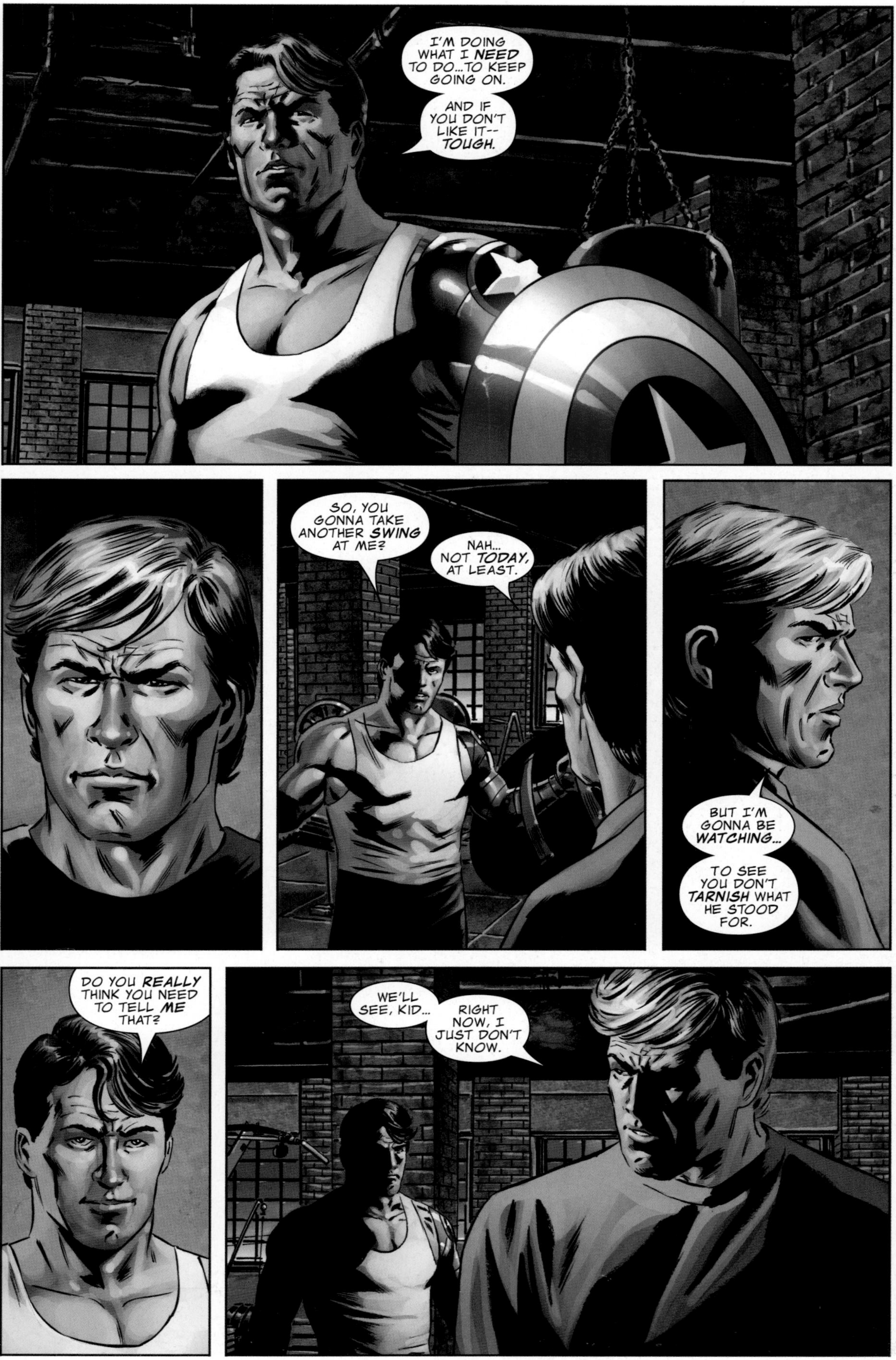
I'M DOING WHAT I NEED TO DO...TO KEEP GOING ON.
AND IF YOU DON'T LIKE IT-- TOUGH.
SO, YOU GONNA TAKE ANOTHER SWING AT ME?
NAH... NOT TODAY, AT LEAST.
BUT I'M GONNA BE WATCHING...
TO SEE YOU DON'T TARNISH WHAT HE STOOD FOR.
DO YOU REALLY THINK YOU NEED TO TELL ME THAT?
WE'LL SEE, KID...
RIGHT NOW, I JUST DON'T KNOW.

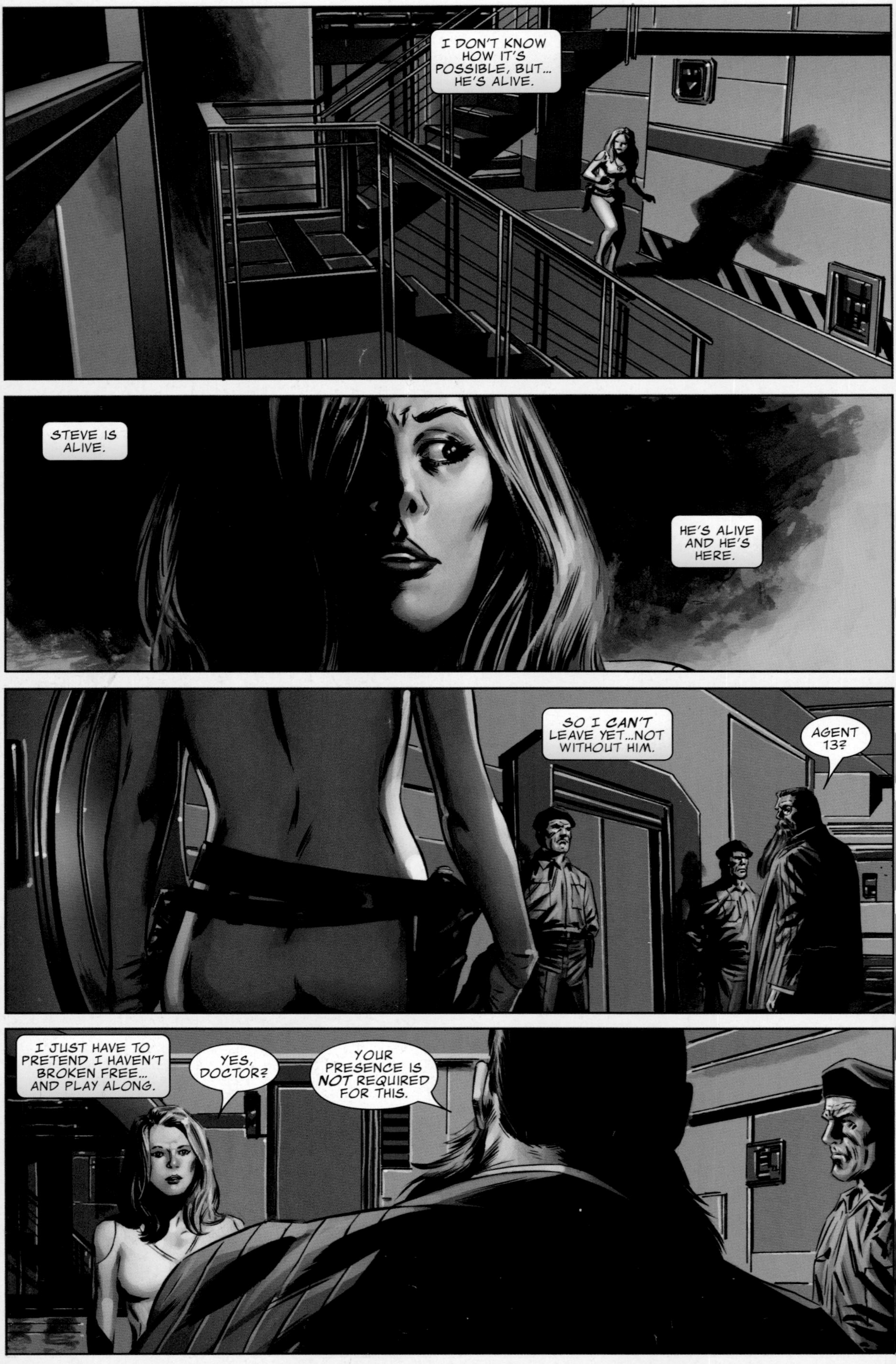
I DON'T KNOW HOW IT'S POSSIBLE, BUT... HE'S ALIVE.
STEVE IS ALIVE.
HE'S ALIVE AND HE'S HERE.
SO I *CAN'T* LEAVE YET...NOT WITHOUT HIM.
AGENT 13?
I JUST HAVE TO PRETEND I HAVEN'T BROKEN FREE... AND PLAY ALONG.
YES, DOCTOR?
YOUR PRESENCE IS *NOT* REQUIRED FOR THIS.

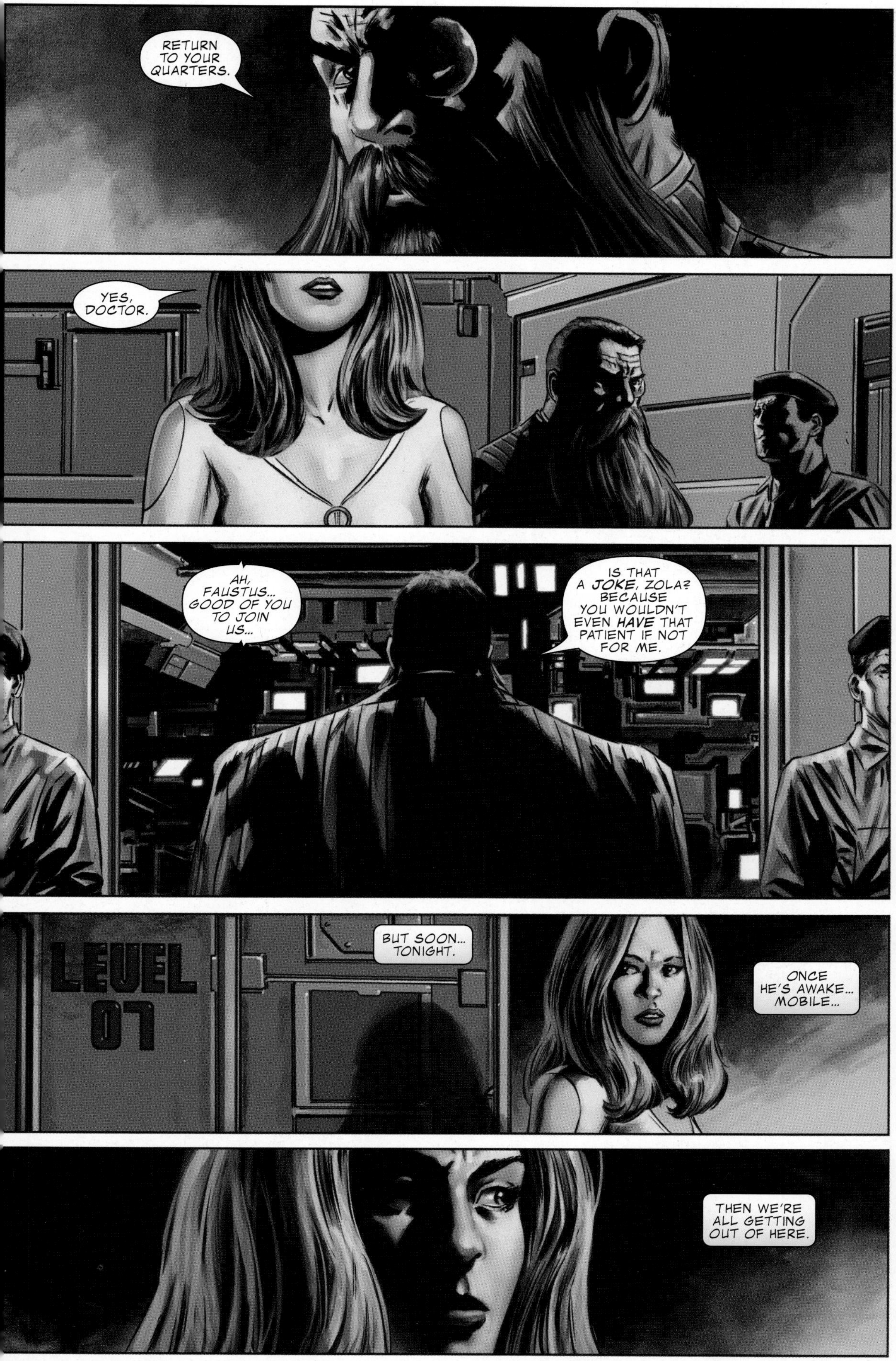
RETURN TO YOUR QUARTERS.
YES, DOCTOR.
AH, FAUSTUS... GOOD OF YOU TO JOIN US...
IS THAT A JOKE, ZOLA? BECAUSE YOU WOULDN'T EVEN HAVE THAT PATIENT IF NOT FOR ME.
LEVEL 07
BUT SOON... TONIGHT.
ONCE HE'S AWAKE... MOBILE...
THEN WE'RE ALL GETTING OUT OF HERE.

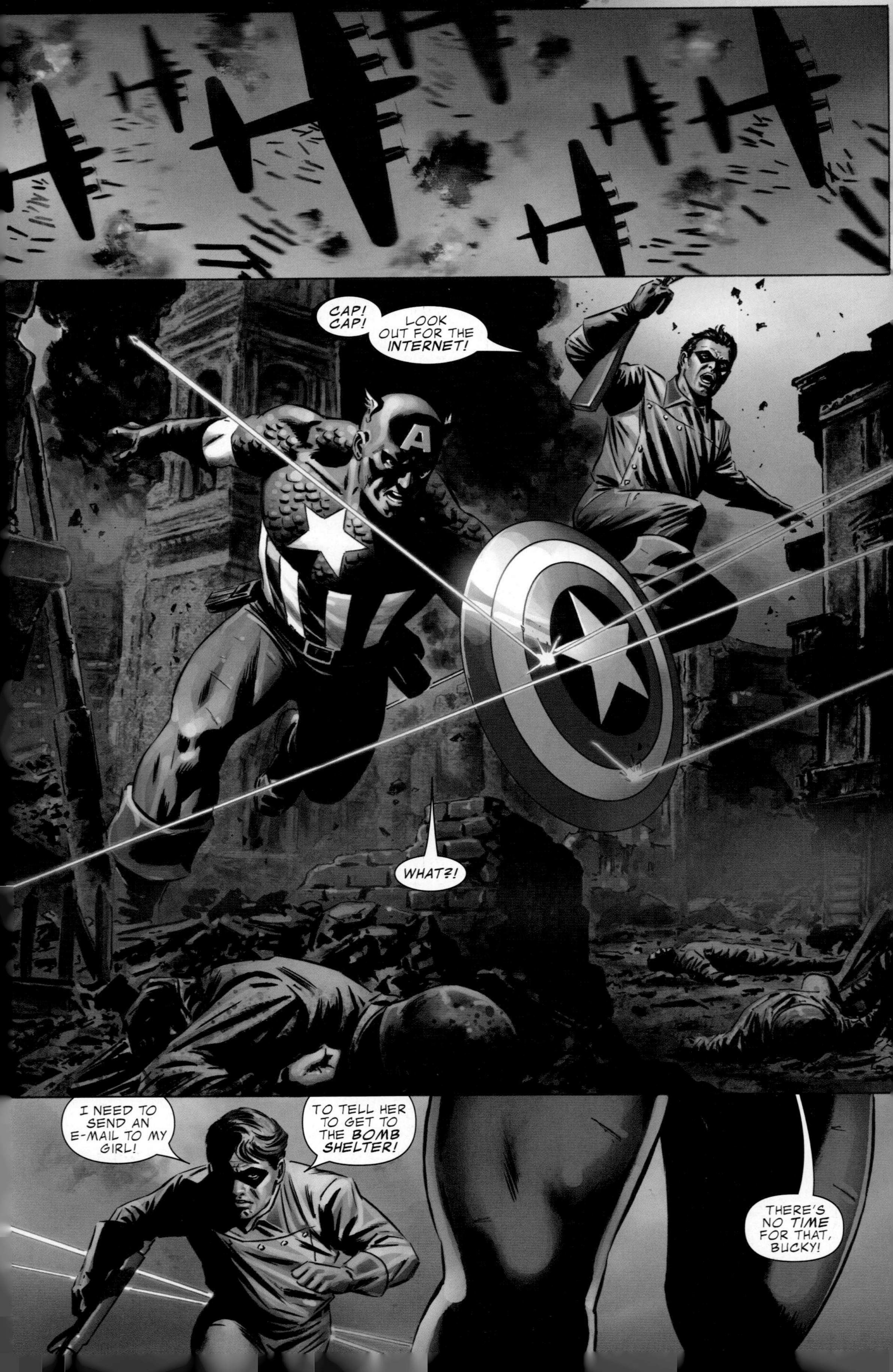
CAP! CAP!
LOOK OUT FOR THE INTERNET!
WHAT?!
I NEED TO SEND AN E-MAIL TO MY GIRL!
TO TELL HER TO GET TO THE BOMB SHELTER!
THERE'S NO TIME FOR THAT, BUCKY!

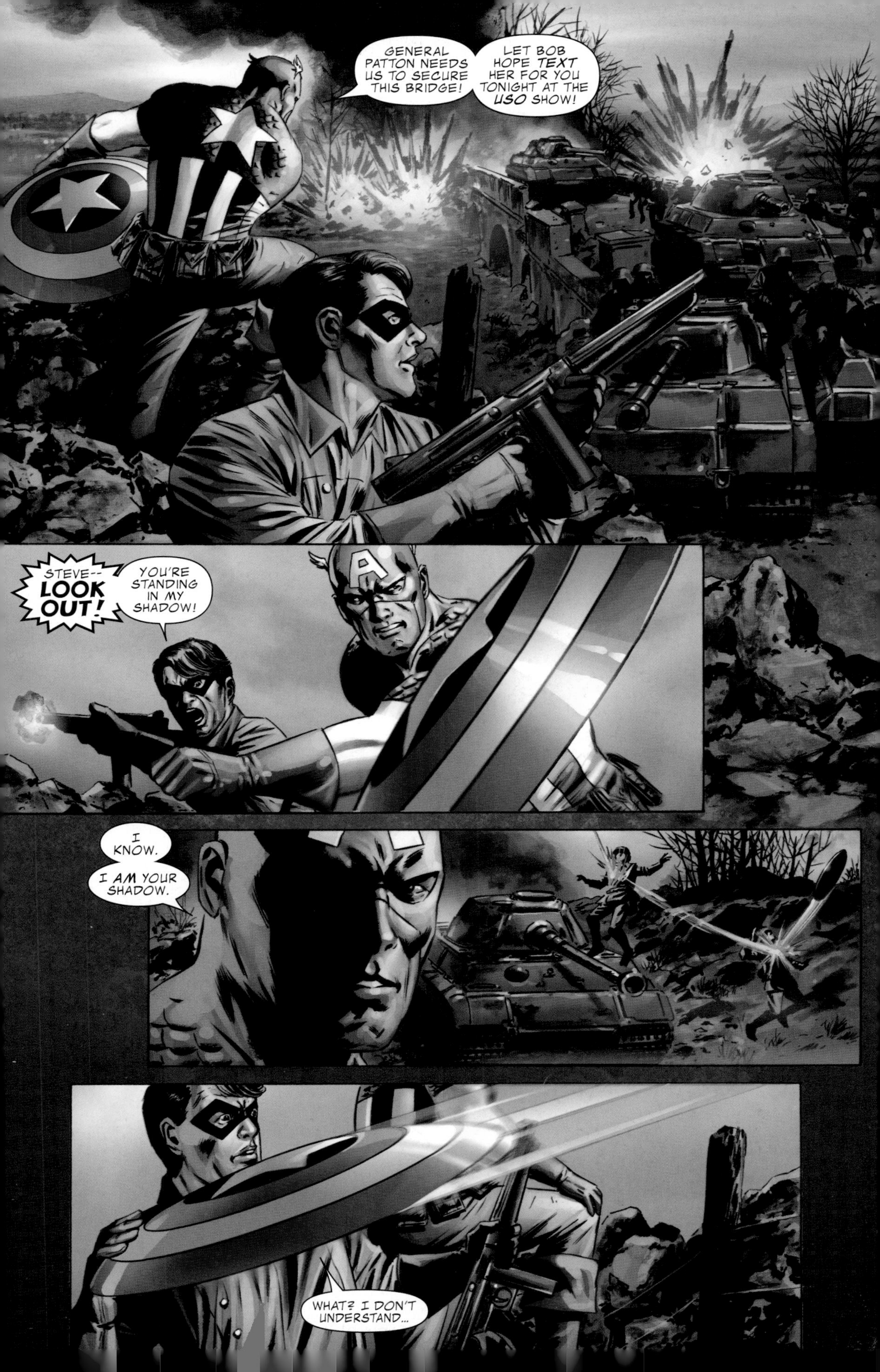
GENERAL PATTON NEEDS US TO SECURE THIS BRIDGE!
LET BOB HOPE TEXT HER FOR YOU TONIGHT AT THE USO SHOW!
STEVE-- LOOK OUT!
YOU'RE STANDING IN MY SHADOW!
I KNOW.
I AM YOUR SHADOW.
WHAT? I DON'T UNDERSTAND...

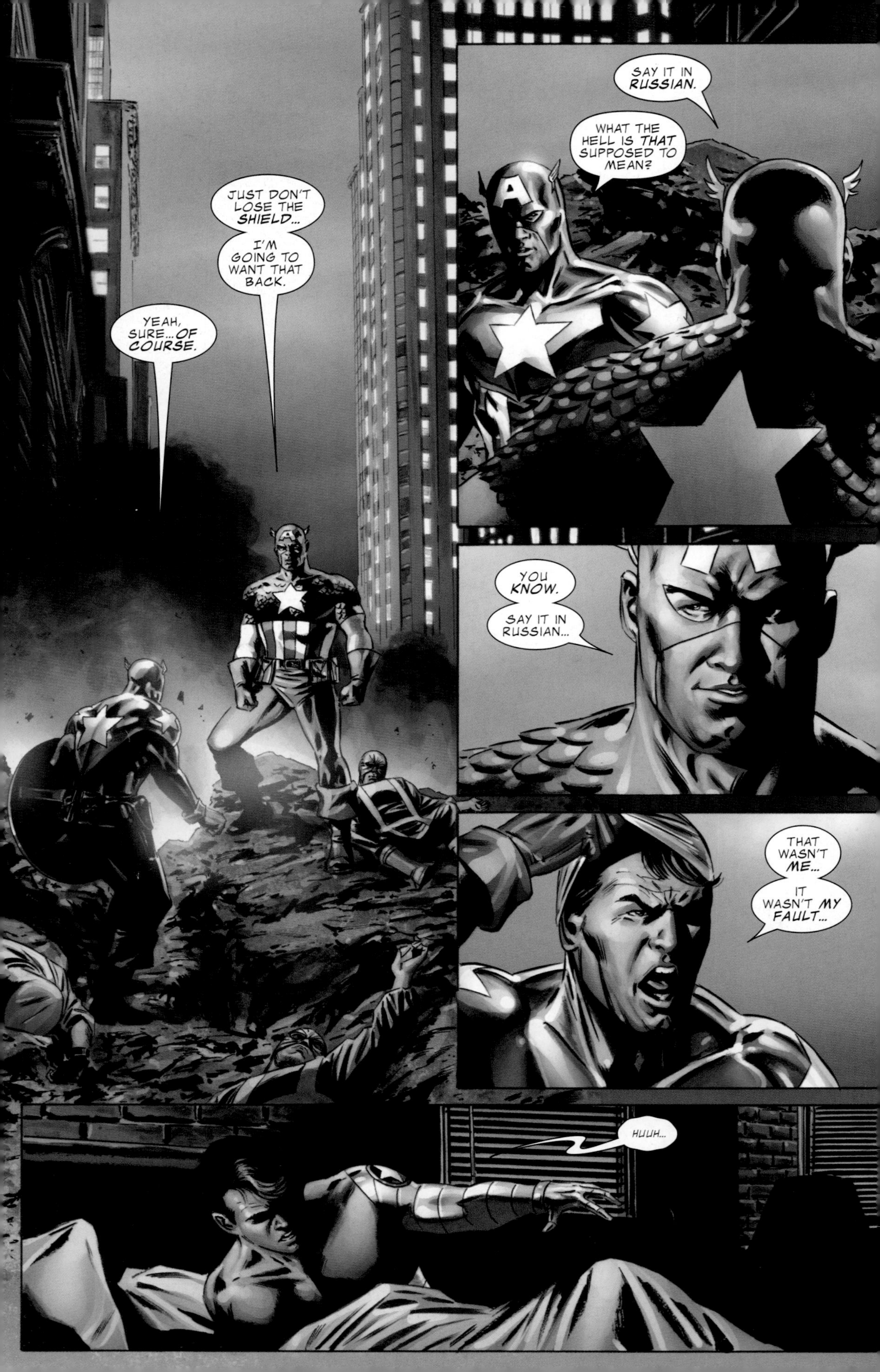
JUST DON'T LOSE THE SHIELD...
I'M GOING TO WANT THAT BACK.
YEAH, SURE... OF COURSE.
SAY IT IN RUSSIAN.
WHAT THE HELL IS THAT SUPPOSED TO MEAN?
YOU KNOW.
SAY IT IN RUSSIAN...
THAT WASN'T ME...
IT WASN'T MY FAULT...
HUUH...

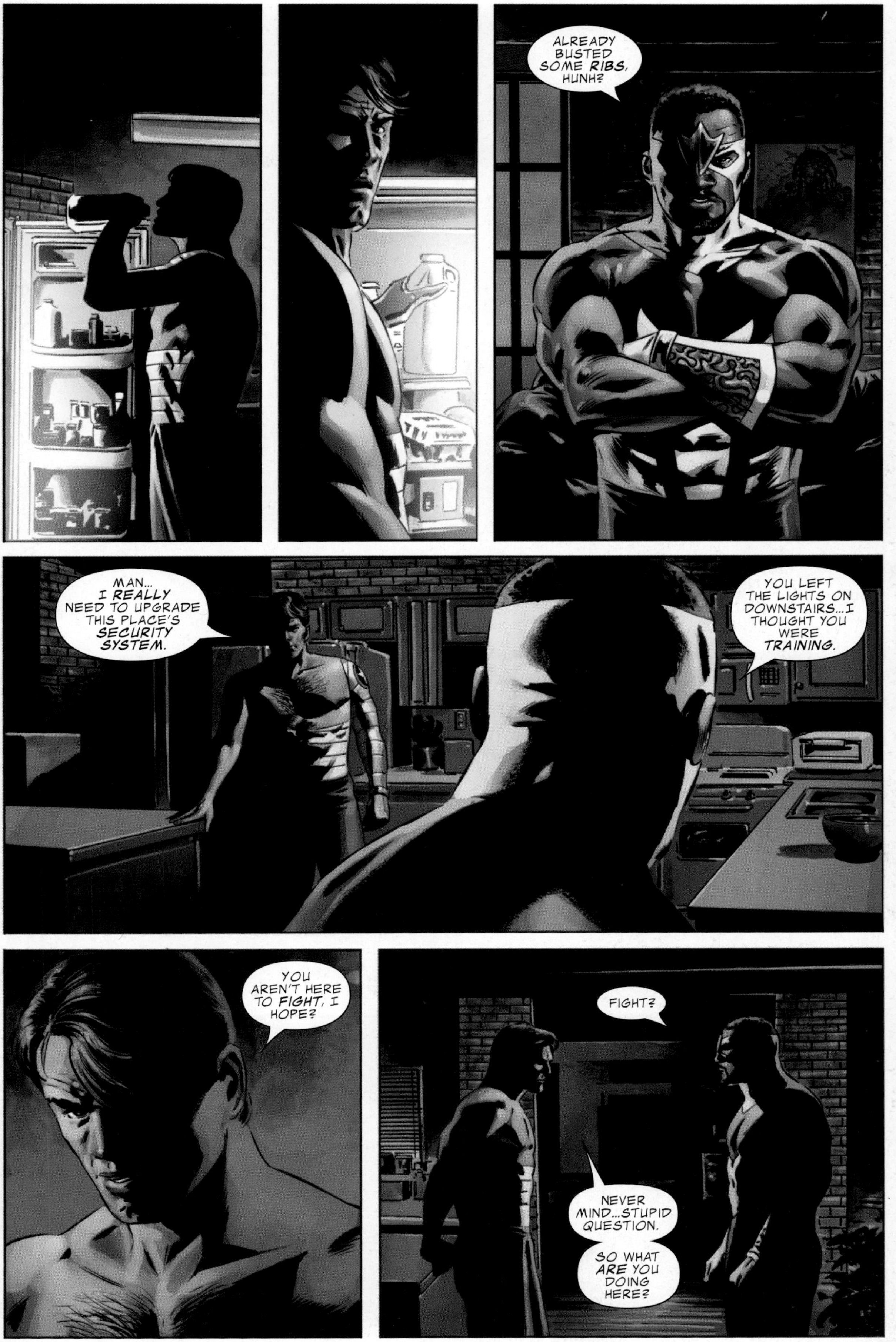
ALREADY BUSTED SOME RIBS, HUNH?
MAN... I REALLY NEED TO UPGRADE THIS PLACE'S SECURITY SYSTEM.
YOU LEFT THE LIGHTS ON DOWNSTAIRS...I THOUGHT YOU WERE TRAINING.
YOU AREN'T HERE TO FIGHT, I HOPE?
FIGHT?
NEVER MIND...STUPID QUESTION.
SO WHAT ARE YOU DOING HERE?

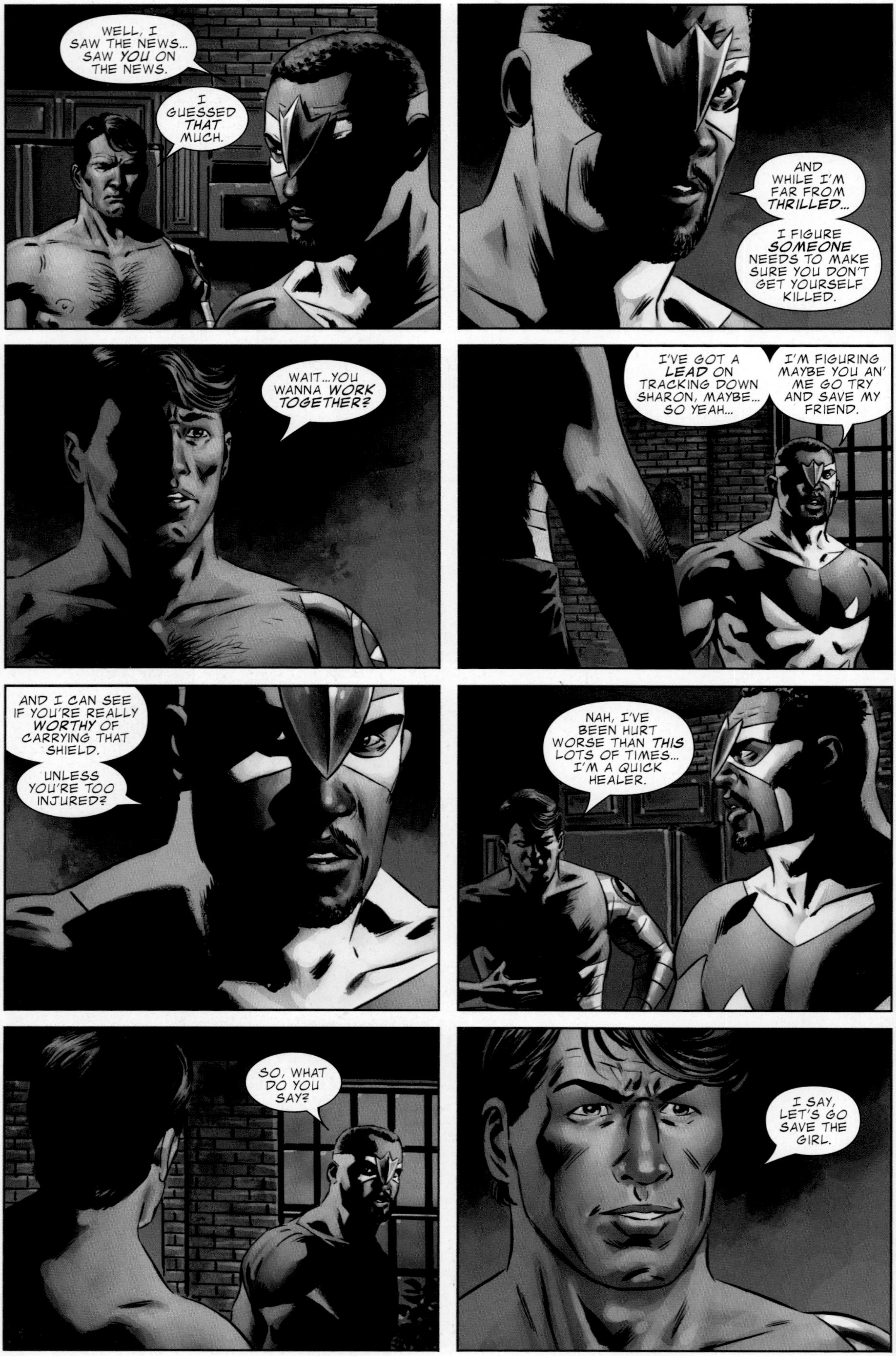
WELL, I SAW THE NEWS... SAW YOU ON THE NEWS.
I GUESSED THAT MUCH.
AND WHILE I'M FAR FROM THRILLED...
I FIGURE SOMEONE NEEDS TO MAKE SURE YOU DON'T GET YOURSELF KILLED.
WAIT...YOU WANNA WORK TOGETHER?
I'VE GOT A LEAD ON TRACKING DOWN SHARON, MAYBE... SO YEAH...
I'M FIGURING MAYBE YOU AN' ME GO TRY AND SAVE MY FRIEND.
AND I CAN SEE IF YOU'RE REALLY WORTHY OF CARRYING THAT SHIELD.
UNLESS YOU'RE TOO INJURED?
NAH, I'VE BEEN HURT WORSE THAN THIS LOTS OF TIMES... I'M A QUICK HEALER.
SO, WHAT DO YOU SAY?
I SAY, LET'S GO SAVE THE GIRL.

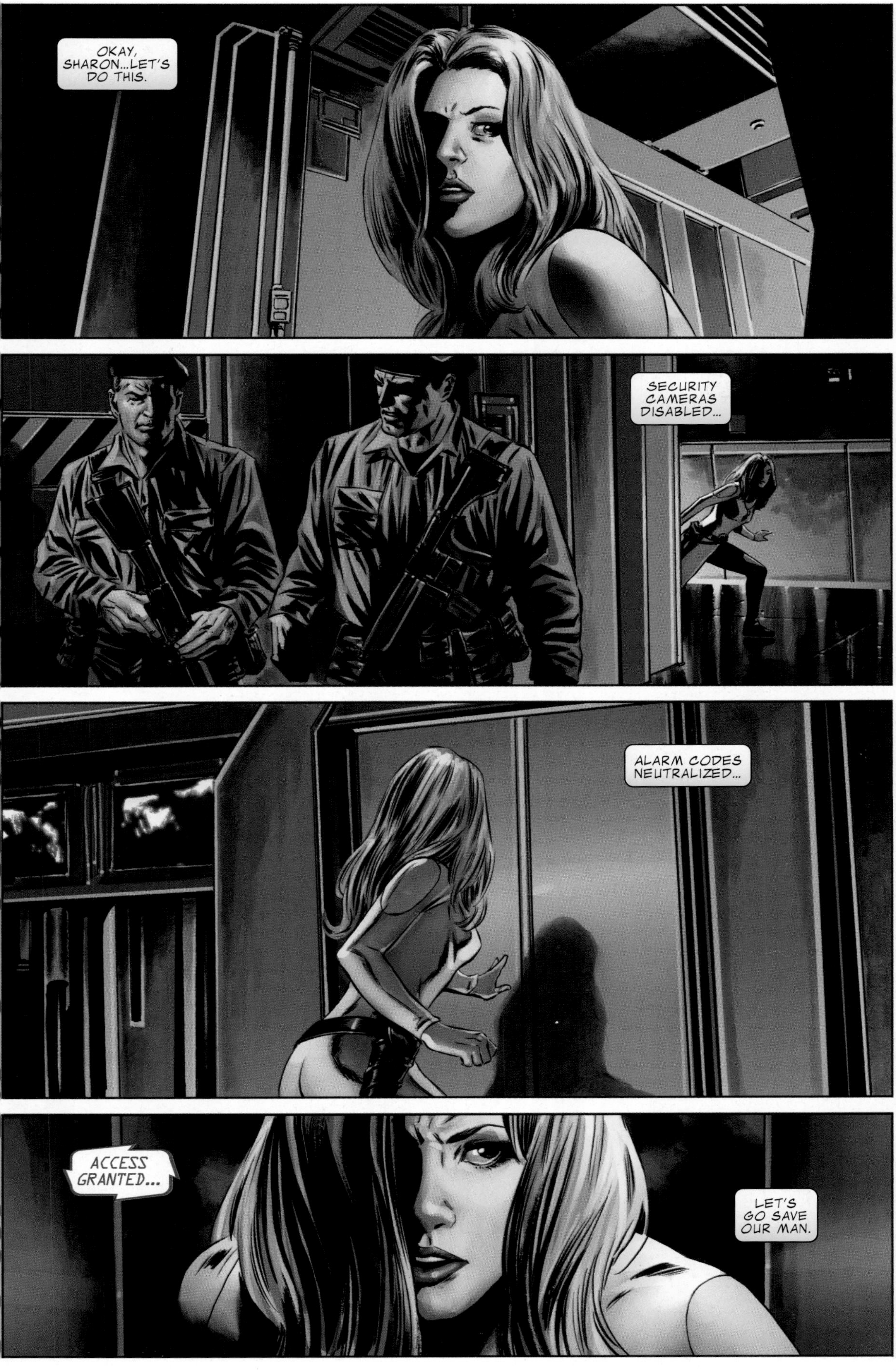
OKAY, SHARON...LET'S DO THIS.
SECURITY CAMERAS DISABLED...
ALARM CODES NEUTRALIZED...
ACCESS GRANTED...
LET'S GO SAVE OUR MAN.

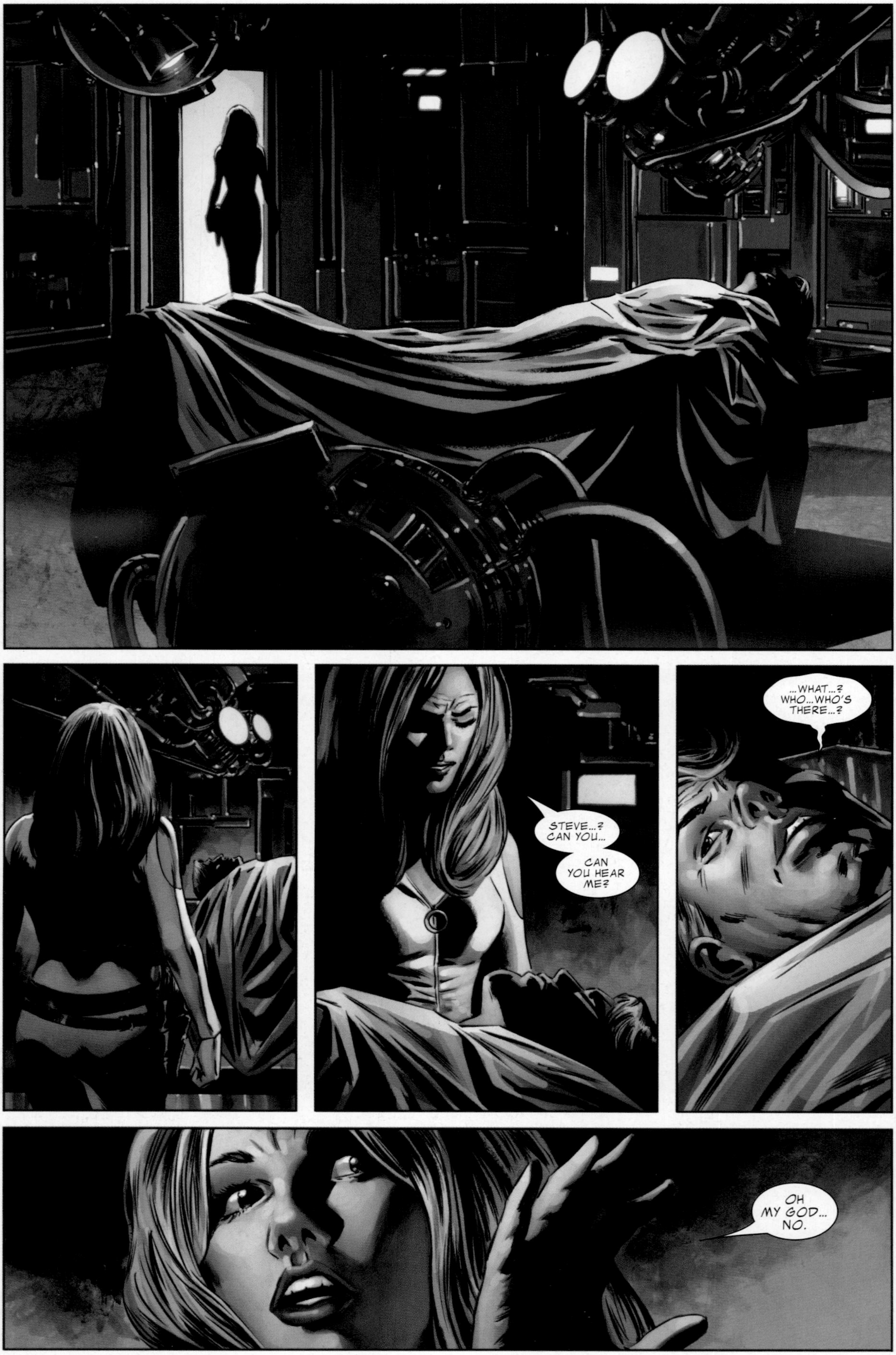
STEVE...? CAN YOU...
CAN YOU HEAR ME?
...WHAT...? WHO...WHO'S THERE...?
OH MY GOD... NO.

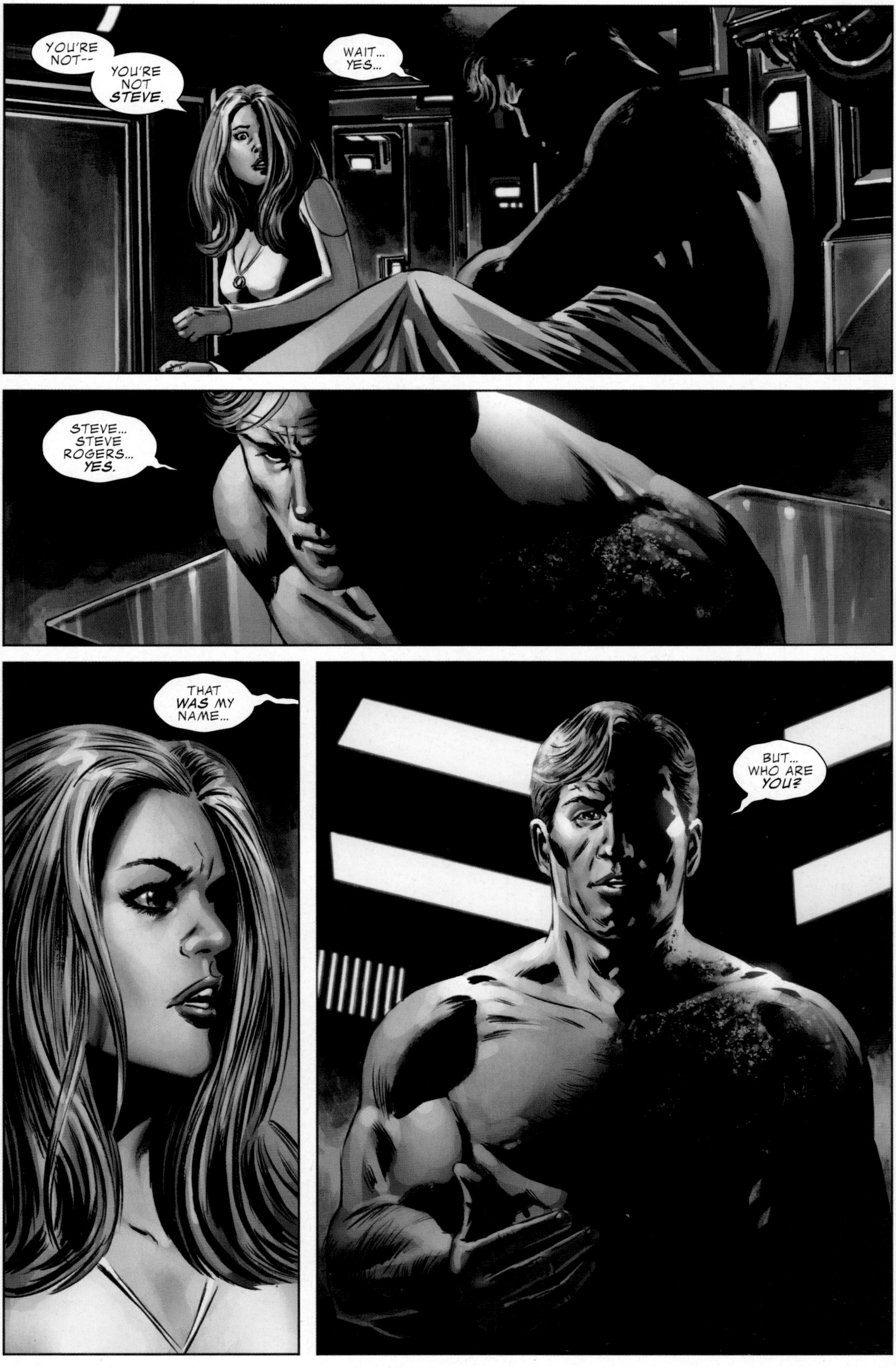
YOU'RE NOT--
YOU'RE NOT STEVE.
WAIT... YES...
STEVE... STEVE ROGERS... YES.
THAT WAS MY NAME...
BUT... WHO ARE YOU?

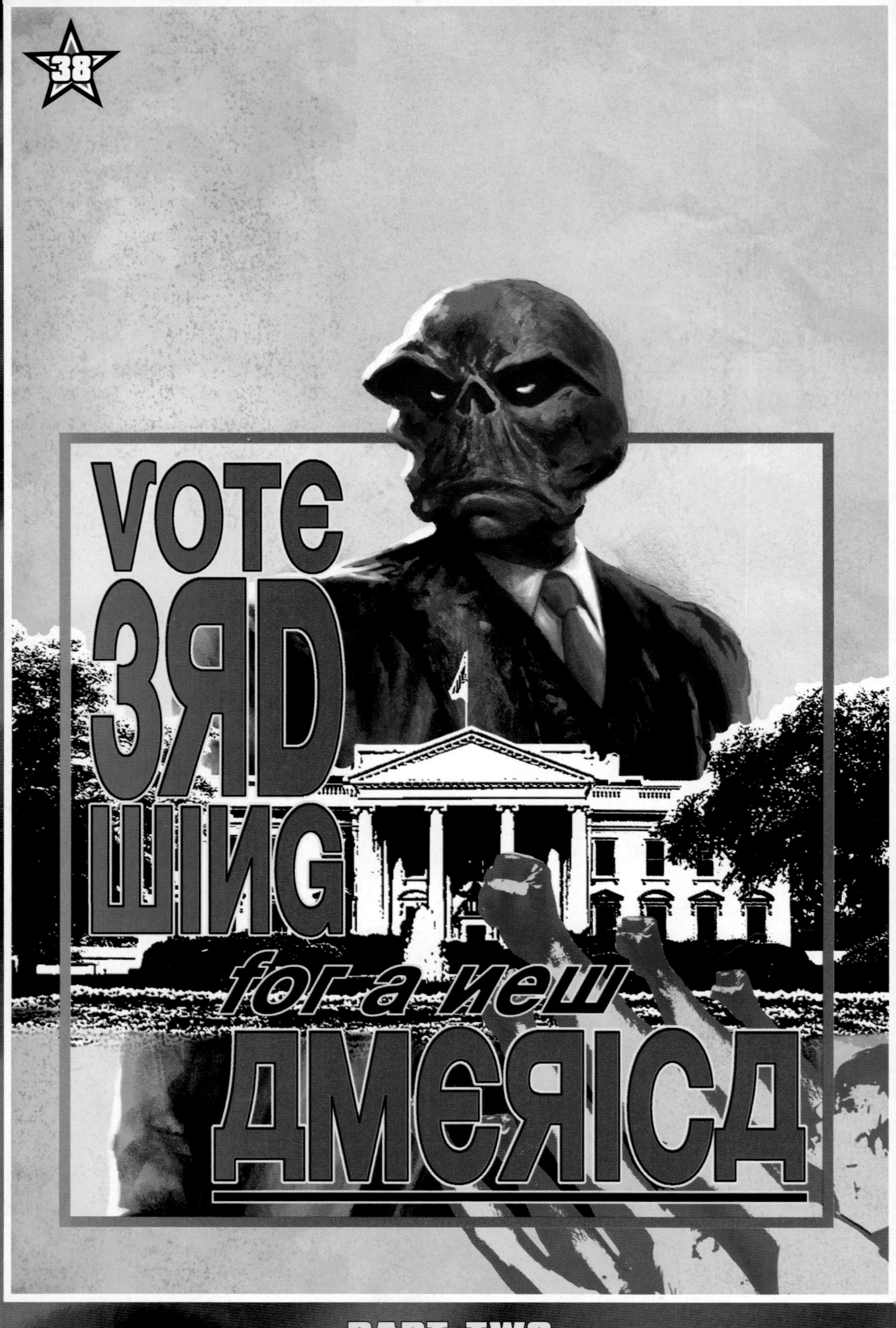
38
VOTE
3RD
WING
for a new
AMERICA

PART TWO

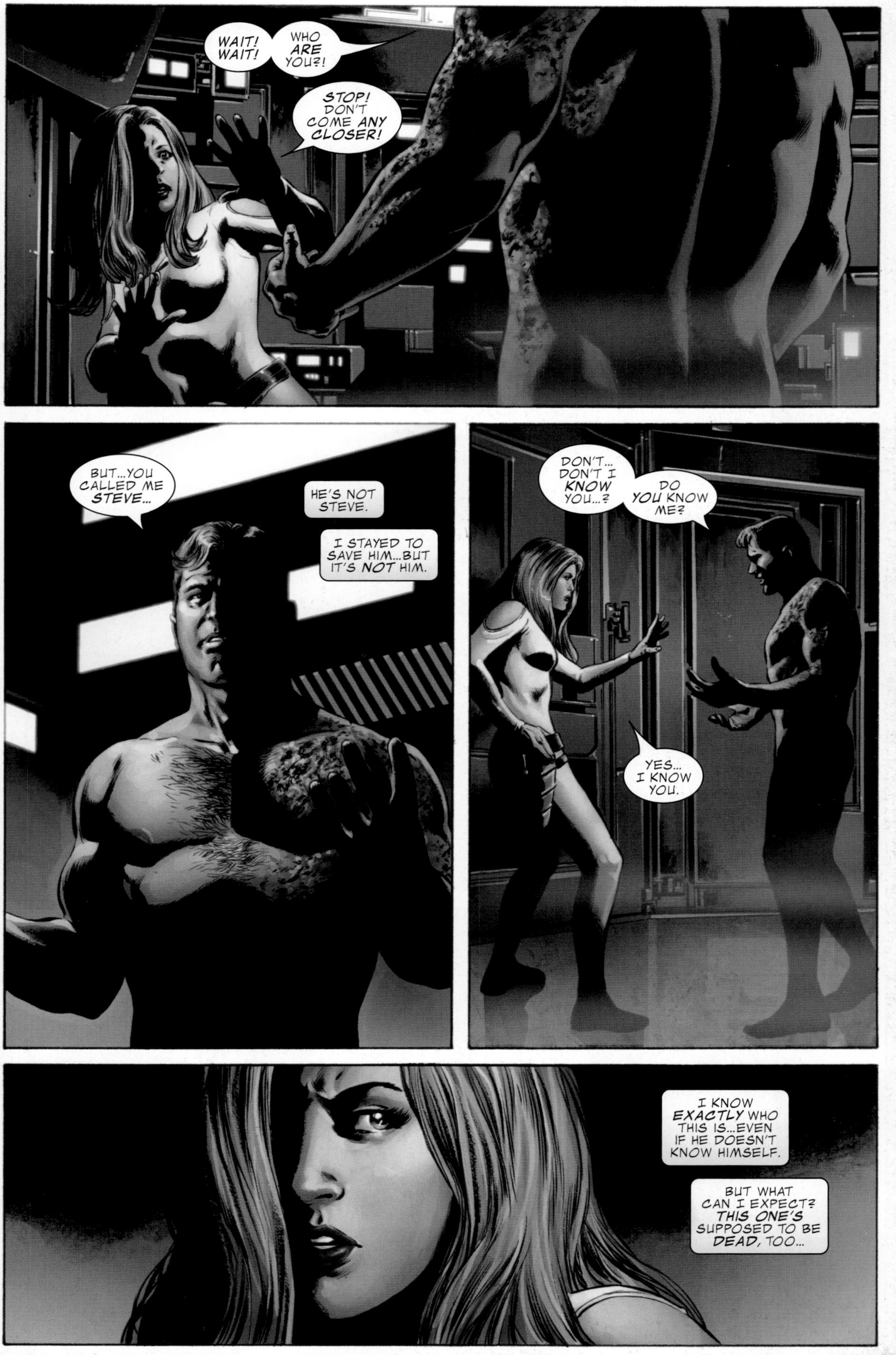

WAIT! WAIT!
WHO ARE YOU?!
STOP! DON'T COME ANY CLOSER!
BUT...YOU CALLED ME STEVE...
HE'S NOT STEVE.
I STAYED TO SAVE HIM...BUT IT'S NOT HIM.
DON'T... DON'T I KNOW YOU...?
DO YOU KNOW ME?
YES... I KNOW YOU.
I KNOW EXACTLY WHO THIS IS...EVEN IF HE DOESN'T KNOW HIMSELF.
BUT WHAT CAN I EXPECT? THIS ONE'S SUPPOSED TO BE DEAD, TOO...

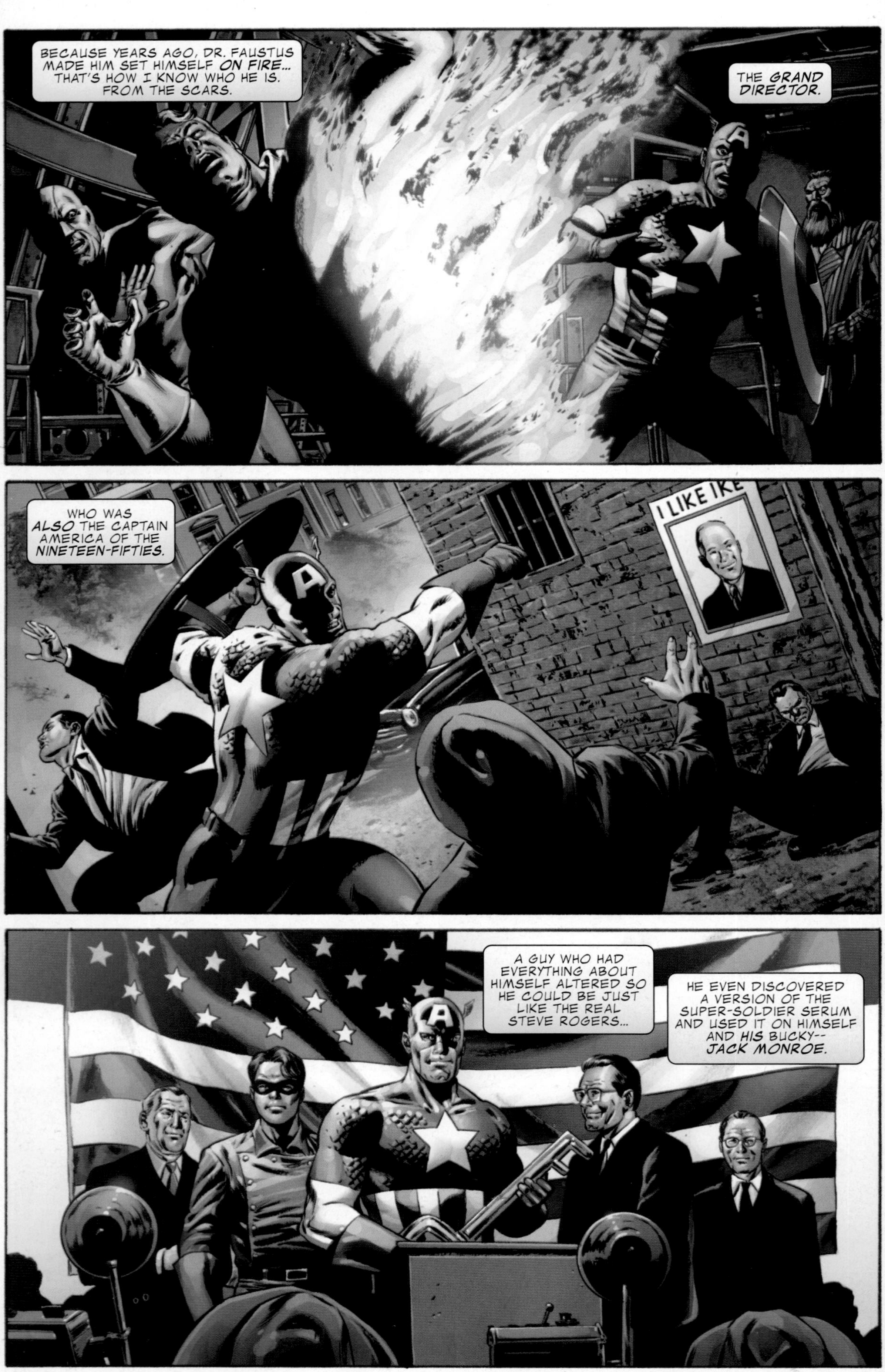
BECAUSE YEARS AGO, DR. FAUSTUS MADE HIM SET HIMSELF ON FIRE... THAT'S HOW I KNOW WHO HE IS. FROM THE SCARS.
THE GRAND DIRECTOR.
WHO WAS ALSO THE CAPTAIN AMERICA OF THE NINETEEN-FIFTIES.
I LIKE IKE
A GUY WHO HAD EVERYTHING ABOUT HIMSELF ALTERED SO HE COULD BE JUST LIKE THE REAL STEVE ROGERS...
HE EVEN DISCOVERED A VERSION OF THE SUPER-SOLDIER SERUM AND USED IT ON HIMSELF AND HIS BUCKY-- JACK MONROE.

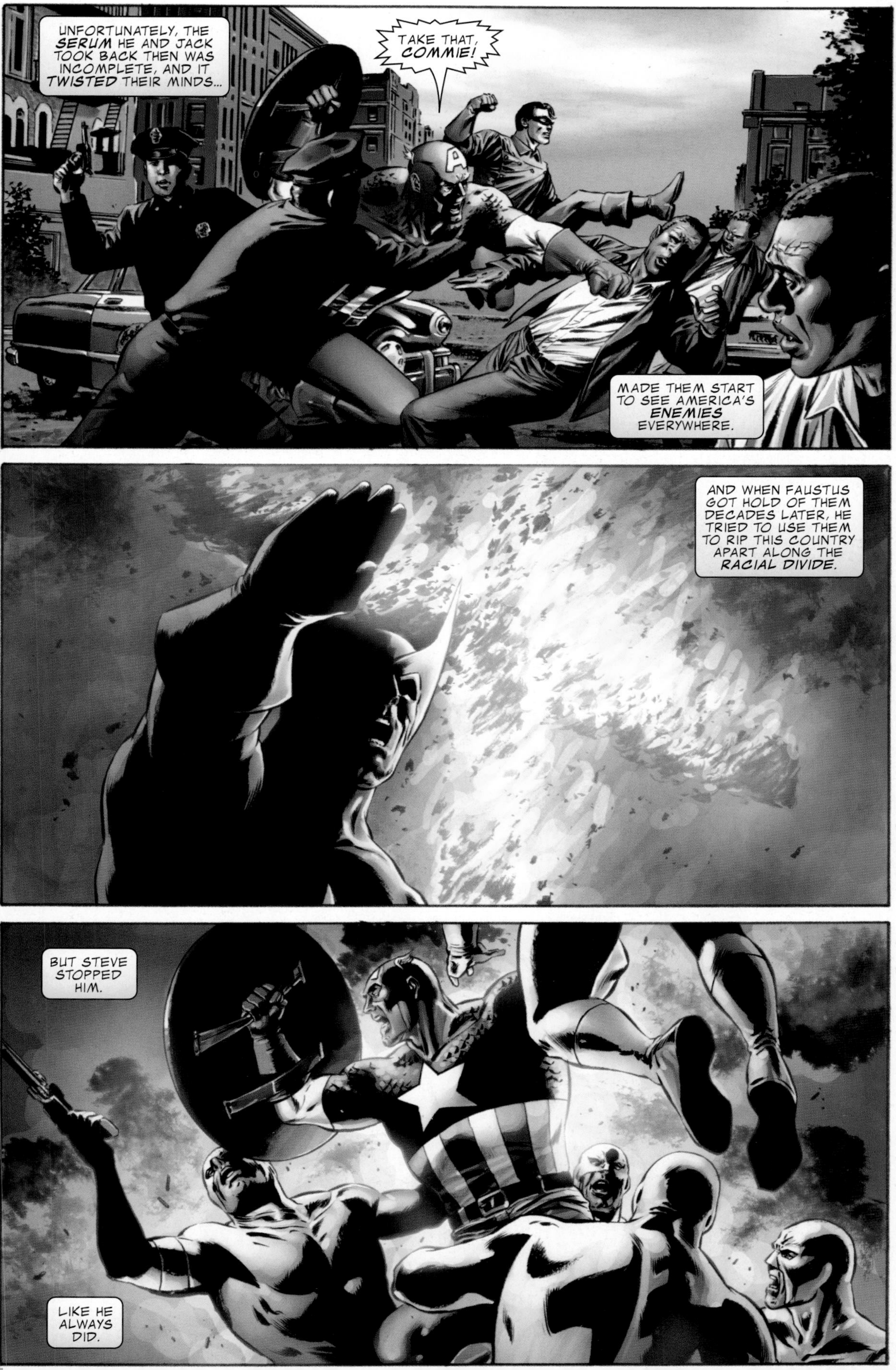
UNFORTUNATELY, THE SERUM HE AND JACK TOOK BACK THEN WAS INCOMPLETE, AND IT TWISTED THEIR MINDS...
TAKE THAT, COMMIE!
MADE THEM START TO SEE AMERICA'S ENEMIES EVERYWHERE.
AND WHEN FAUSTUS GOT HOLD OF THEM DECADES LATER, HE TRIED TO USE THEM TO RIP THIS COUNTRY APART ALONG THE RACIAL DIVIDE.
BUT STEVE STOPPED HIM.
LIKE HE ALWAYS DID.

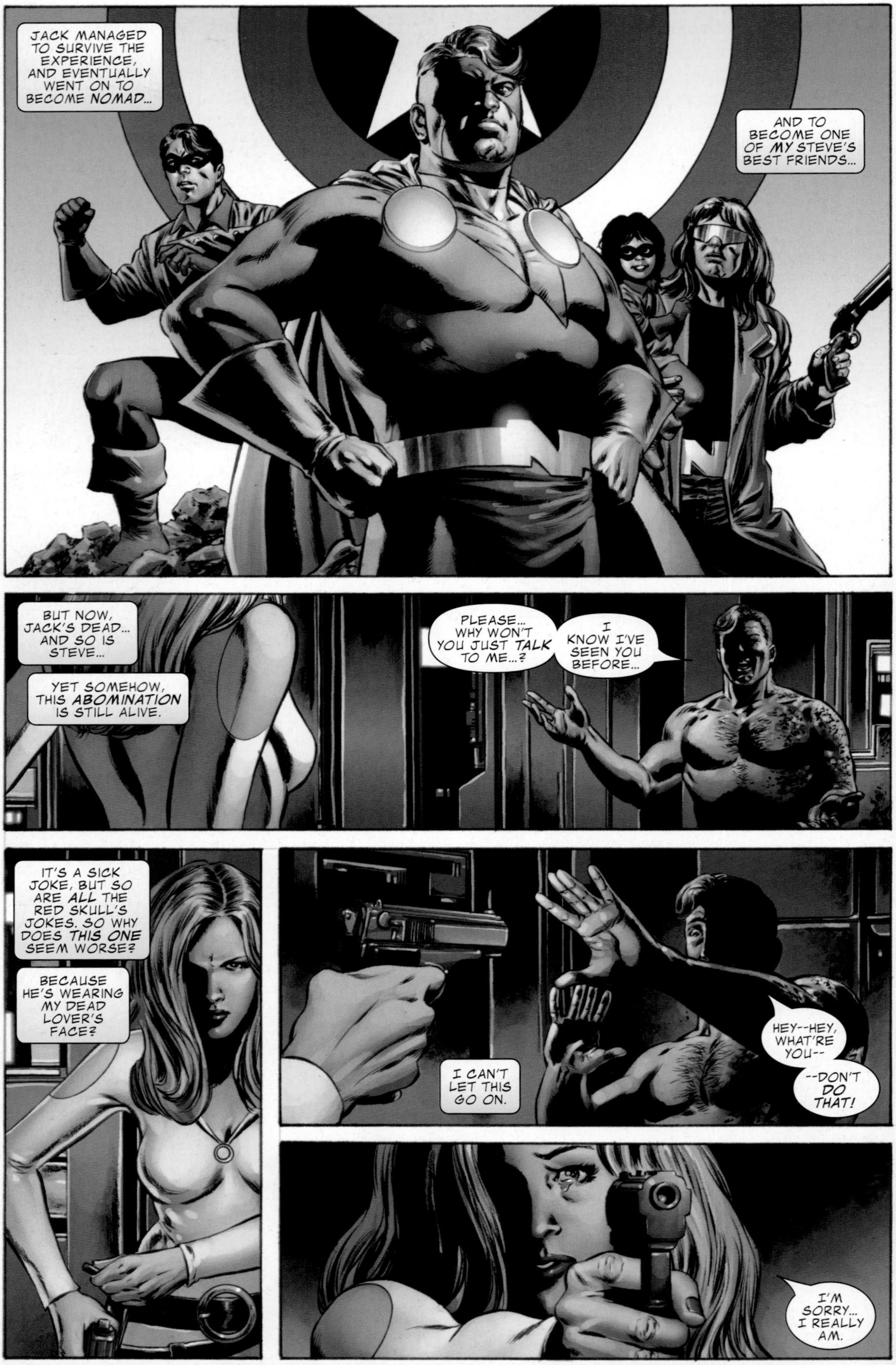
JACK MANAGED TO SURVIVE THE EXPERIENCE, AND EVENTUALLY WENT ON TO BECOME NOMAD...
AND TO BECOME ONE OF MY STEVE'S BEST FRIENDS...
BUT NOW, JACK'S DEAD... AND SO IS STEVE...
YET SOMEHOW, THIS ABOMINATION IS STILL ALIVE.
PLEASE... WHY WON'T YOU JUST TALK TO ME...?
I KNOW I'VE SEEN YOU BEFORE...
IT'S A SICK JOKE, BUT SO ARE ALL THE RED SKULL'S JOKES. SO WHY DOES THIS ONE SEEM WORSE?
BECAUSE HE'S WEARING MY DEAD LOVER'S FACE?
I CAN'T LET THIS GO ON.
HEY--HEY, WHAT'RE YOU--
--DON'T DO THAT!
I'M SORRY... I REALLY AM.

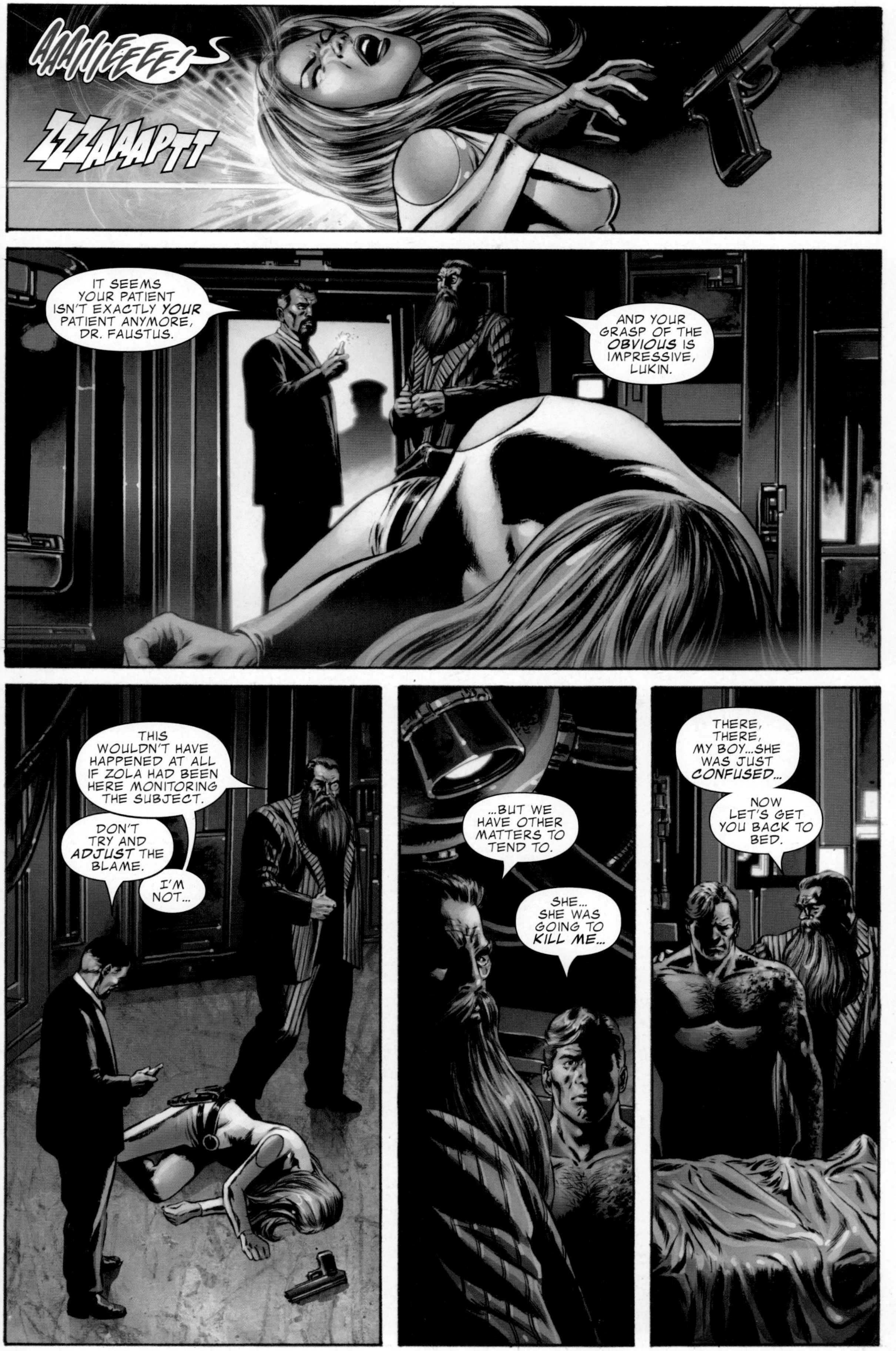
AAAIIIEEEE!
ZZZAAAPTT
IT SEEMS YOUR PATIENT ISN'T EXACTLY YOUR PATIENT ANYMORE, DR. FAUSTUS.
AND YOUR GRASP OF THE OBVIOUS IS IMPRESSIVE, LUKIN.
THIS WOULDN'T HAVE HAPPENED AT ALL IF ZOLA HAD BEEN HERE MONITORING THE SUBJECT.
DON'T TRY AND ADJUST THE BLAME.
I'M NOT...
...BUT WE HAVE OTHER MATTERS TO TEND TO.
SHE... SHE WAS GOING TO KILL ME...
THERE, THERE, MY BOY...SHE WAS JUST CONFUSED...
NOW LET'S GET YOU BACK TO BED.

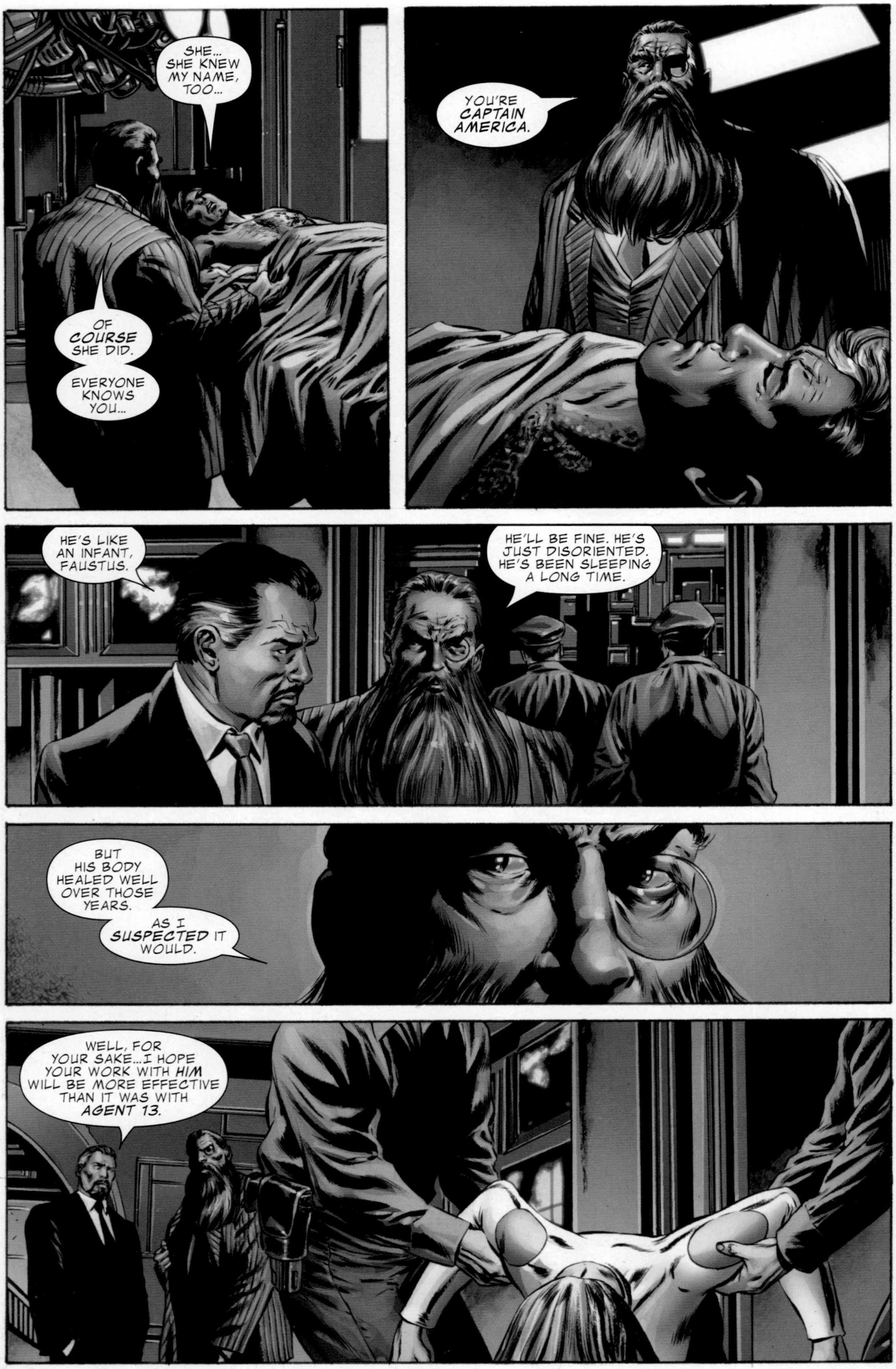

SHE... SHE KNEW MY NAME, TOO...
OF COURSE SHE DID.
EVERYONE KNOWS YOU...
YOU'RE CAPTAIN AMERICA.
HE'S LIKE AN INFANT, FAUSTUS.
HE'LL BE FINE. HE'S JUST DISORIENTED. HE'S BEEN SLEEPING A LONG TIME.
BUT HIS BODY HEALED WELL OVER THOSE YEARS.
AS I SUSPECTED IT WOULD.
WELL, FOR YOUR SAKE...I HOPE YOUR WORK WITH HIM WILL BE MORE EFFECTIVE THAN IT WAS WITH AGENT 13.

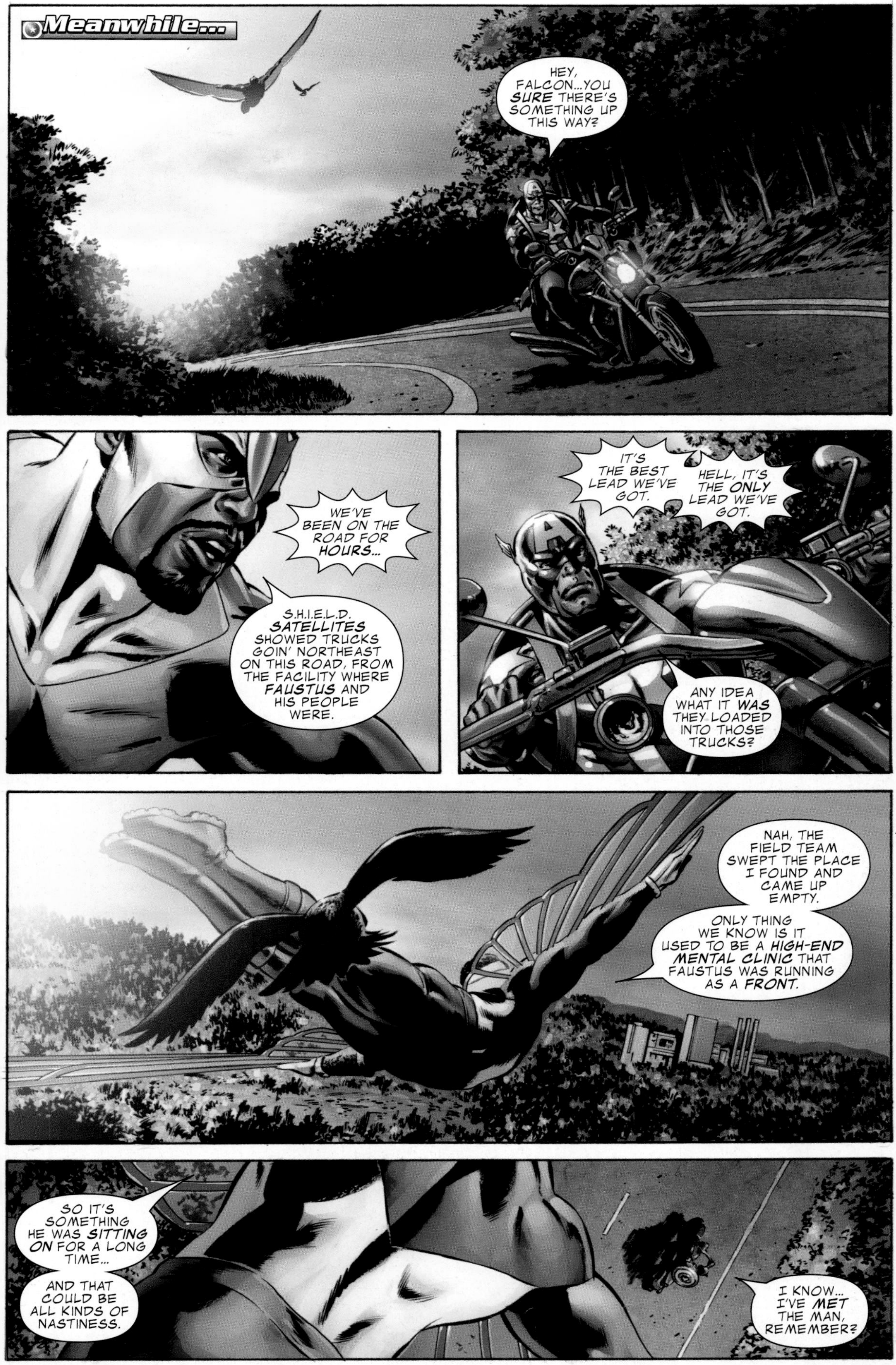
Meanwhile...
HEY, FALCON...YOU SURE THERE'S SOMETHING UP THIS WAY?
WE'VE BEEN ON THE ROAD FOR HOURS...
S.H.I.E.L.D. SATELLITES SHOWED TRUCKS GOIN' NORTHEAST ON THIS ROAD, FROM THE FACILITY WHERE FAUSTUS AND HIS PEOPLE WERE.
IT'S THE BEST LEAD WE'VE GOT.
HELL, IT'S THE ONLY LEAD WE'VE GOT.
ANY IDEA WHAT IT WAS THEY LOADED INTO THOSE TRUCKS?
NAH, THE FIELD TEAM SWEPT THE PLACE I FOUND AND CAME UP EMPTY.
ONLY THING WE KNOW IS IT USED TO BE A HIGH-END MENTAL CLINIC THAT FAUSTUS WAS RUNNING AS A FRONT.
SO IT'S SOMETHING HE WAS SITTING ON FOR A LONG TIME...
AND THAT COULD BE ALL KINDS OF NASTINESS.
I KNOW... I'VE MET THE MAN, REMEMBER?

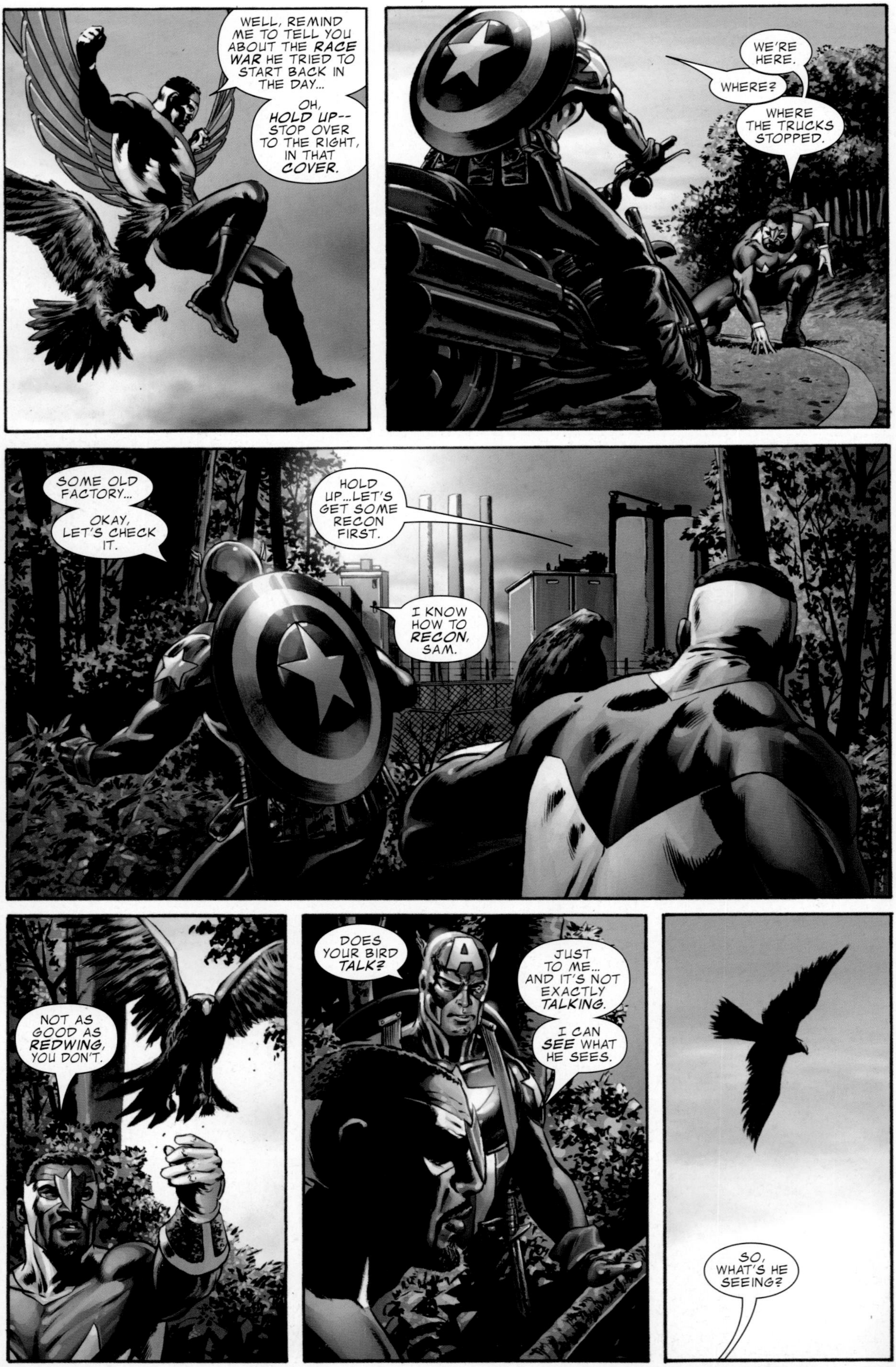
WELL, REMIND ME TO TELL YOU ABOUT THE RACE WAR HE TRIED TO START BACK IN THE DAY...
OH, HOLD UP-- STOP OVER TO THE RIGHT, IN THAT COVER.
WE'RE HERE.
WHERE?
WHERE THE TRUCKS STOPPED.
SOME OLD FACTORY...
OKAY, LET'S CHECK IT.
HOLD UP...LET'S GET SOME RECON FIRST.
I KNOW HOW TO RECON, SAM.
NOT AS GOOD AS REDWING, YOU DON'T.
DOES YOUR BIRD TALK?
JUST TO ME... AND IT'S NOT EXACTLY TALKING.
I CAN SEE WHAT HE SEES.
SO, WHAT'S HE SEEING?

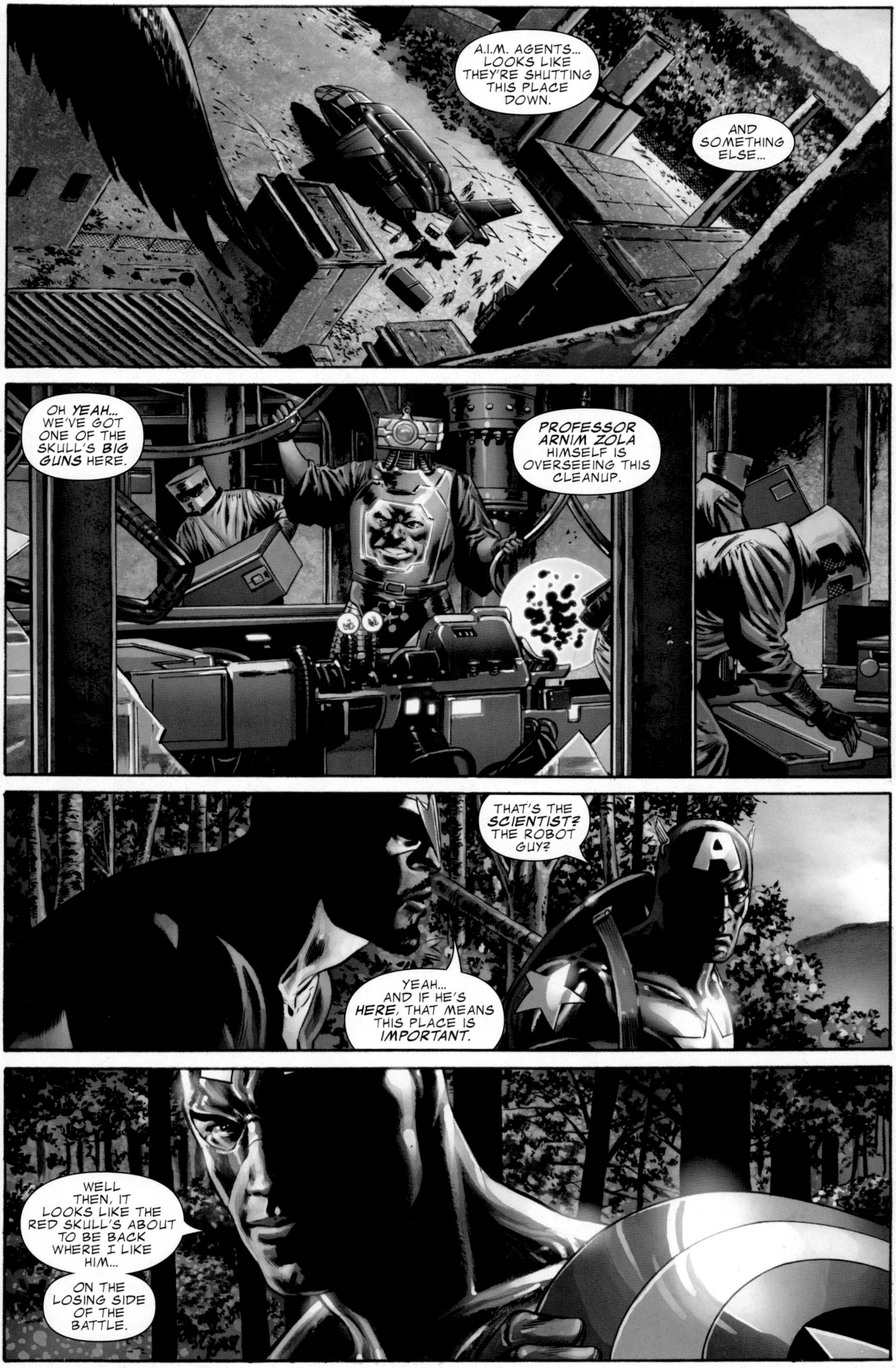
A.I.M. AGENTS... LOOKS LIKE THEY'RE SHUTTING THIS PLACE DOWN.
AND SOMETHING ELSE...
OH *YEAH*... WE'VE GOT ONE OF THE SKULL'S ***BIG GUNS*** HERE.
PROFESSOR ARNIM ZOLA HIMSELF IS OVERSEEING THIS CLEANUP.
THAT'S THE ***SCIENTIST?*** THE ROBOT GUY?
YEAH... AND IF HE'S ***HERE***, THAT MEANS THIS PLACE IS ***IMPORTANT***.
WELL THEN, IT LOOKS LIKE THE RED SKULL'S ABOUT TO BE BACK WHERE I LIKE HIM...
ON THE LOSING SIDE OF THE BATTLE.

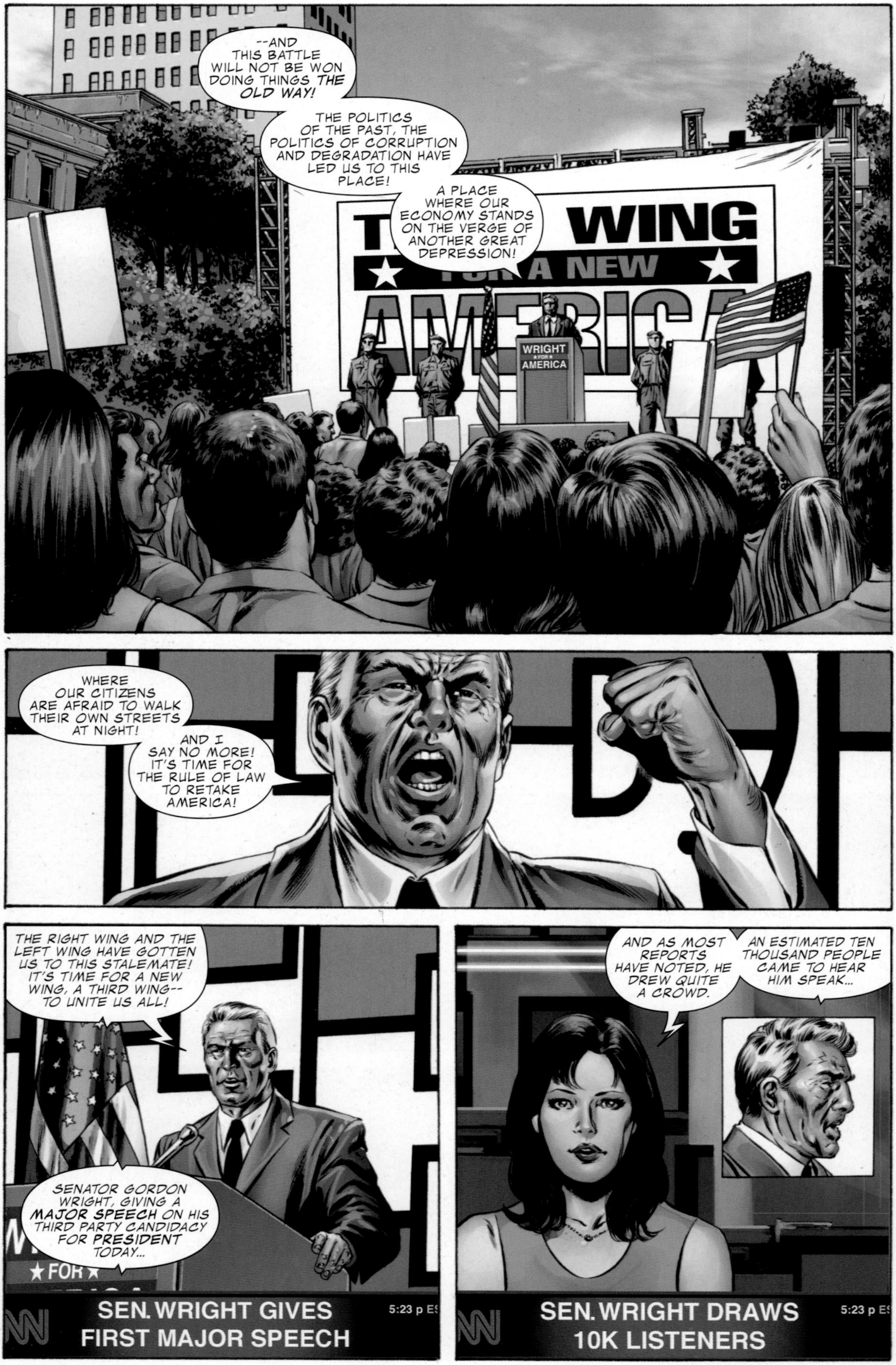
--AND THIS BATTLE WILL NOT BE WON DOING THINGS THE OLD WAY!
THE POLITICS OF THE PAST, THE POLITICS OF CORRUPTION AND DEGRADATION HAVE LED US TO THIS PLACE!
A PLACE WHERE OUR ECONOMY STANDS ON THE VERGE OF ANOTHER GREAT DEPRESSION!
WING
A NEW
WRIGHT FOR AMERICA
WHERE OUR CITIZENS ARE AFRAID TO WALK THEIR OWN STREETS AT NIGHT!
AND I SAY NO MORE! IT'S TIME FOR THE RULE OF LAW TO RETAKE AMERICA!
THE RIGHT WING AND THE LEFT WING HAVE GOTTEN US TO THIS STALEMATE! IT'S TIME FOR A NEW WING, A THIRD WING-- TO UNITE US ALL!
SENATOR GORDON WRIGHT, GIVING A MAJOR SPEECH ON HIS THIRD PARTY CANDIDACY FOR PRESIDENT TODAY...
★FOR★
SEN. WRIGHT GIVES FIRST MAJOR SPEECH
5:23 p ES
AND AS MOST REPORTS HAVE NOTED, HE DREW QUITE A CROWD.
AN ESTIMATED TEN THOUSAND PEOPLE CAME TO HEAR HIM SPEAK...
SEN. WRIGHT DRAWS 10K LISTENERS
5:23 p ES

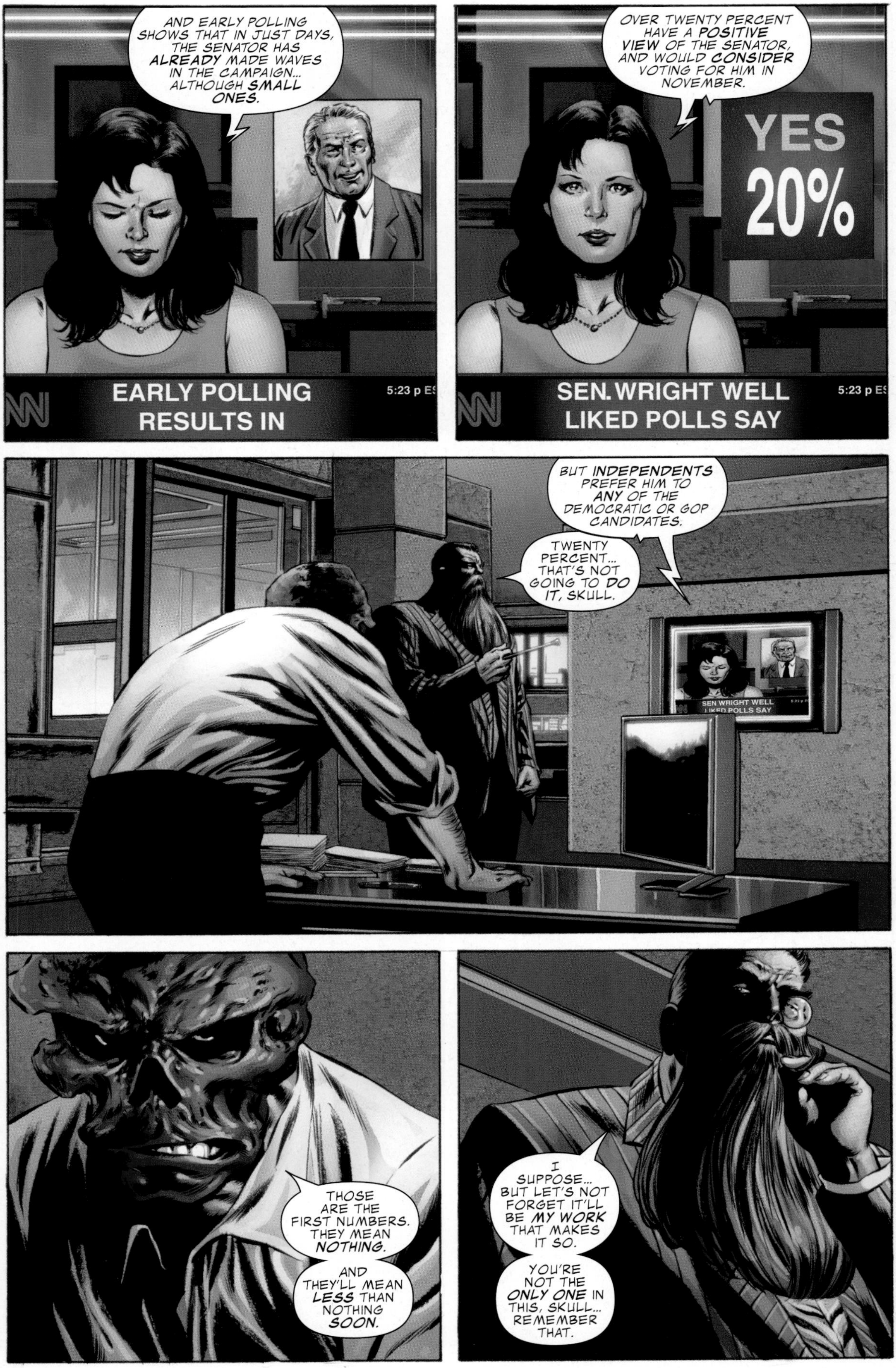
AND EARLY POLLING SHOWS THAT IN JUST DAYS, THE SENATOR HAS ALREADY MADE WAVES IN THE CAMPAIGN... ALTHOUGH SMALL ONES.
EARLY POLLING RESULTS IN
5:23 p ES
OVER TWENTY PERCENT HAVE A POSITIVE VIEW OF THE SENATOR, AND WOULD CONSIDER VOTING FOR HIM IN NOVEMBER.
YES
20%
SEN. WRIGHT WELL LIKED POLLS SAY
5:23 p ES
BUT INDEPENDENTS PREFER HIM TO ANY OF THE DEMOCRATIC OR GOP CANDIDATES.
TWENTY PERCENT... THAT'S NOT GOING TO DO IT, SKULL.
SEN WRIGHT WELL LIKED POLLS SAY
THOSE ARE THE FIRST NUMBERS. THEY MEAN NOTHING.
AND THEY'LL MEAN LESS THAN NOTHING SOON.
I SUPPOSE... BUT LET'S NOT FORGET IT'LL BE MY WORK THAT MAKES IT SO.
YOU'RE NOT THE ONLY ONE IN THIS, SKULL... REMEMBER THAT.

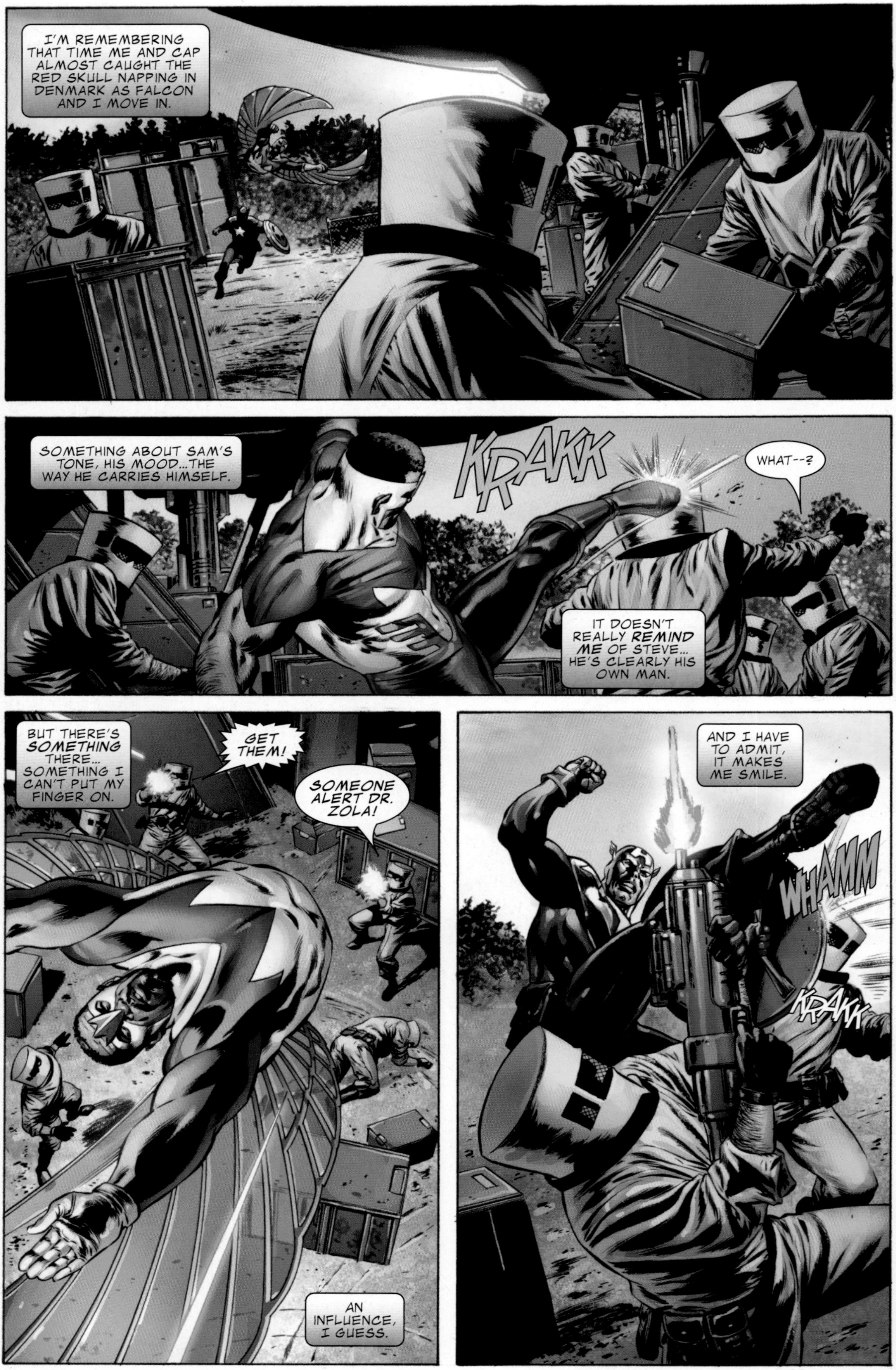
I'M REMEMBERING THAT TIME ME AND CAP ALMOST CAUGHT THE RED SKULL NAPPING IN DENMARK AS FALCON AND I MOVE IN.
SOMETHING ABOUT SAM'S TONE, HIS MOOD...THE WAY HE CARRIES HIMSELF.
KRAKK
WHAT--?
IT DOESN'T REALLY REMIND ME OF STEVE... HE'S CLEARLY HIS OWN MAN.
BUT THERE'S SOMETHING THERE... SOMETHING I CAN'T PUT MY FINGER ON.
GET THEM!
SOMEONE ALERT DR. ZOLA!
AN INFLUENCE, I GUESS.
AND I HAVE TO ADMIT, IT MAKES ME SMILE.
WHAMM
KRAKK

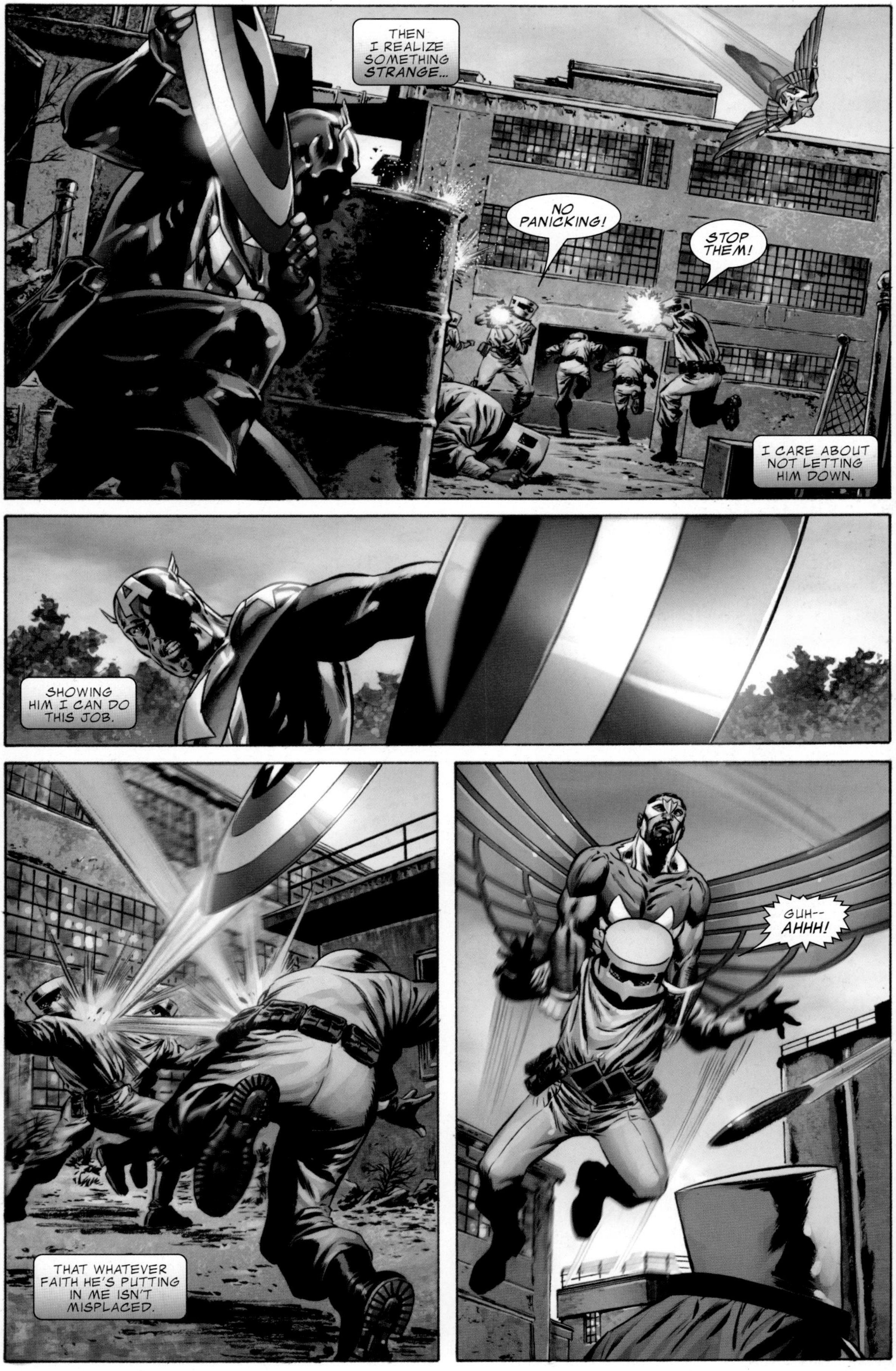
THEN I REALIZE SOMETHING STRANGE...
NO PANICKING!
STOP THEM!
I CARE ABOUT NOT LETTING HIM DOWN.
SHOWING HIM I CAN DO THIS JOB.
THAT WHATEVER FAITH HE'S PUTTING IN ME ISN'T MISPLACED.
GUH-- AHHH!

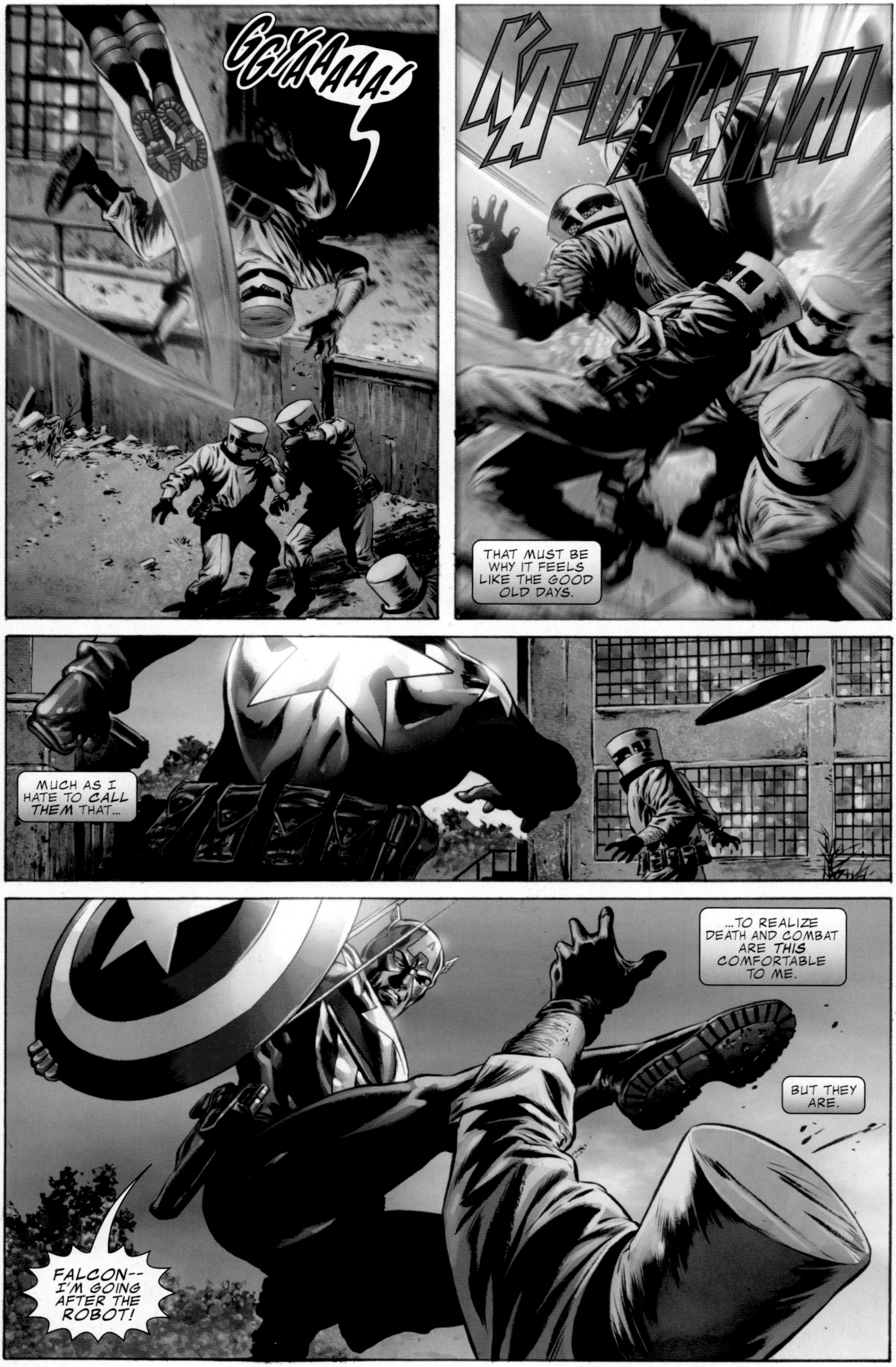
GGYAAAAAA!
KA-WHOOM
THAT MUST BE WHY IT FEELS LIKE THE GOOD OLD DAYS.
MUCH AS I HATE TO CALL THEM THAT...
...TO REALIZE DEATH AND COMBAT ARE THIS COMFORTABLE TO ME.
BUT THEY ARE.
FALCON-- I'M GOING AFTER THE ROBOT!

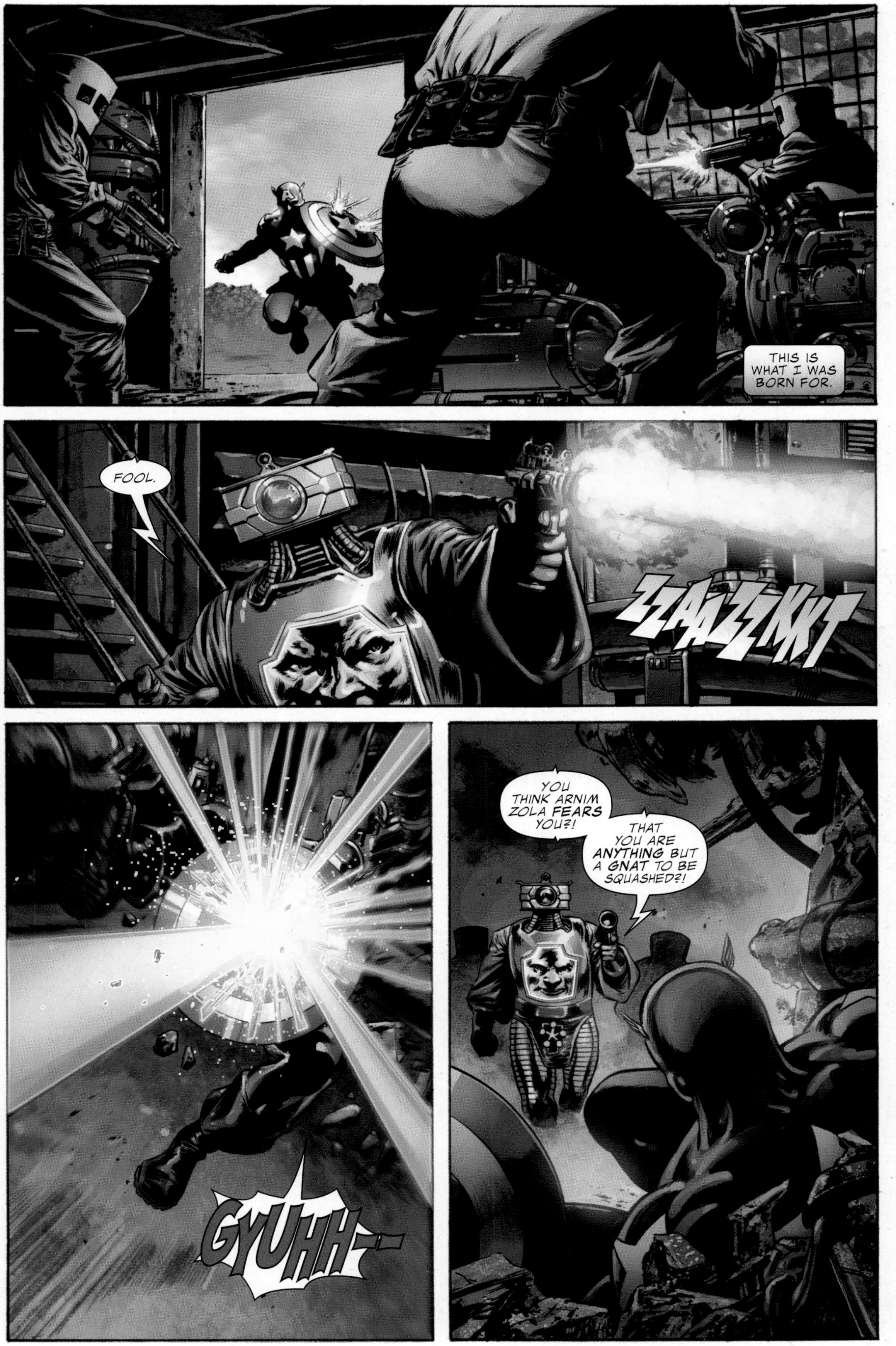
THIS IS WHAT I WAS BORN FOR.
FOOL.
ZZAAZZKKT
GYUHH--
YOU THINK ARNIM ZOLA FEARS YOU?!
THAT YOU ARE ANYTHING BUT A GNAT TO BE SQUASHED?!

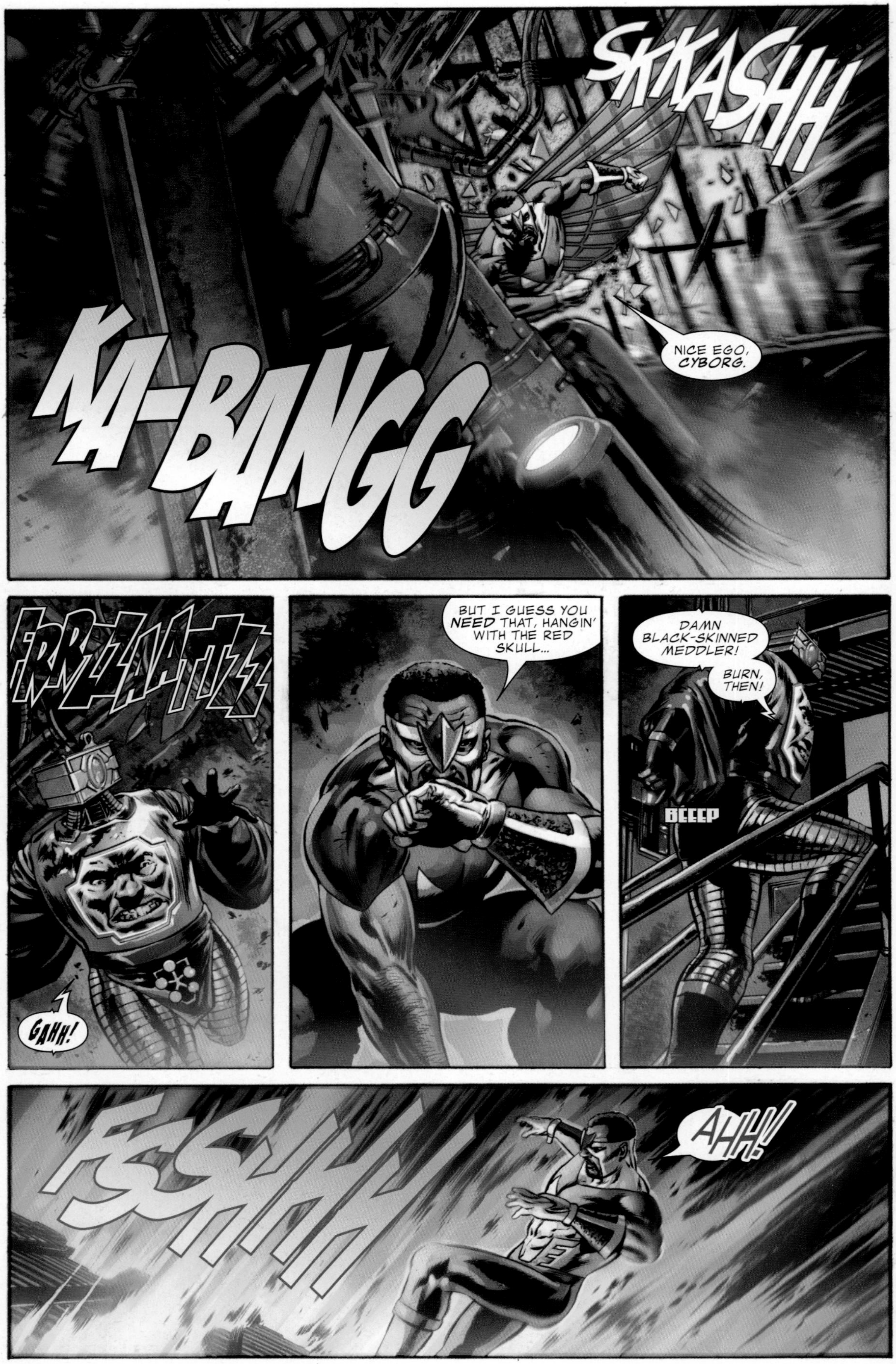
SKKASHH
NICE EGO, CYBORG.
KA-BANGG
GAHH!
BUT I GUESS YOU NEED THAT, HANGIN' WITH THE RED SKULL...
DAMN BLACK-SKINNED MEDDLER!
BURN, THEN!
BEEEP
AHH!

HOLD THEM BACK! ALL OF YOU!

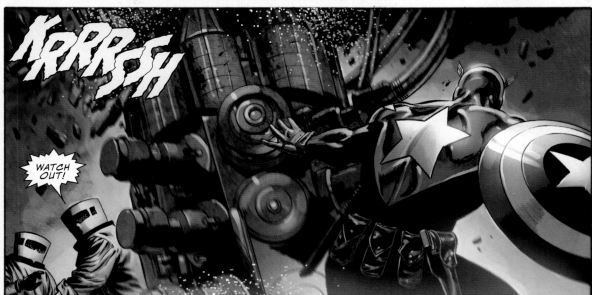

KRRRSSH

WATCH OUT!

I GOT THESE GUYS!

DON'T LET ZOLA GET AWAY!

RIGHT-- YEAH!

SHUK

THEY THINK THEY'VE ACCOMPLISHED SOMETHING. FOOLS.

I'LL TAKE EVERYTHING IMPORTANT HERE WITH ME.

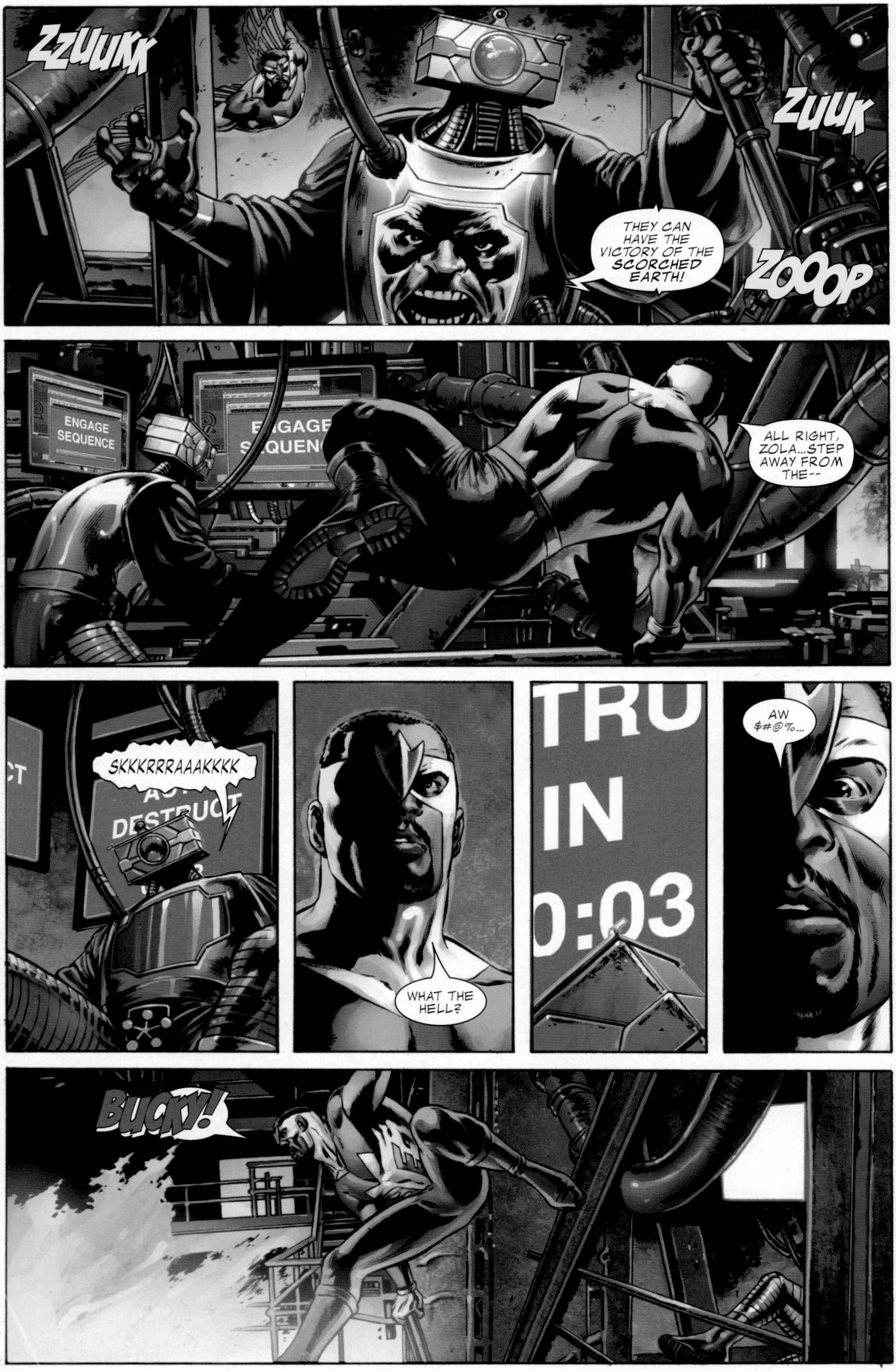

ZZUUKK
ZUUK
THEY CAN HAVE THE VICTORY OF THE SCORCHED EARTH!
ZOOOP
ENGAGE SEQUENCE
ALL RIGHT, ZOLA...STEP AWAY FROM THE--
SKKKRRRAAAKKKK
DESTRUCT
WHAT THE HELL?
TRU
IN
0:03
AW $#@%...
BUCKY!

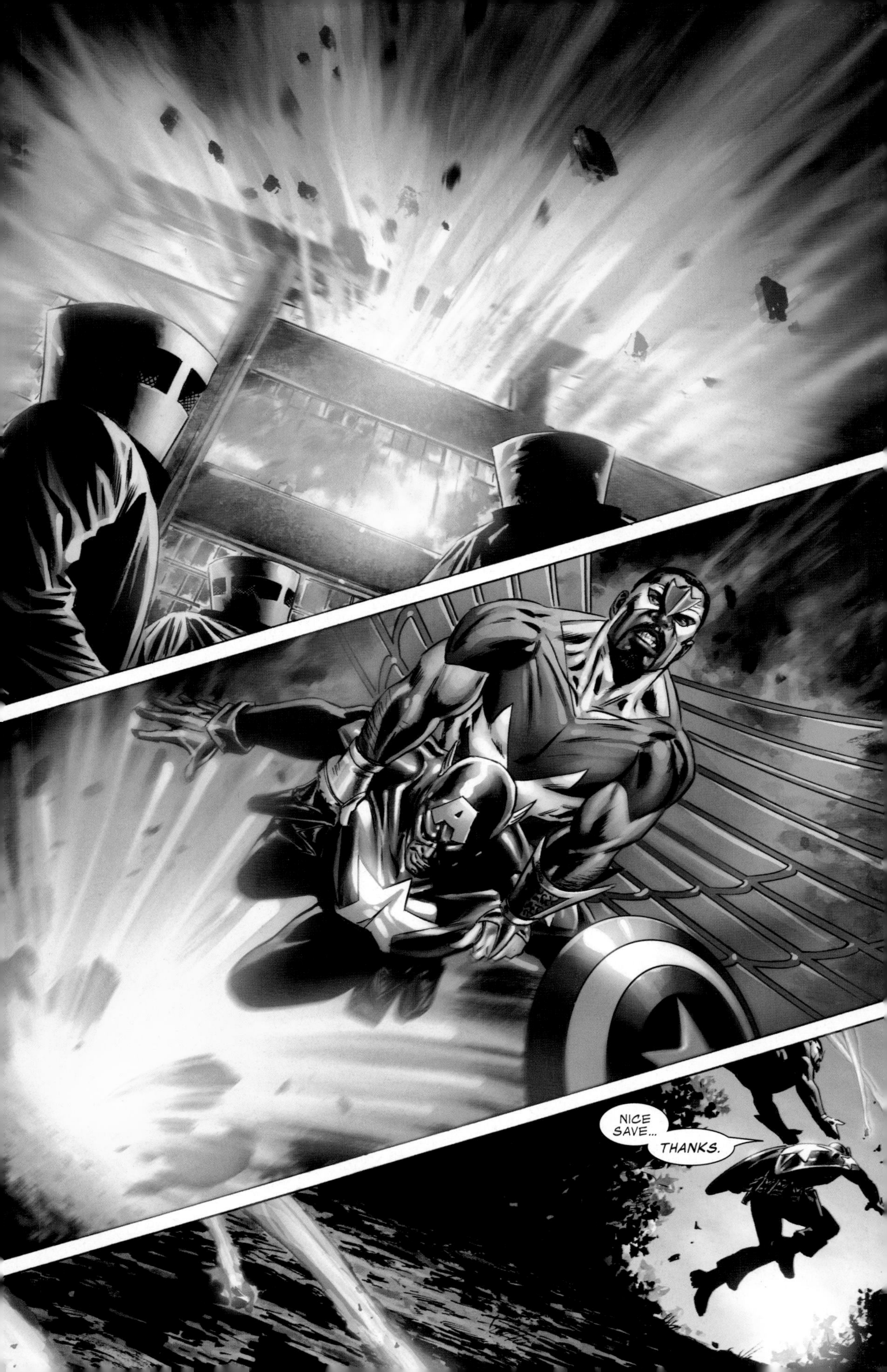
NICE SAVE...
THANKS.

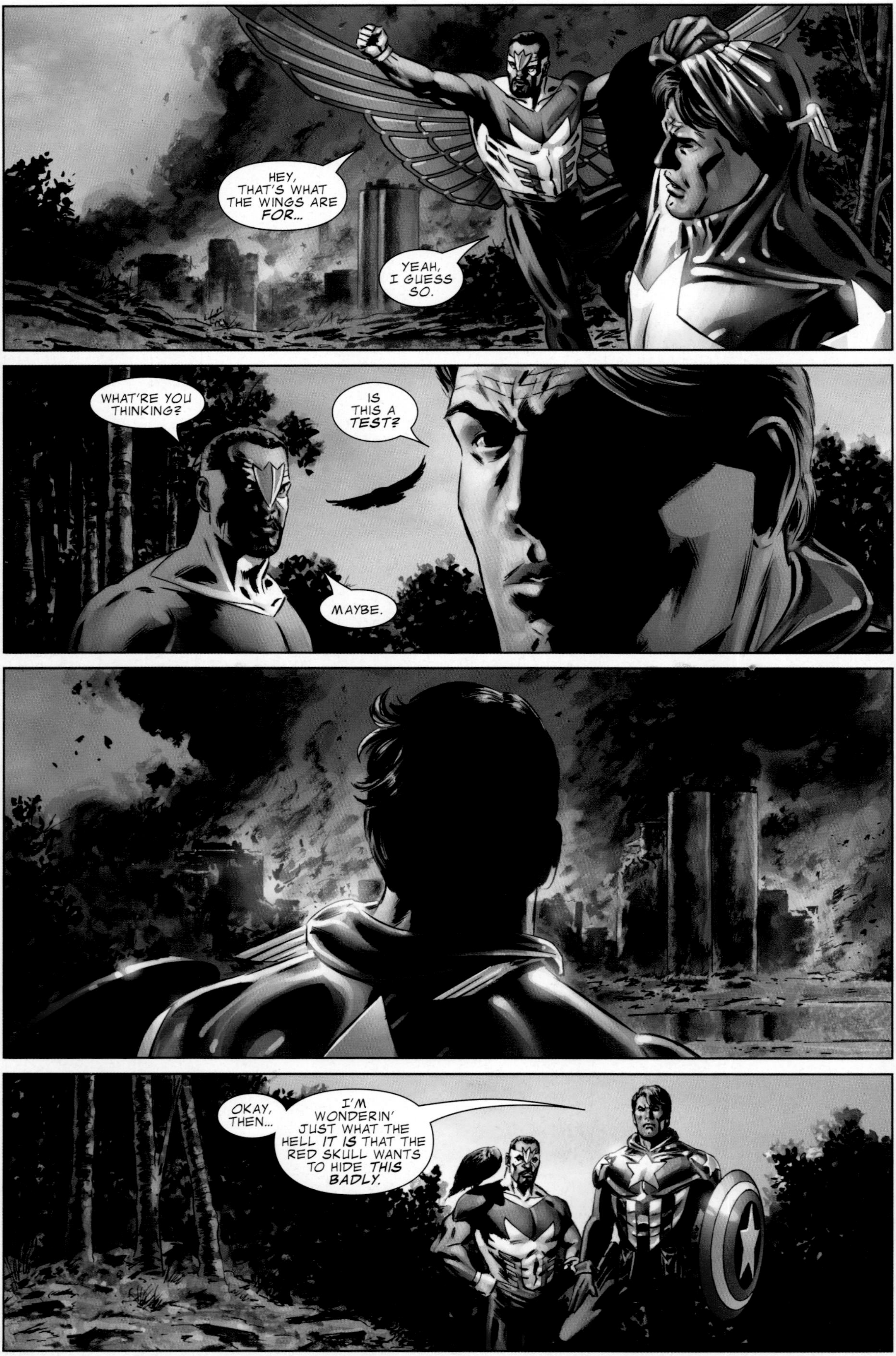
HEY, THAT'S WHAT THE WINGS ARE FOR...
YEAH, I GUESS SO.
WHAT'RE YOU THINKING?
IS THIS A TEST?
MAYBE.
OKAY, THEN...
I'M WONDERIN' JUST WHAT THE HELL IT IS THAT THE RED SKULL WANTS TO HIDE THIS BADLY.

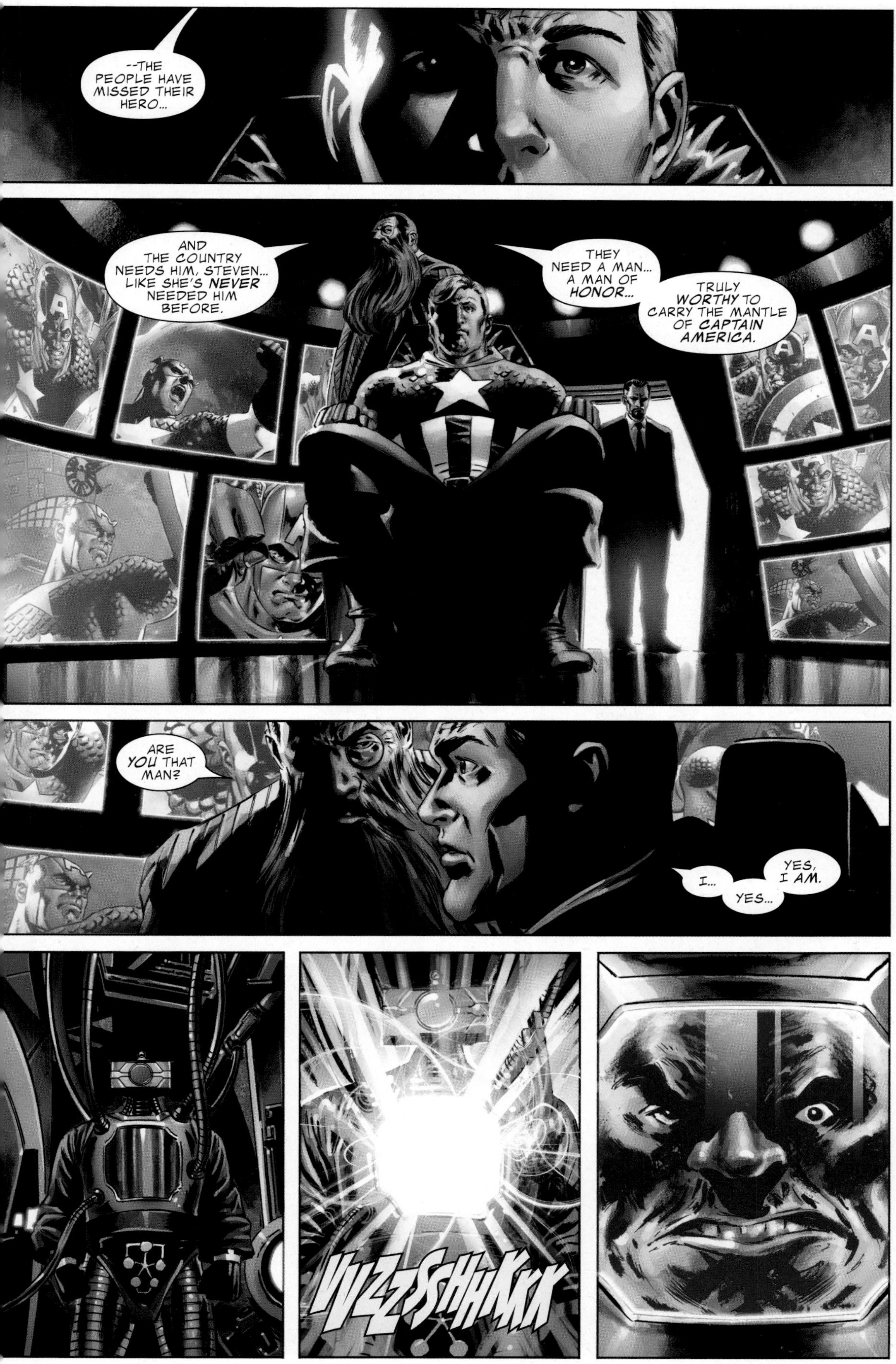
--THE PEOPLE HAVE MISSED THEIR HERO...
AND THE COUNTRY NEEDS HIM, STEVEN... LIKE SHE'S NEVER NEEDED HIM BEFORE.
THEY NEED A MAN... A MAN OF HONOR...
TRULY WORTHY TO CARRY THE MANTLE OF CAPTAIN AMERICA.
ARE YOU THAT MAN?
I...
YES...
YES, I AM.
VVZZSSHHKKKK

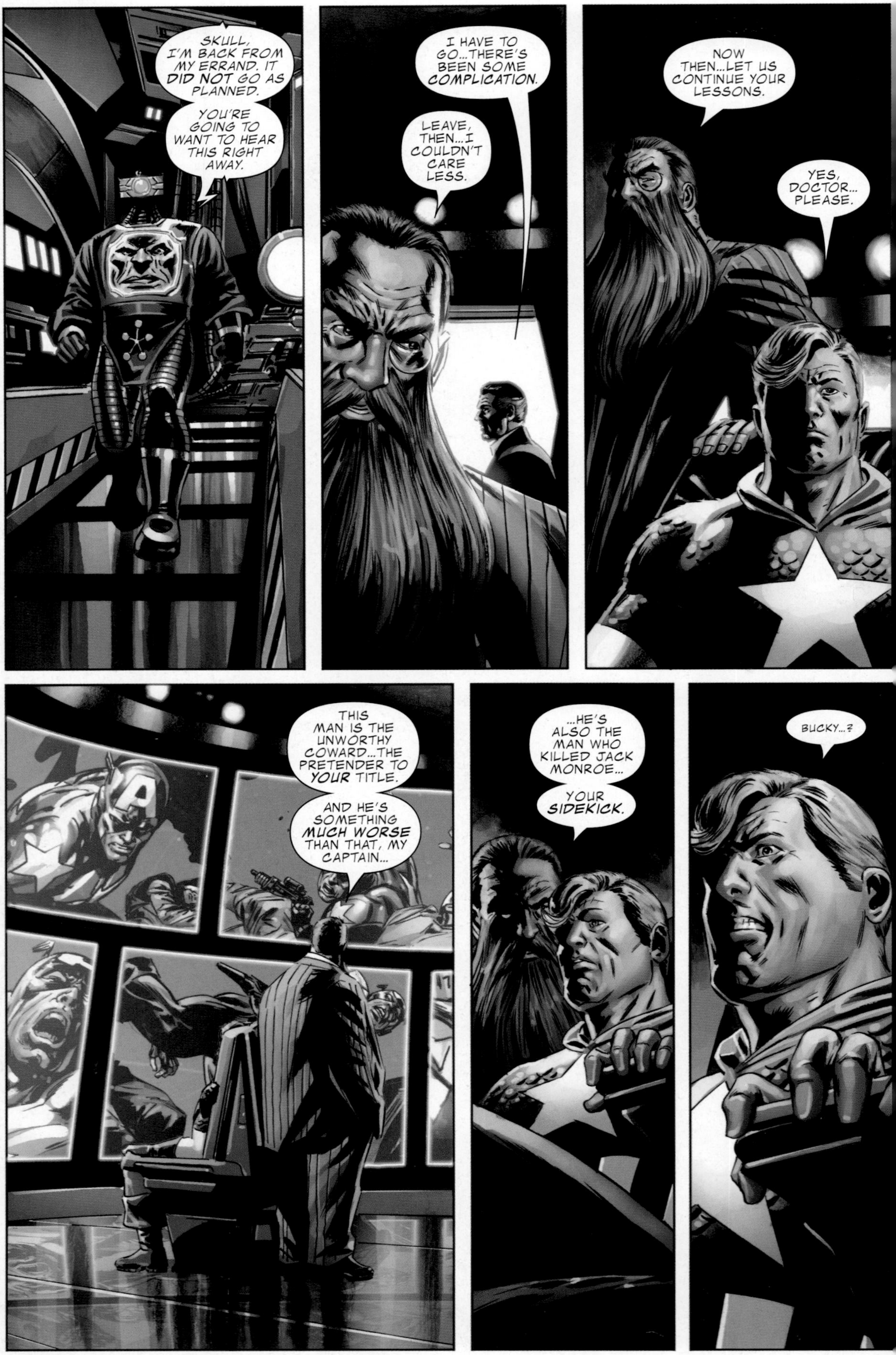
SKULL, I'M BACK FROM MY ERRAND. IT DID NOT GO AS PLANNED.
YOU'RE GOING TO WANT TO HEAR THIS RIGHT AWAY.
I HAVE TO GO...THERE'S BEEN SOME COMPLICATION.
LEAVE, THEN...I COULDN'T CARE LESS.
NOW THEN...LET US CONTINUE YOUR LESSONS.
YES, DOCTOR... PLEASE.
THIS MAN IS THE UNWORTHY COWARD...THE PRETENDER TO YOUR TITLE.
AND HE'S SOMETHING MUCH WORSE THAN THAT, MY CAPTAIN...
...HE'S ALSO THE MAN WHO KILLED JACK MONROE...
YOUR SIDEKICK.
BUCKY...?

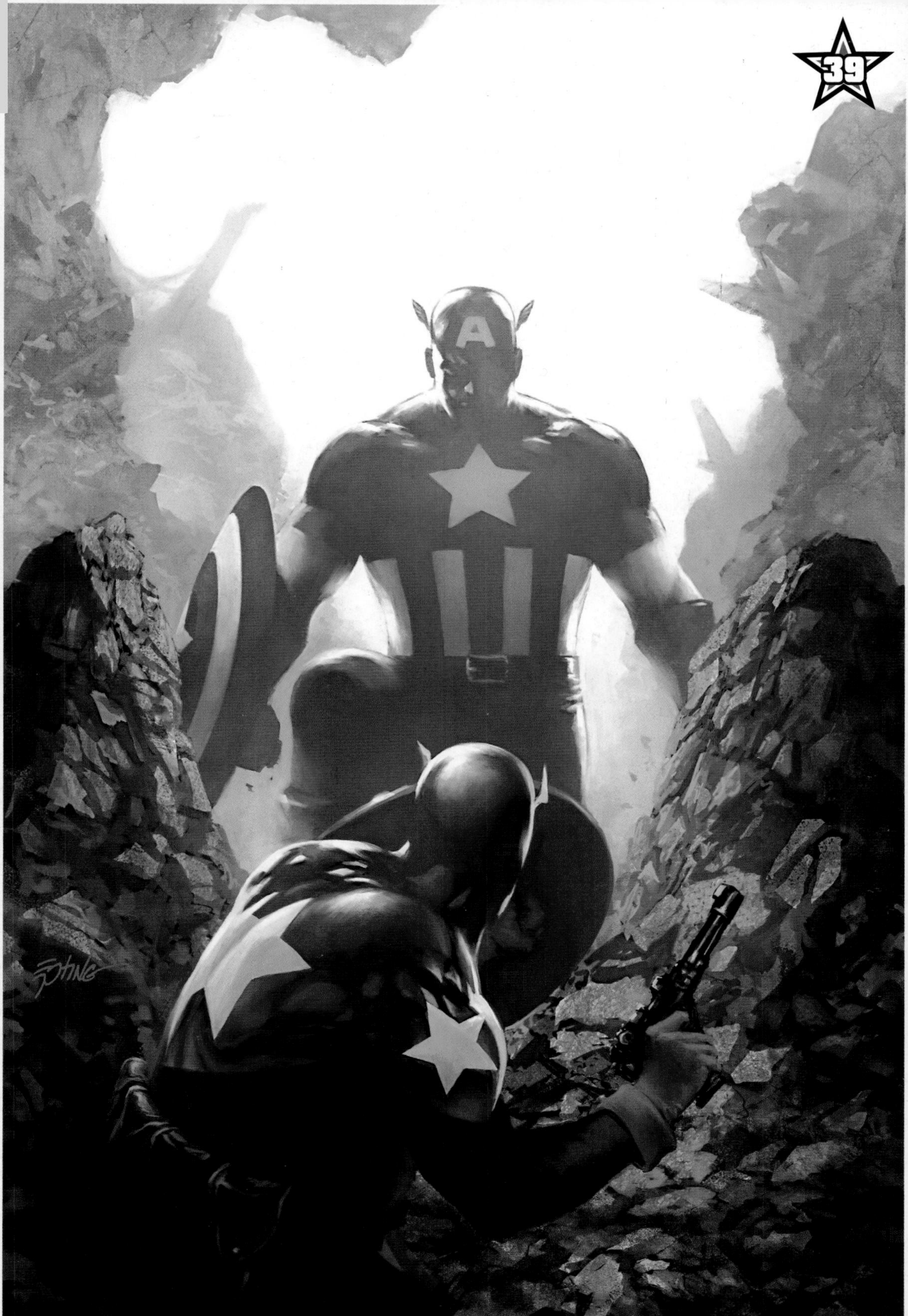
39

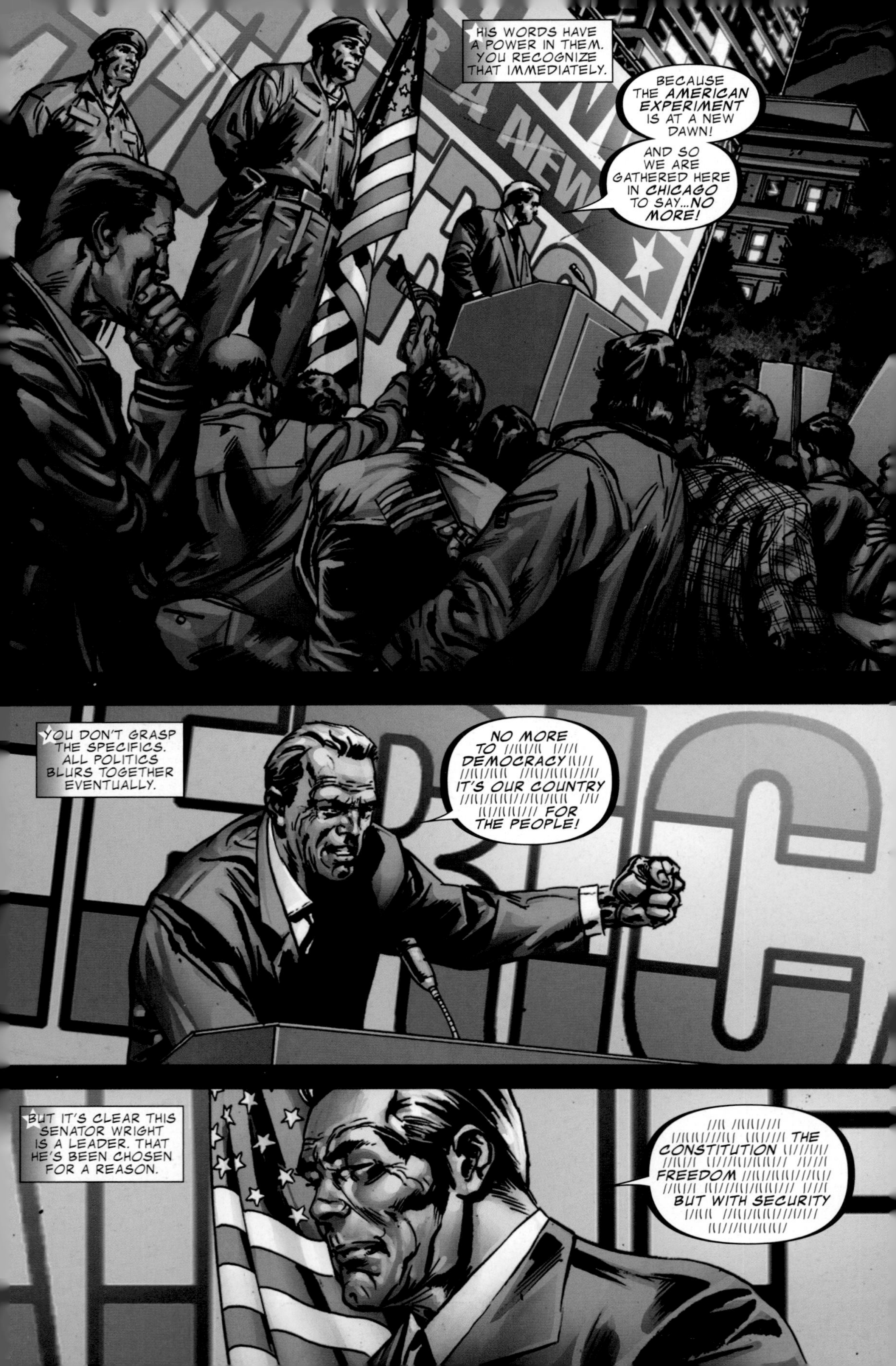
HIS WORDS HAVE A POWER IN THEM. YOU RECOGNIZE THAT IMMEDIATELY.
BECAUSE THE AMERICAN EXPERIMENT IS AT A NEW DAWN!
AND SO WE ARE GATHERED HERE IN CHICAGO TO SAY...NO MORE!
YOU DON'T GRASP THE SPECIFICS. ALL POLITICS BLURS TOGETHER EVENTUALLY.
NO MORE TO DEMOCRACY IT'S OUR COUNTRY FOR THE PEOPLE!
BUT IT'S CLEAR THIS SENATOR WRIGHT IS A LEADER. THAT HE'S BEEN CHOSEN FOR A REASON.
THE CONSTITUTION FREEDOM BUT WITH SECURITY

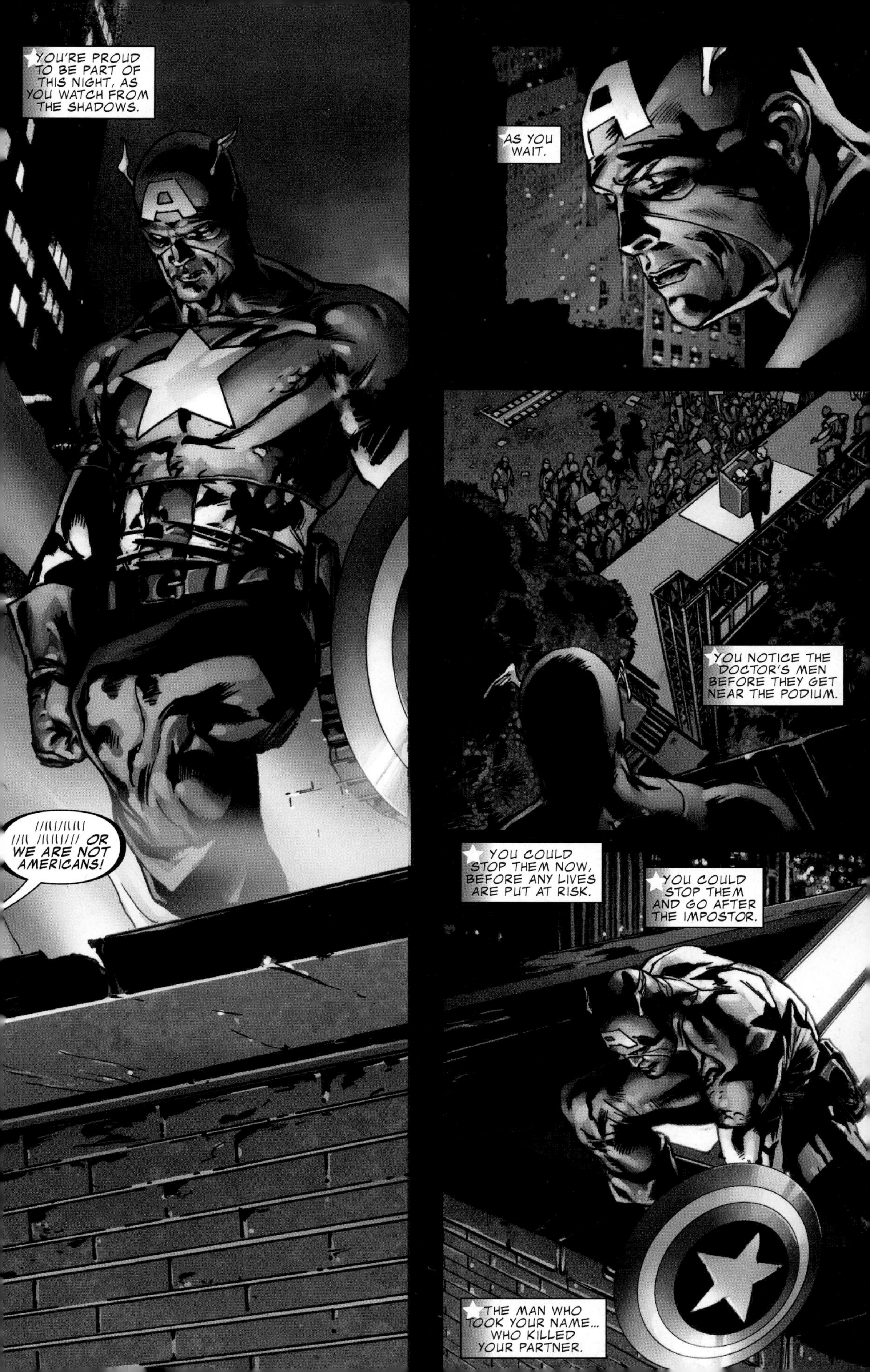
YOU'RE PROUD TO BE PART OF THIS NIGHT, AS YOU WATCH FROM THE SHADOWS.
//////// /// //////// OR WE ARE NOT AMERICANS!
AS YOU WAIT.
YOU NOTICE THE DOCTOR'S MEN BEFORE THEY GET NEAR THE PODIUM.
YOU COULD STOP THEM NOW, BEFORE ANY LIVES ARE PUT AT RISK.
YOU COULD STOP THEM AND GO AFTER THE IMPOSTOR.
THE MAN WHO TOOK YOUR NAME... WHO KILLED YOUR PARTNER.

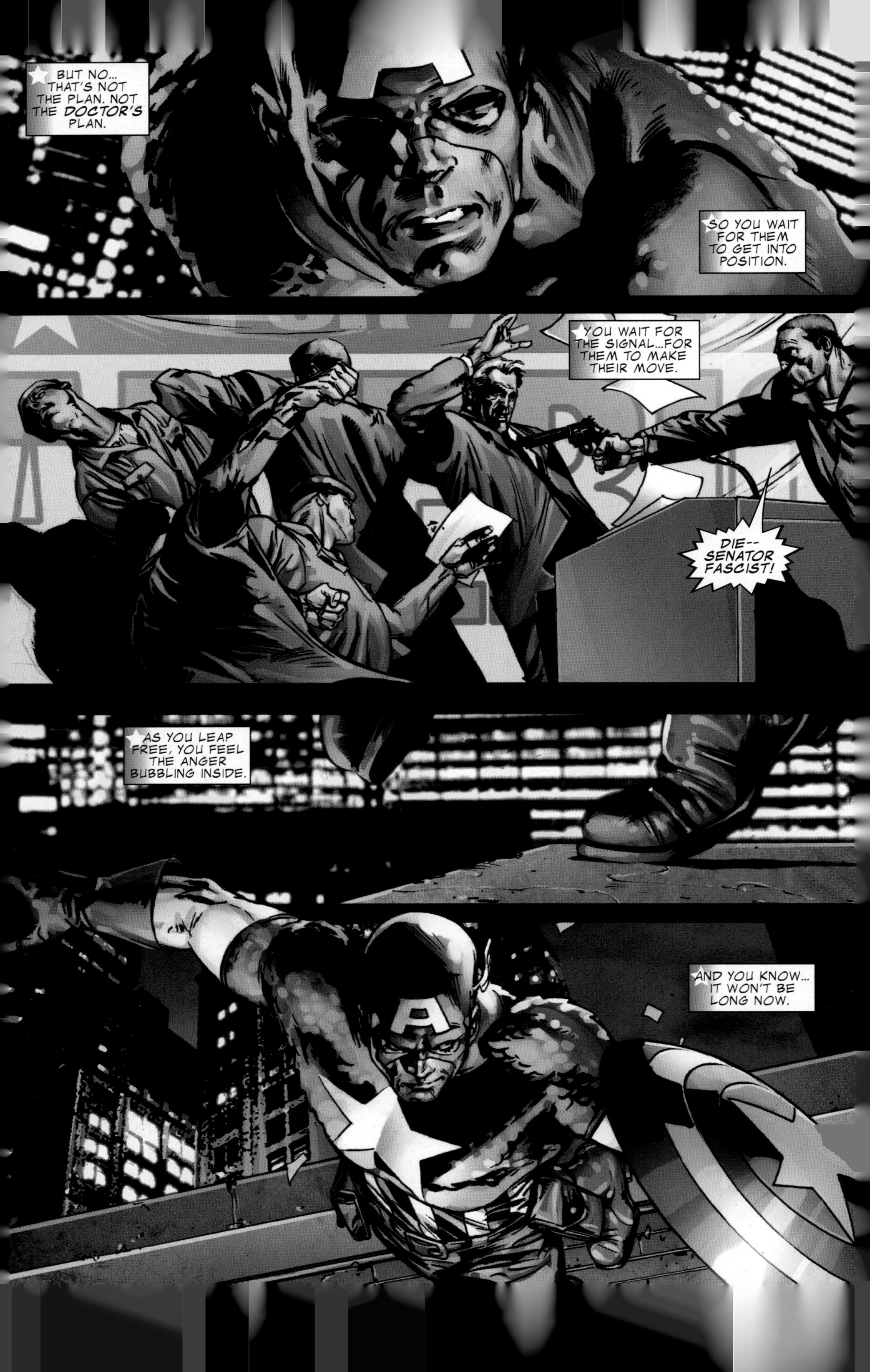
BUT NO... THAT'S NOT THE PLAN. NOT THE ***DOCTOR'S*** PLAN.
SO YOU WAIT FOR THEM TO GET INTO POSITION.
YOU WAIT FOR THE SIGNAL...FOR THEM TO MAKE THEIR MOVE.
DIE-- SENATOR FASCIST!
AS YOU LEAP FREE, YOU FEEL THE ANGER BUBBLING INSIDE.
AND YOU KNOW... IT WON'T BE LONG NOW.

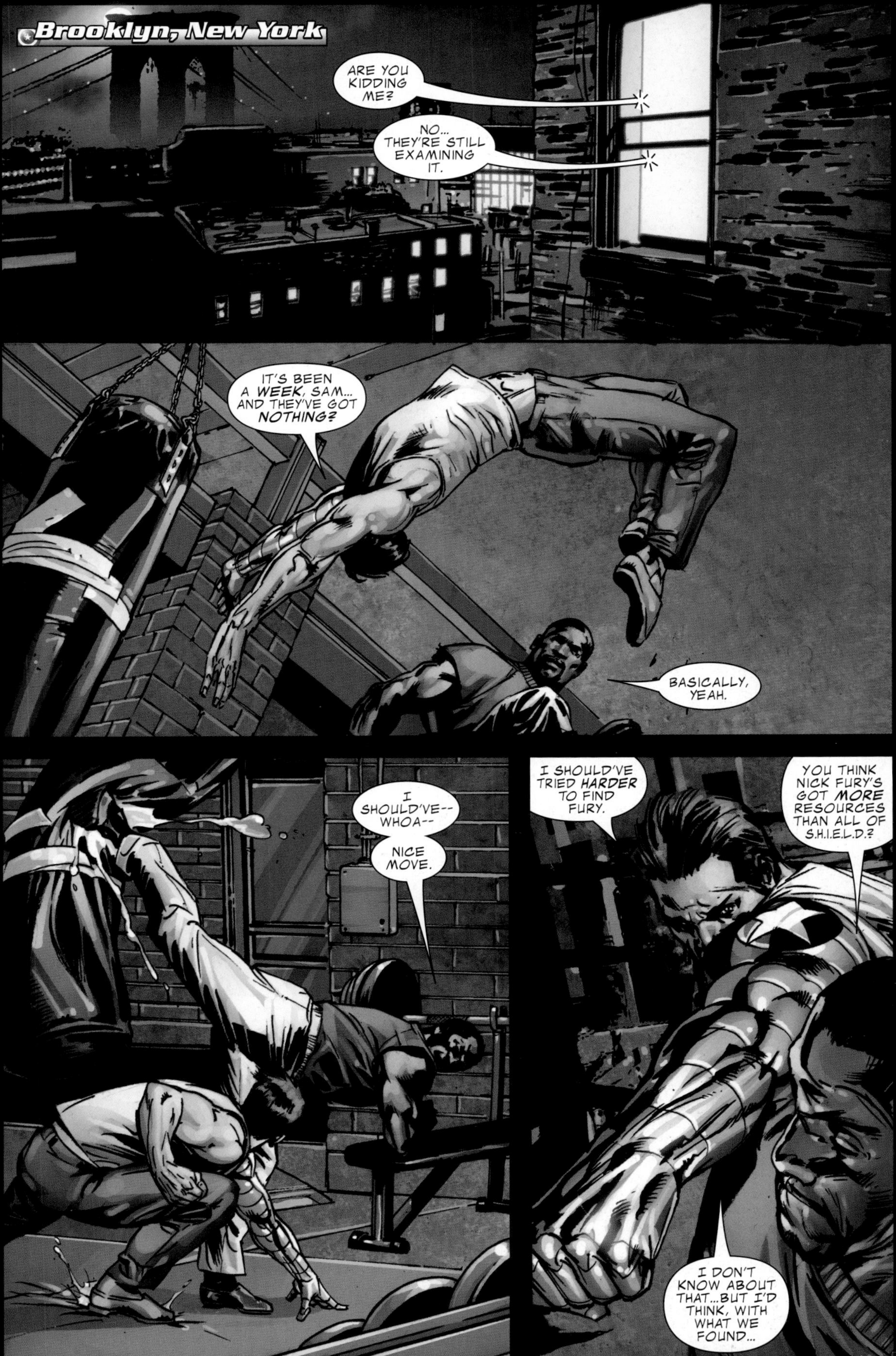
Brooklyn, New York
ARE YOU KIDDING ME?
NO... THEY'RE STILL EXAMINING IT.
IT'S BEEN A WEEK, SAM... AND THEY'VE GOT NOTHING?
BASICALLY, YEAH.
I SHOULD'VE-- WHOA--
NICE MOVE.
I SHOULD'VE TRIED HARDER TO FIND FURY.
YOU THINK NICK FURY'S GOT MORE RESOURCES THAN ALL OF S.H.I.E.L.D.?
I DON'T KNOW ABOUT THAT...BUT I'D THINK, WITH WHAT WE FOUND...

"...I MEAN, THAT THING WASN'T ALL JUNK."

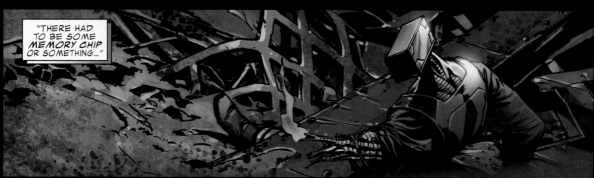

"THERE HAD TO BE SOME MEMORY CHIP OR SOMETHING..."

SOMETHING USEFUL.

BUT WITH S.H.I.E.L.D. SPREAD SO THIN LIKE THEY'VE BEEN...

THEY'RE DOING THEIR BEST, BUCKY.

BUT ARNIM ZOLA IS A GENIUS ON THE DOCTOR DOOM LEVEL...

GETTING ANY CLUE OUT OF ONE OF HIS HALF-DESTROYED ROBOT BODIES ISN'T GONNA BE EASY.

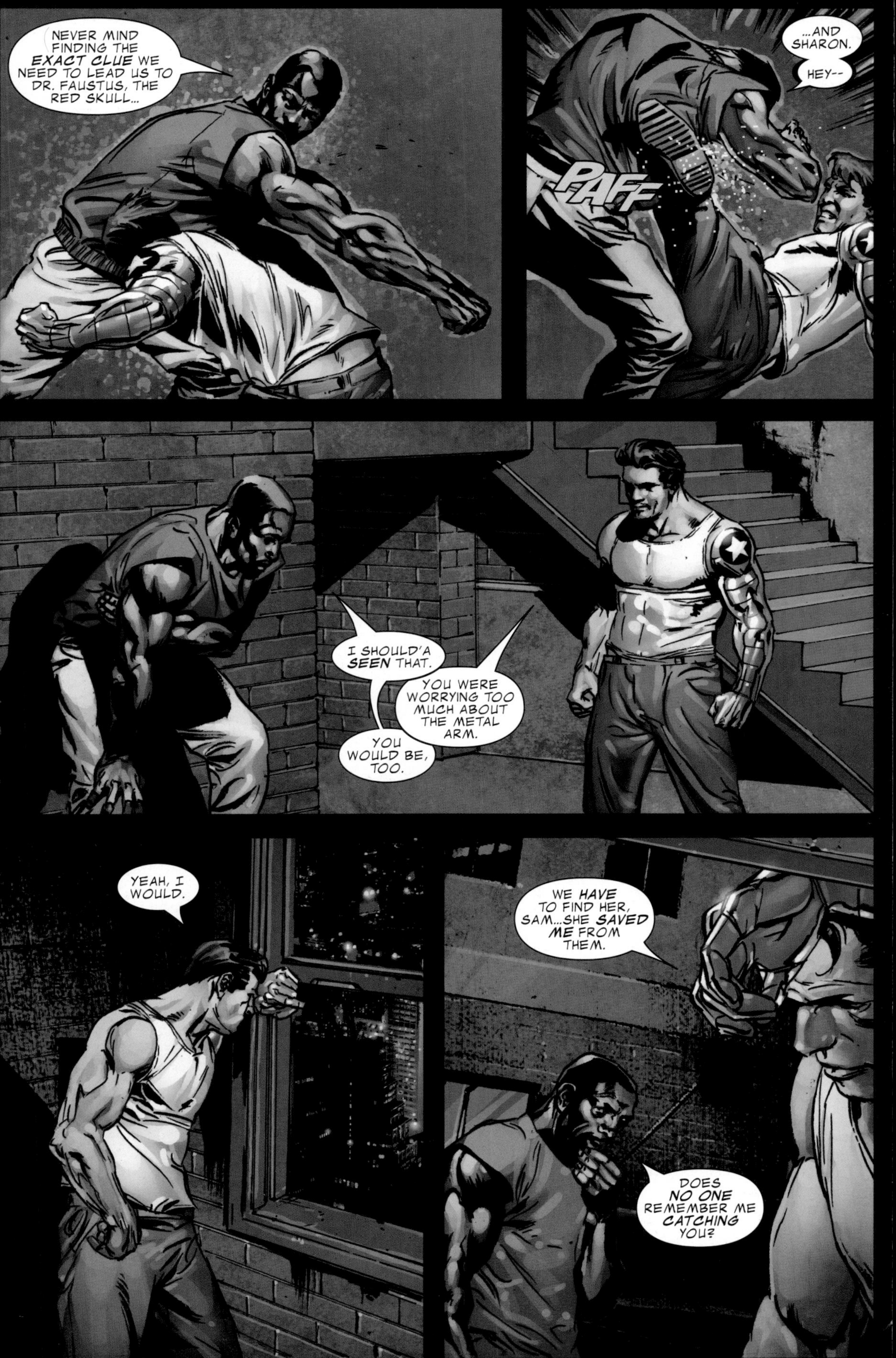
NEVER MIND FINDING THE EXACT CLUE WE NEED TO LEAD US TO DR. FAUSTUS, THE RED SKULL...
...AND SHARON.
HEY--
PAFF
I SHOULD'A SEEN THAT.
YOU WERE WORRYING TOO MUCH ABOUT THE METAL ARM.
YOU WOULD BE, TOO.
YEAH, I WOULD.
WE HAVE TO FIND HER, SAM...SHE SAVED ME FROM THEM.
DOES NO ONE REMEMBER ME CATCHING YOU?

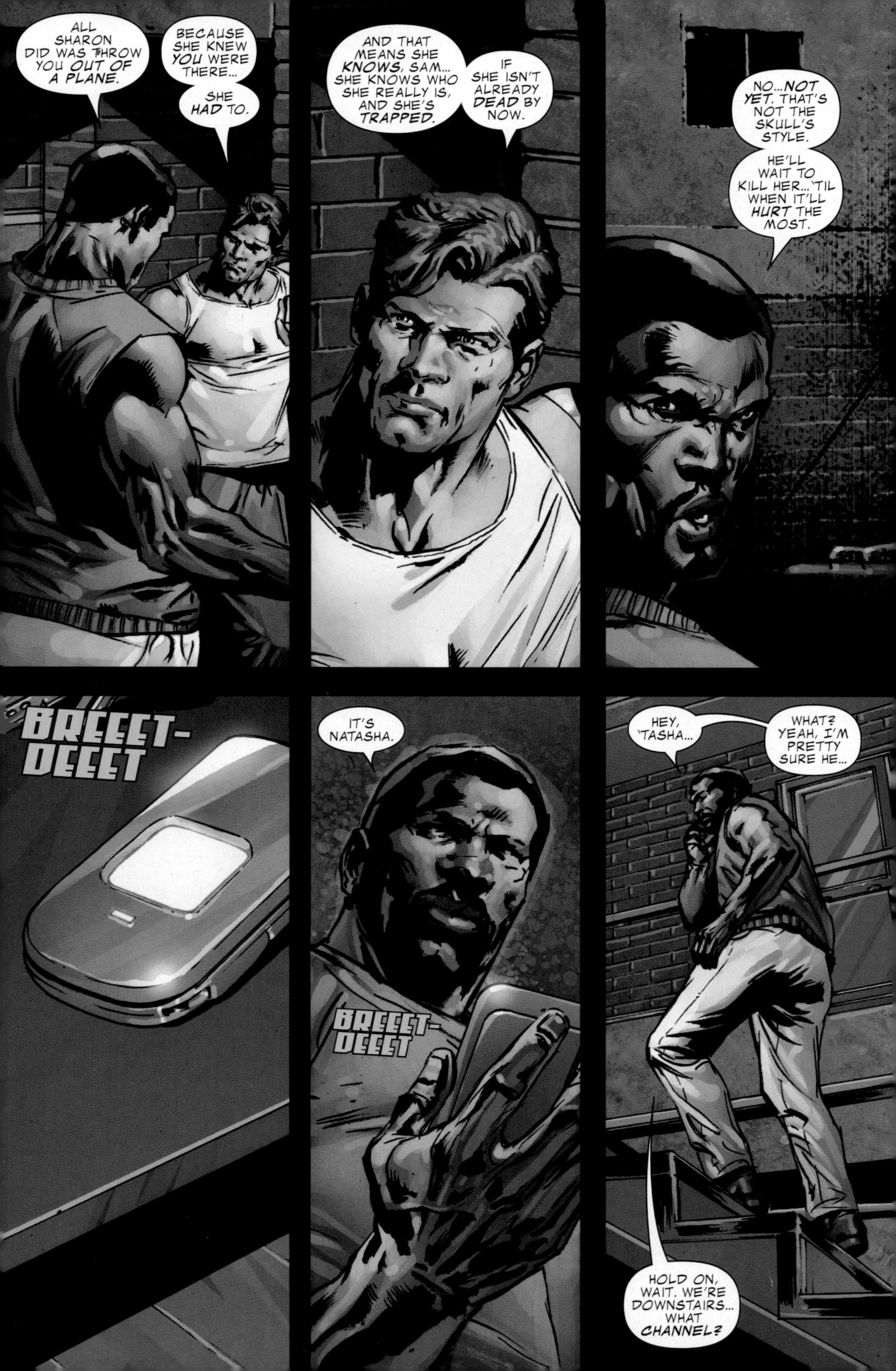
ALL SHARON DID WAS THROW YOU OUT OF A PLANE.
BECAUSE SHE KNEW YOU WERE THERE...
SHE HAD TO.
AND THAT MEANS SHE KNOWS, SAM... SHE KNOWS WHO SHE REALLY IS, AND SHE'S TRAPPED.
IF SHE ISN'T ALREADY DEAD BY NOW.
NO...NOT YET. THAT'S NOT THE SKULL'S STYLE.
HE'LL WAIT TO KILL HER...'TIL WHEN IT'LL HURT THE MOST.
BREEET-DEEET
IT'S NATASHA.
BREEET-DEEET
HEY, 'TASHA...
WHAT? YEAH, I'M PRETTY SURE HE...
HOLD ON, WAIT. WE'RE DOWNSTAIRS... WHAT CHANNEL?

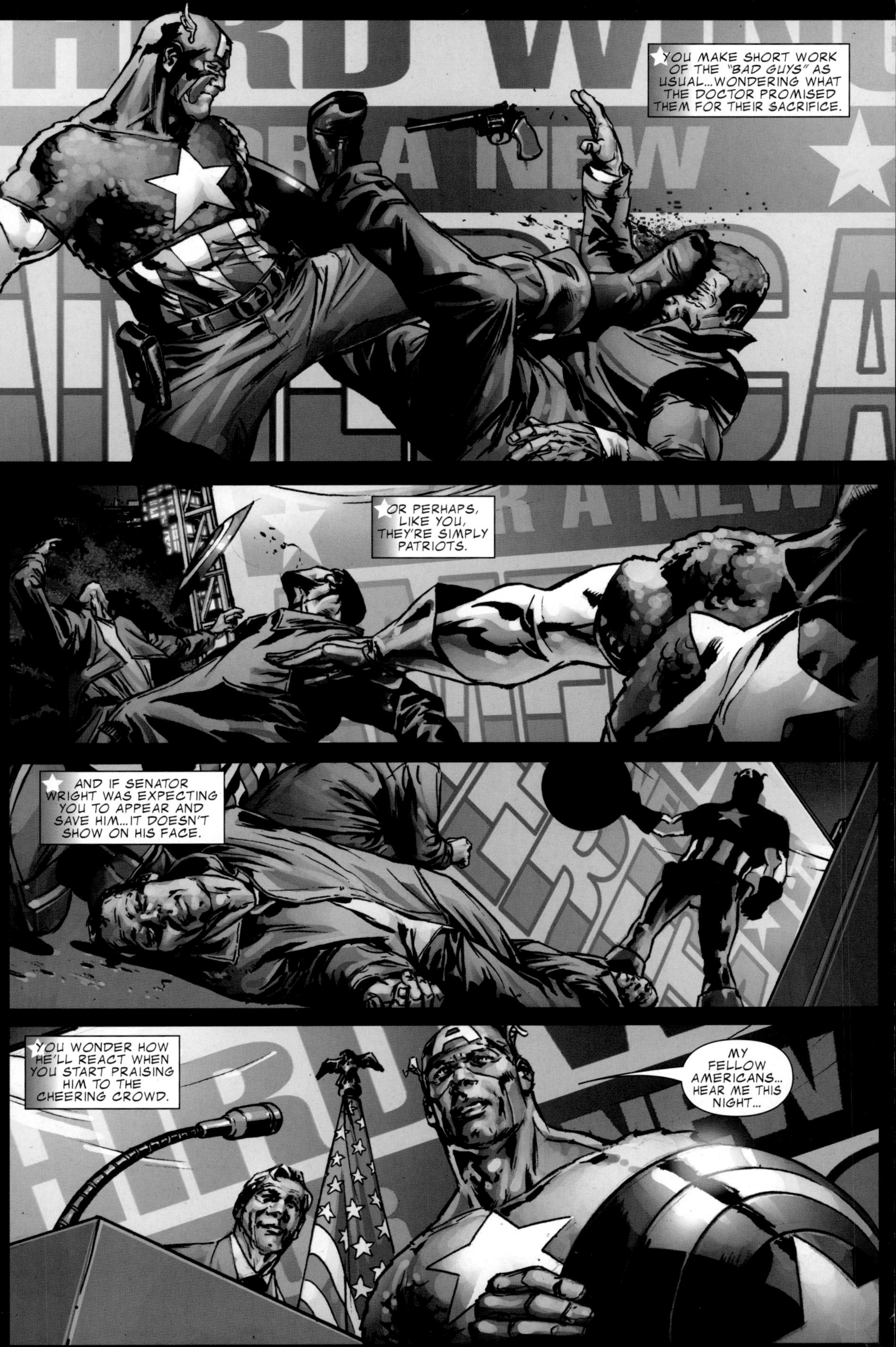
YOU MAKE SHORT WORK OF THE "BAD GUYS" AS USUAL...WONDERING WHAT THE DOCTOR PROMISED THEM FOR THEIR SACRIFICE.
OR PERHAPS, LIKE YOU, THEY'RE SIMPLY PATRIOTS.
AND IF SENATOR WRIGHT WAS EXPECTING YOU TO APPEAR AND SAVE HIM...IT DOESN'T SHOW ON HIS FACE.
YOU WONDER HOW HE'LL REACT WHEN YOU START PRAISING HIM TO THE CHEERING CROWD.
MY FELLOW AMERICANS... HEAR ME THIS NIGHT...

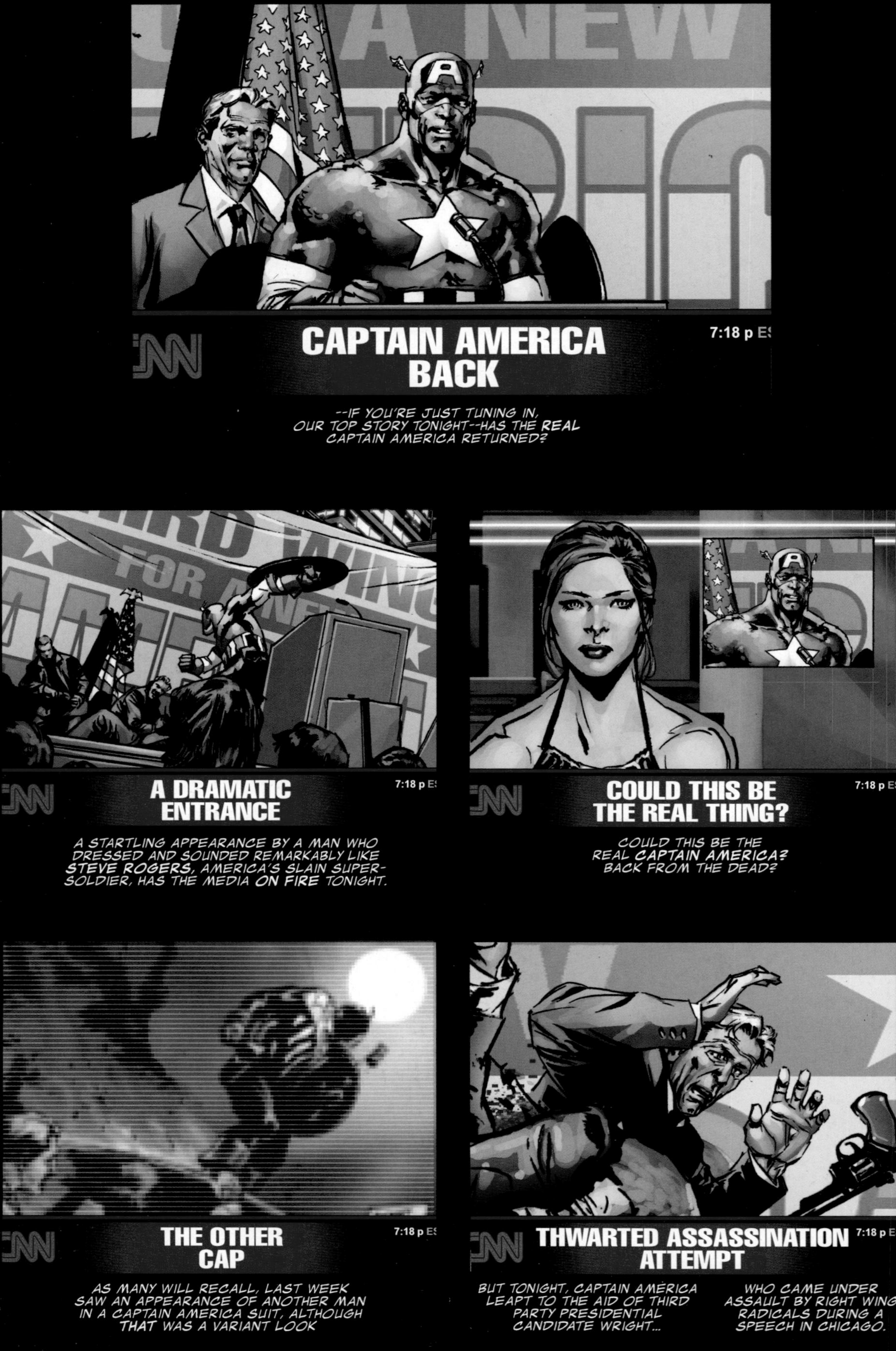
CAPTAIN AMERICA BACK
7:18 p
--IF YOU'RE JUST TUNING IN, OUR TOP STORY TONIGHT--HAS THE REAL CAPTAIN AMERICA RETURNED?
A DRAMATIC ENTRANCE
7:18 p
A STARTLING APPEARANCE BY A MAN WHO DRESSED AND SOUNDED REMARKABLY LIKE STEVE ROGERS, AMERICA'S SLAIN SUPER-SOLDIER, HAS THE MEDIA ON FIRE TONIGHT.
COULD THIS BE THE REAL THING?
7:18 p
COULD THIS BE THE REAL CAPTAIN AMERICA? BACK FROM THE DEAD?
THE OTHER CAP
7:18 p
AS MANY WILL RECALL, LAST WEEK SAW AN APPEARANCE OF ANOTHER MAN IN A CAPTAIN AMERICA SUIT, ALTHOUGH THAT WAS A VARIANT LOOK
THWARTED ASSASSINATION ATTEMPT
7:18 p
BUT TONIGHT, CAPTAIN AMERICA LEAPT TO THE AID OF THIRD PARTY PRESIDENTIAL CANDIDATE WRIGHT...
WHO CAME UNDER ASSAULT BY RIGHT WING RADICALS DURING A SPEECH IN CHICAGO.

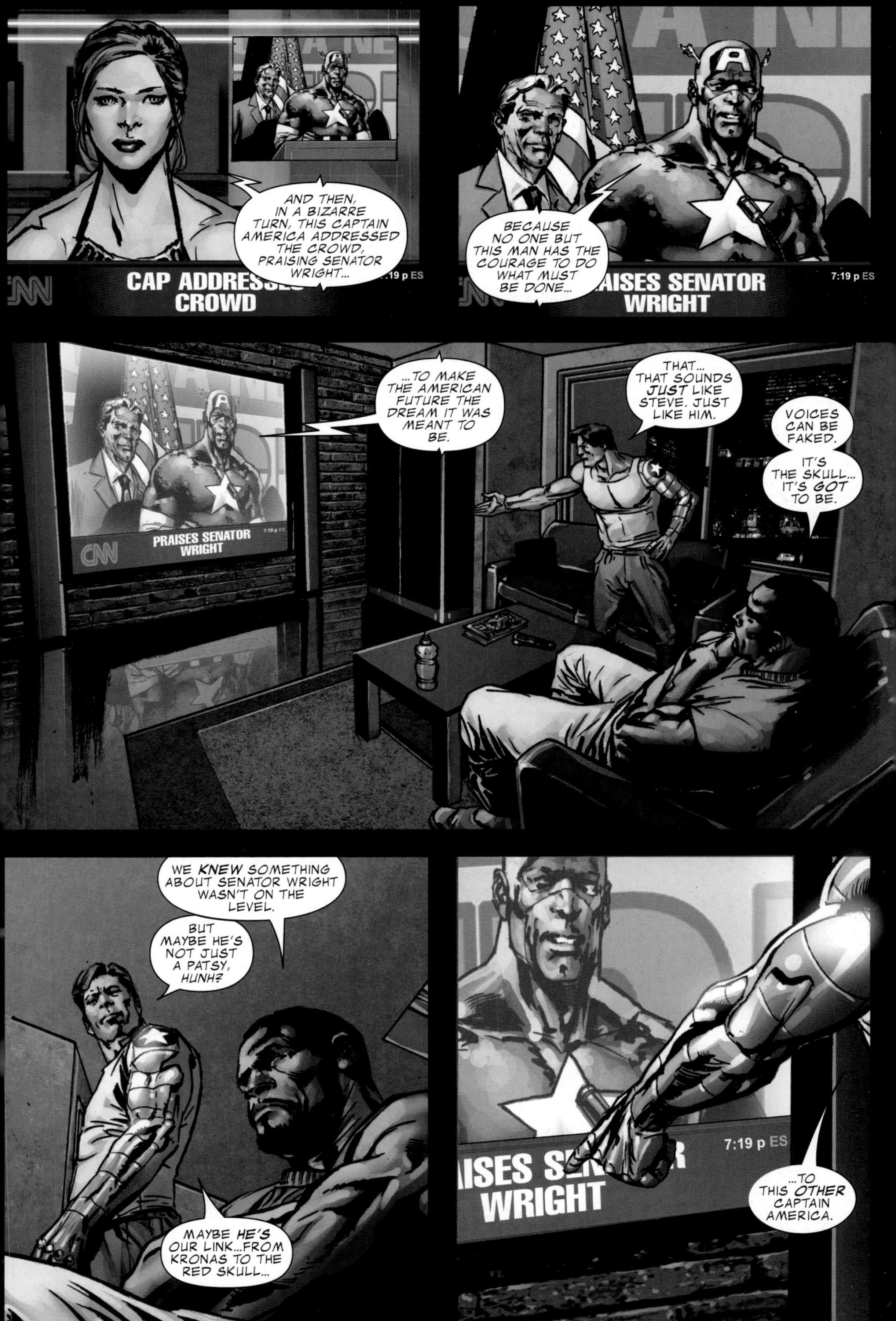
CAP ADDRESSES CROWD
7:19 p ES
AND THEN, IN A BIZARRE TURN, THIS CAPTAIN AMERICA ADDRESSED THE CROWD, PRAISING SENATOR WRIGHT...
PRAISES SENATOR WRIGHT
7:19 p ES
BECAUSE NO ONE BUT THIS MAN HAS THE COURAGE TO DO WHAT MUST BE DONE...
PRAISES SENATOR WRIGHT
...TO MAKE THE AMERICAN FUTURE THE DREAM IT WAS MEANT TO BE.
THAT... THAT SOUNDS JUST LIKE STEVE. JUST LIKE HIM.
VOICES CAN BE FAKED.
IT'S THE SKULL... IT'S GOT TO BE.
WE KNEW SOMETHING ABOUT SENATOR WRIGHT WASN'T ON THE LEVEL.
BUT MAYBE HE'S NOT JUST A PATSY, HUNH?
MAYBE HE'S OUR LINK...FROM KRONAS TO THE RED SKULL...
7:19 p ES
...TO THIS OTHER CAPTAIN AMERICA.

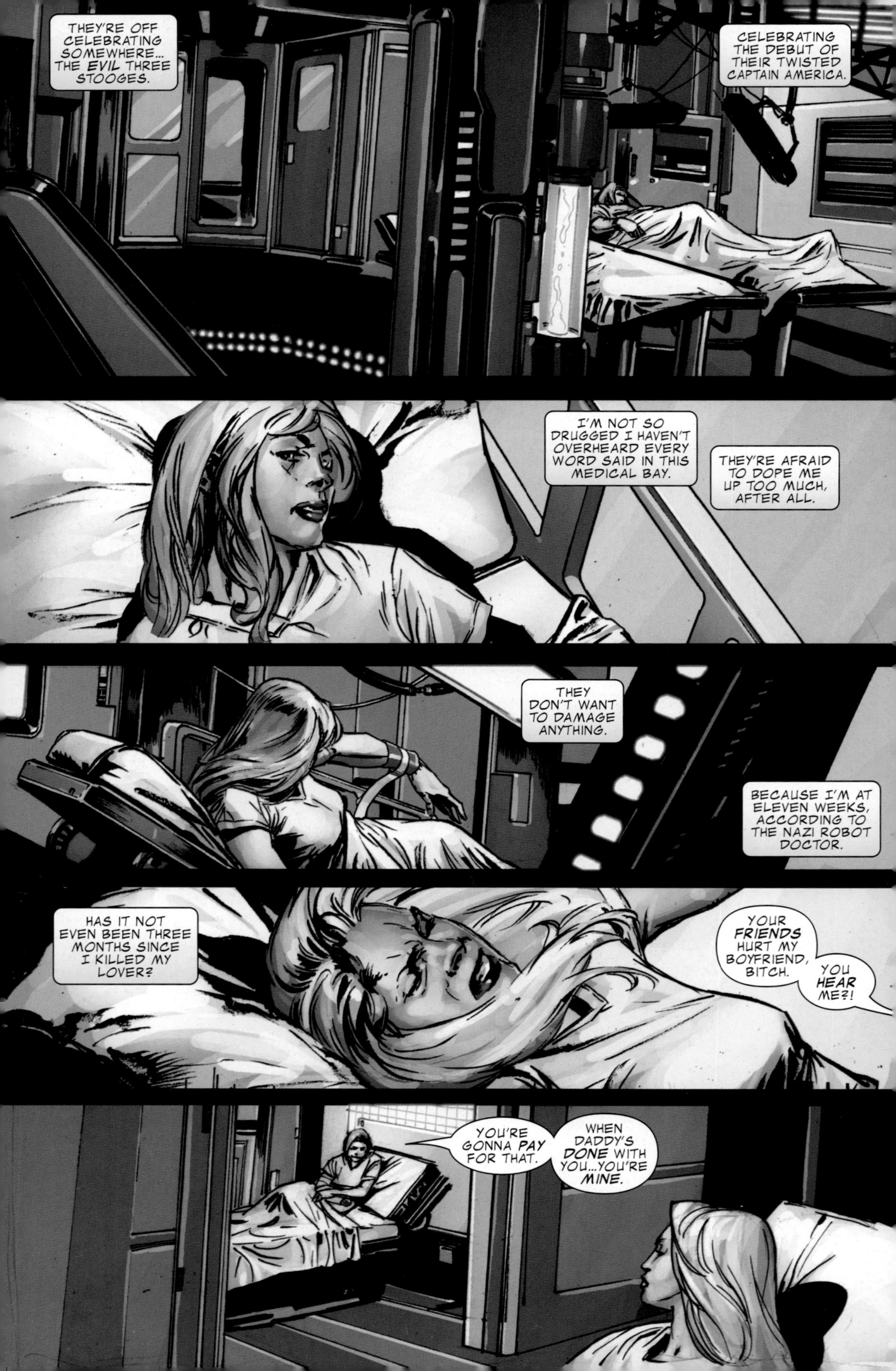
THEY'RE OFF CELEBRATING SOMEWHERE... THE EVIL THREE STOOGES.
CELEBRATING THE DEBUT OF THEIR TWISTED CAPTAIN AMERICA.
I'M NOT SO DRUGGED I HAVEN'T OVERHEARD EVERY WORD SAID IN THIS MEDICAL BAY.
THEY'RE AFRAID TO DOPE ME UP TOO MUCH, AFTER ALL.
THEY DON'T WANT TO DAMAGE ANYTHING.
BECAUSE I'M AT ELEVEN WEEKS, ACCORDING TO THE NAZI ROBOT DOCTOR.
HAS IT NOT EVEN BEEN THREE MONTHS SINCE I KILLED MY LOVER?
YOUR FRIENDS HURT MY BOYFRIEND, BITCH.
YOU HEAR ME?!
YOU'RE GONNA PAY FOR THAT.
WHEN DADDY'S DONE WITH YOU...YOU'RE MINE.

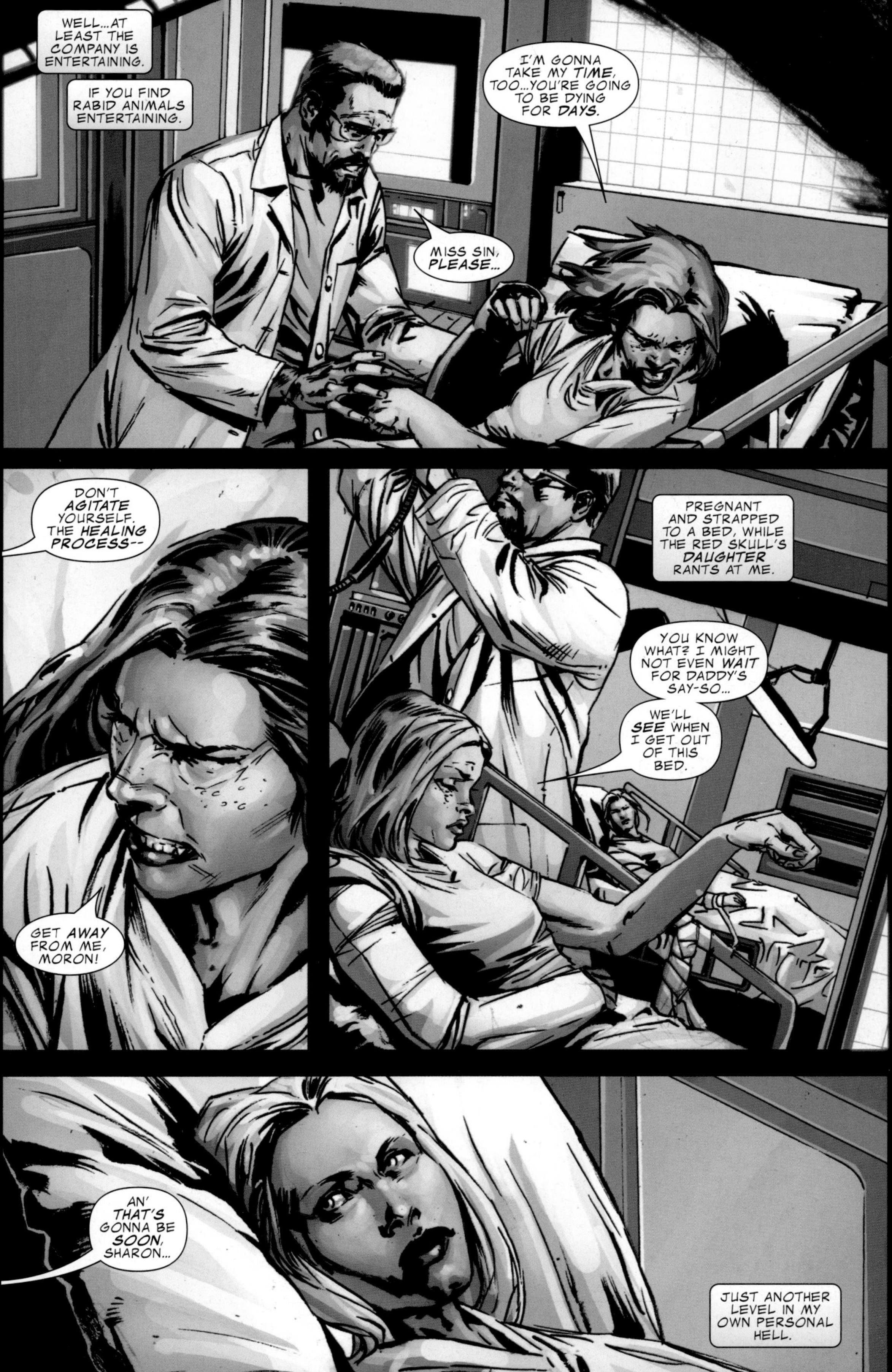
WELL...AT LEAST THE COMPANY IS ENTERTAINING.
IF YOU FIND RABID ANIMALS ENTERTAINING.
I'M GONNA TAKE MY TIME, TOO...YOU'RE GOING TO BE DYING FOR DAYS.
MISS SIN, PLEASE...
DON'T AGITATE YOURSELF. THE HEALING PROCESS--
GET AWAY FROM ME, MORON!
PREGNANT AND STRAPPED TO A BED, WHILE THE RED SKULL'S DAUGHTER RANTS AT ME.
YOU KNOW WHAT? I MIGHT NOT EVEN WAIT FOR DADDY'S SAY-SO...
WE'LL SEE WHEN I GET OUT OF THIS BED.
AN' THAT'S GONNA BE SOON, SHARON...
JUST ANOTHER LEVEL IN MY OWN PERSONAL HELL.

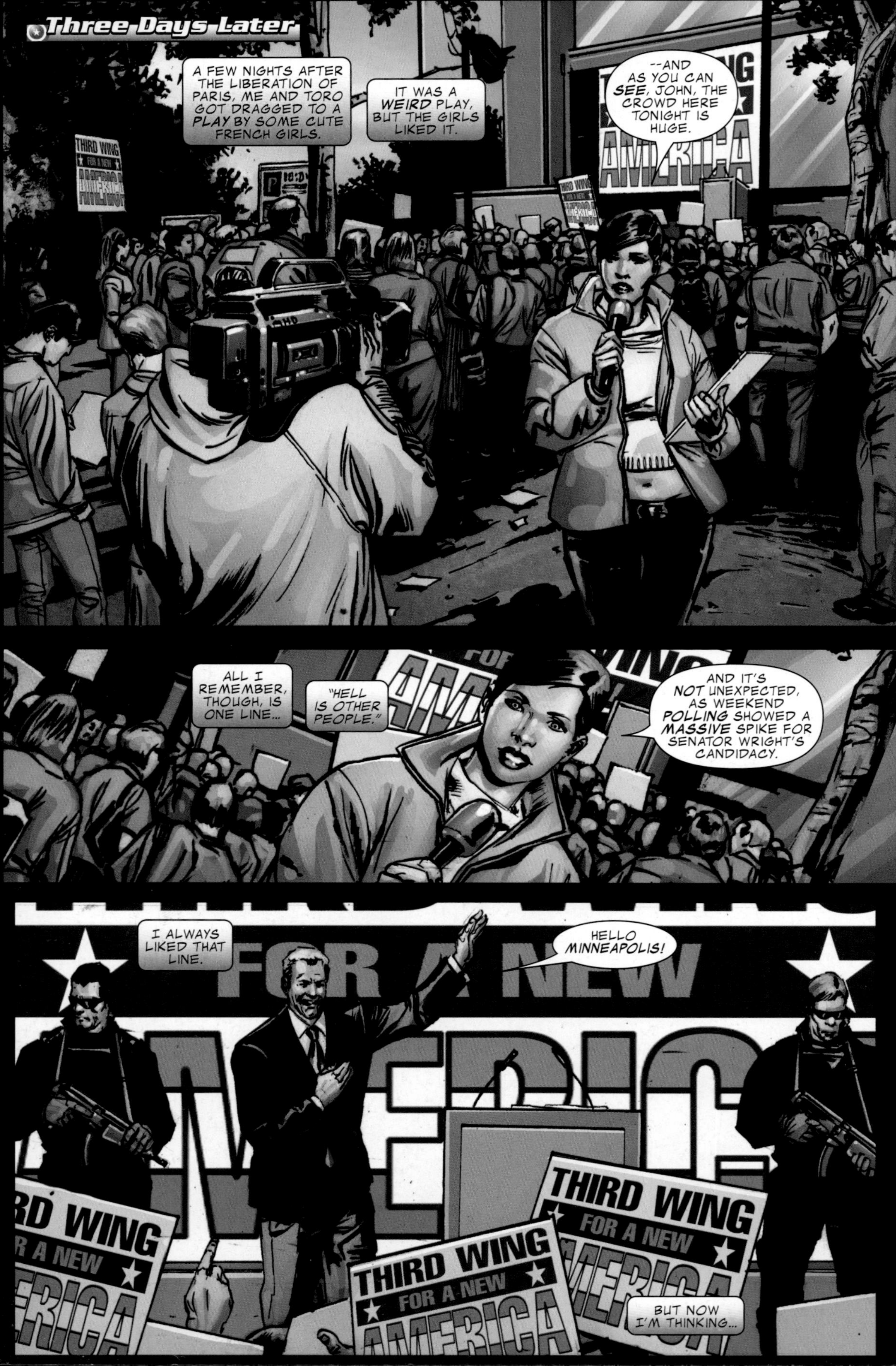
Three Days Later
A FEW NIGHTS AFTER THE LIBERATION OF PARIS, ME AND TORO GOT DRAGGED TO A PLAY BY SOME CUTE FRENCH GIRLS.
IT WAS A WEIRD PLAY, BUT THE GIRLS LIKED IT.
--AND AS YOU CAN SEE, JOHN, THE CROWD HERE TONIGHT IS HUGE.
THIRD WING ★ FOR A NEW AMERICA
ALL I REMEMBER, THOUGH, IS ONE LINE...
"HELL IS OTHER PEOPLE."
AND IT'S NOT UNEXPECTED, AS WEEKEND POLLING SHOWED A MASSIVE SPIKE FOR SENATOR WRIGHT'S CANDIDACY.
I ALWAYS LIKED THAT LINE.
HELLO MINNEAPOLIS!
FOR A NEW
THIRD WING FOR A NEW AMERICA
BUT NOW I'M THINKING...

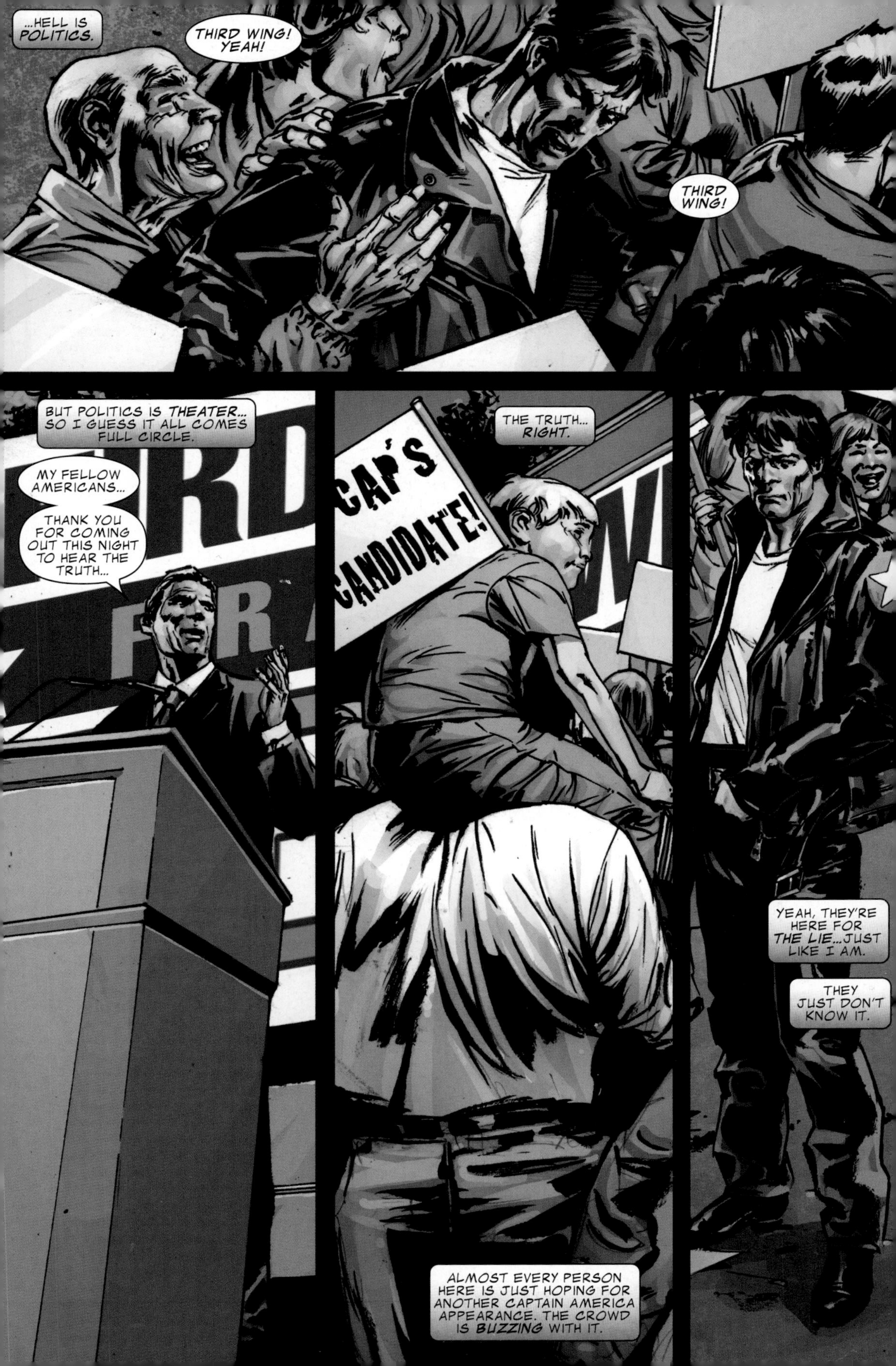
...HELL IS POLITICS.
THIRD WING! YEAH!
THIRD WING!
BUT POLITICS IS THEATER... SO I GUESS IT ALL COMES FULL CIRCLE.
MY FELLOW AMERICANS...
THANK YOU FOR COMING OUT THIS NIGHT TO HEAR THE TRUTH...
CAP'S CANDIDATE!
THE TRUTH... RIGHT.
ALMOST EVERY PERSON HERE IS JUST HOPING FOR ANOTHER CAPTAIN AMERICA APPEARANCE. THE CROWD IS BUZZING WITH IT.
YEAH, THEY'RE HERE FOR THE LIE...JUST LIKE I AM.
THEY JUST DON'T KNOW IT.

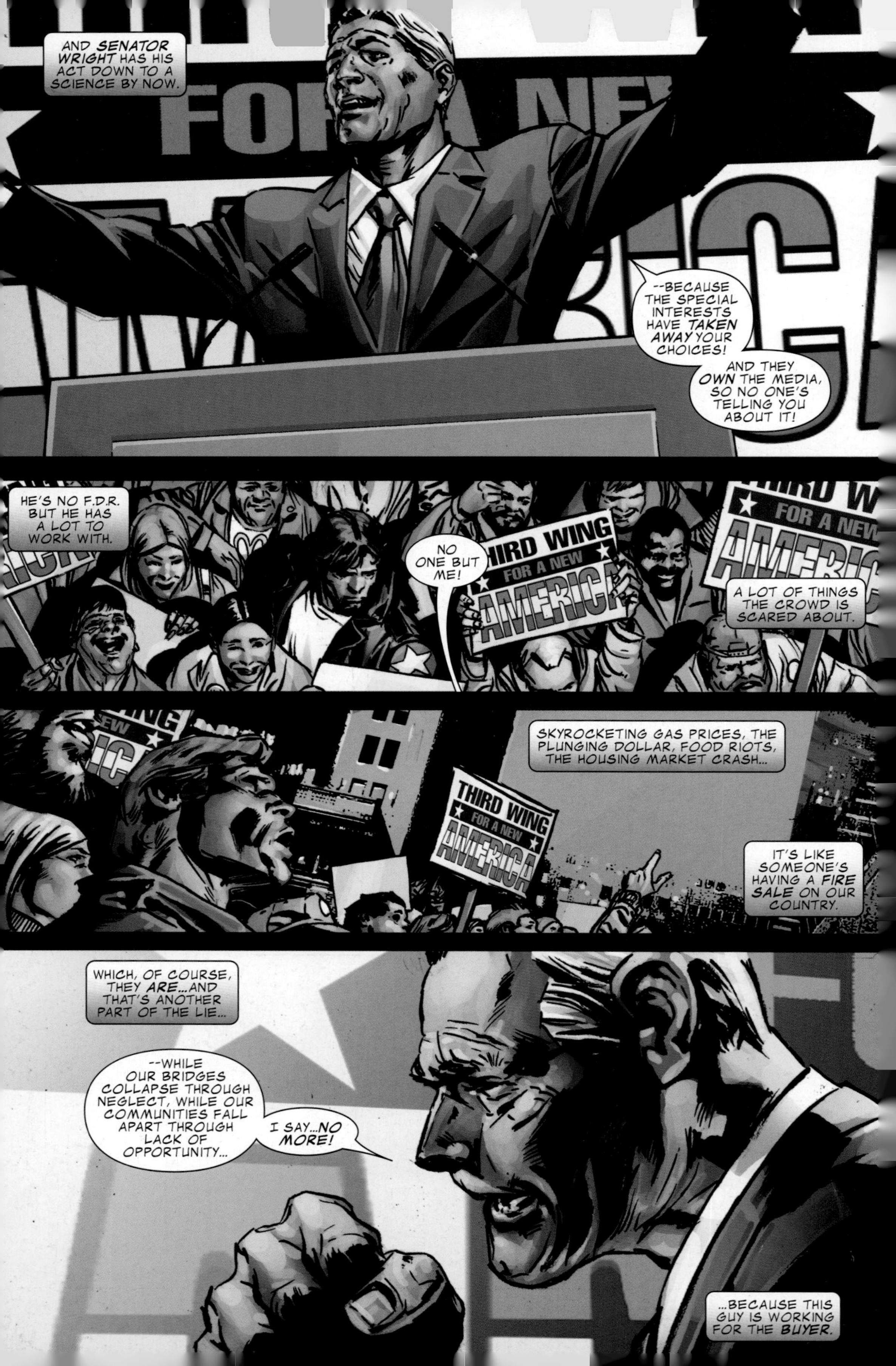

FOR A NEW
AMERICA
AND SENATOR WRIGHT HAS HIS ACT DOWN TO A SCIENCE BY NOW.
--BECAUSE THE SPECIAL INTERESTS HAVE TAKEN AWAY YOUR CHOICES!
AND THEY OWN THE MEDIA, SO NO ONE'S TELLING YOU ABOUT IT!
HE'S NO F.D.R. BUT HE HAS A LOT TO WORK WITH.
NO ONE BUT ME!
THIRD WING FOR A NEW AMERICA
A LOT OF THINGS THE CROWD IS SCARED ABOUT.
SKYROCKETING GAS PRICES, THE PLUNGING DOLLAR, FOOD RIOTS, THE HOUSING MARKET CRASH...
THIRD WING FOR A NEW AMERICA
IT'S LIKE SOMEONE'S HAVING A FIRE SALE ON OUR COUNTRY.
WHICH, OF COURSE, THEY ARE...AND THAT'S ANOTHER PART OF THE LIE...
--WHILE OUR BRIDGES COLLAPSE THROUGH NEGLECT, WHILE OUR COMMUNITIES FALL APART THROUGH LACK OF OPPORTUNITY...
I SAY...NO MORE!
...BECAUSE THIS GUY IS WORKING FOR THE BUYER.

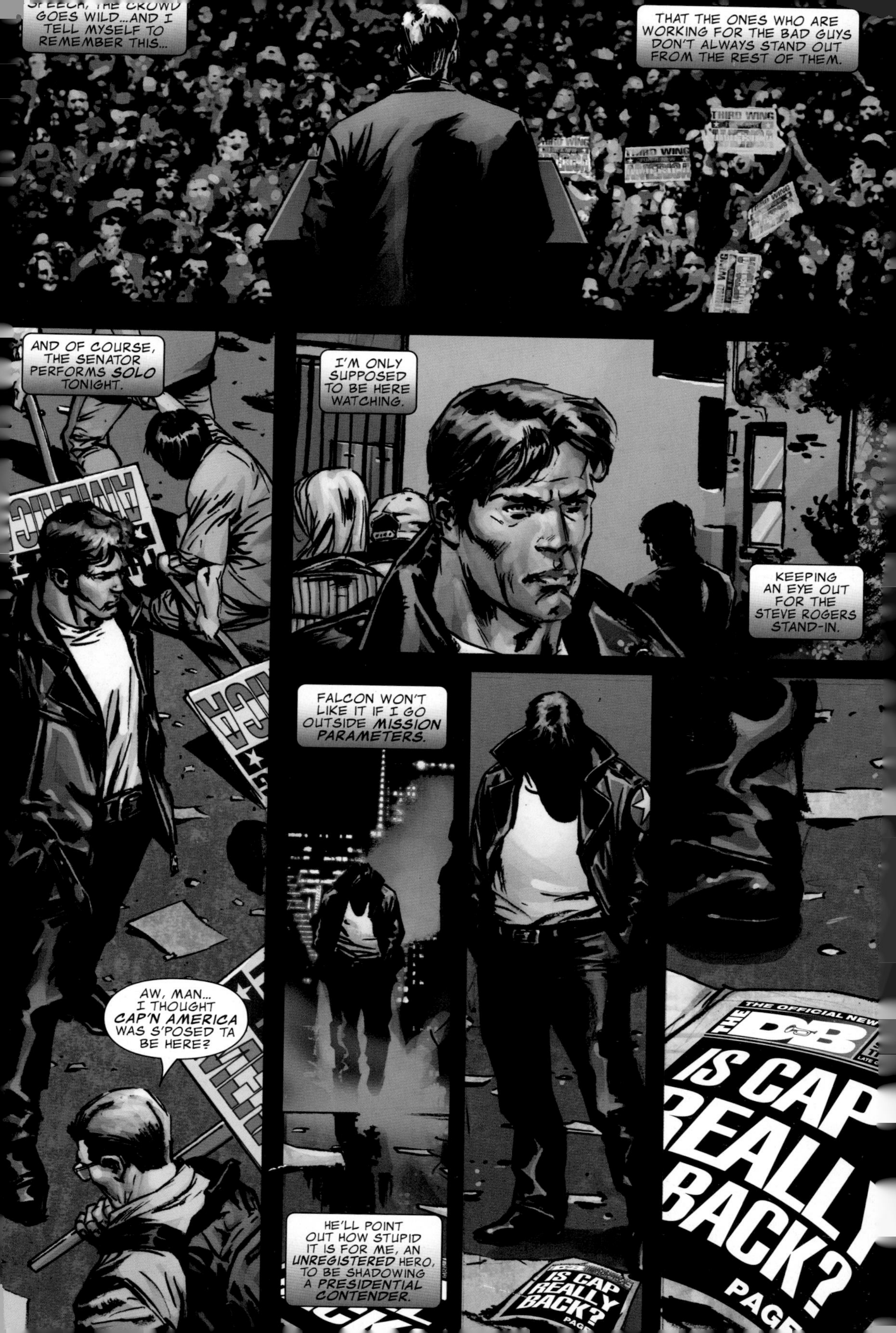
SPEECH, THE CROWD GOES WILD...AND I TELL MYSELF TO REMEMBER THIS...
THAT THE ONES WHO ARE WORKING FOR THE BAD GUYS DON'T ALWAYS STAND OUT FROM THE REST OF THEM.
THIRD WING
AND OF COURSE, THE SENATOR PERFORMS SOLO TONIGHT.
I'M ONLY SUPPOSED TO BE HERE WATCHING.
KEEPING AN EYE OUT FOR THE STEVE ROGERS STAND-IN.
AW, MAN... I THOUGHT CAP'N AMERICA WAS S'POSED TA BE HERE?
FALCON WON'T LIKE IT IF I GO OUTSIDE MISSION PARAMETERS.
HE'LL POINT OUT HOW STUPID IT IS FOR ME, AN UNREGISTERED HERO, TO BE SHADOWING A PRESIDENTIAL CONTENDER.
IS CAP REALLY BACK?
THE OFFICIAL NEW
THE DB
IS CAP REALLY BACK?
PAGE

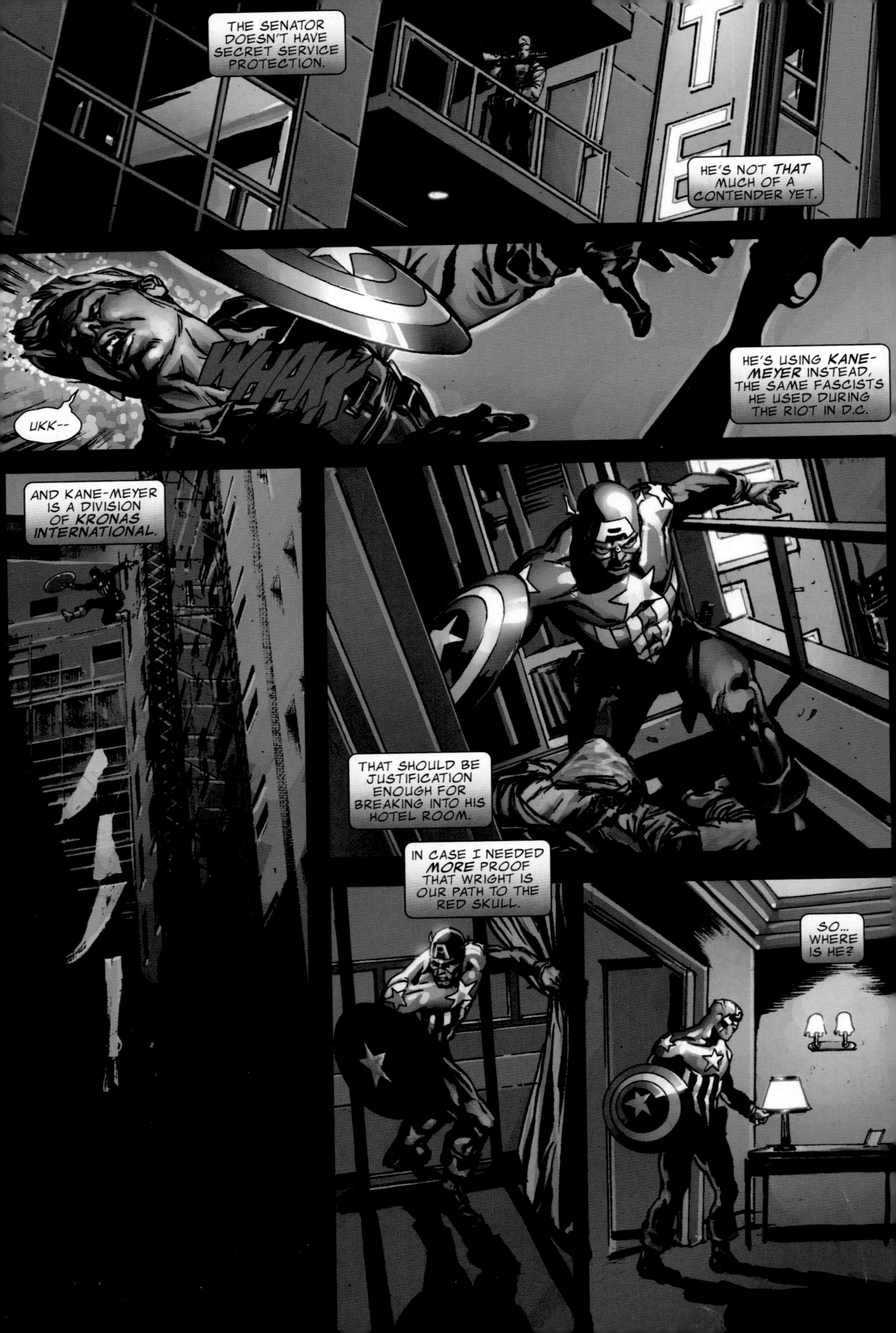
THE SENATOR DOESN'T HAVE SECRET SERVICE PROTECTION.
HE'S NOT THAT MUCH OF A CONTENDER YET.
WHAKK
UKK--
HE'S USING KANE-MEYER INSTEAD, THE SAME FASCISTS HE USED DURING THE RIOT IN D.C.
AND KANE-MEYER IS A DIVISION OF KRONAS INTERNATIONAL.
THAT SHOULD BE JUSTIFICATION ENOUGH FOR BREAKING INTO HIS HOTEL ROOM.
IN CASE I NEEDED MORE PROOF THAT WRIGHT IS OUR PATH TO THE RED SKULL.
SO... WHERE IS HE?

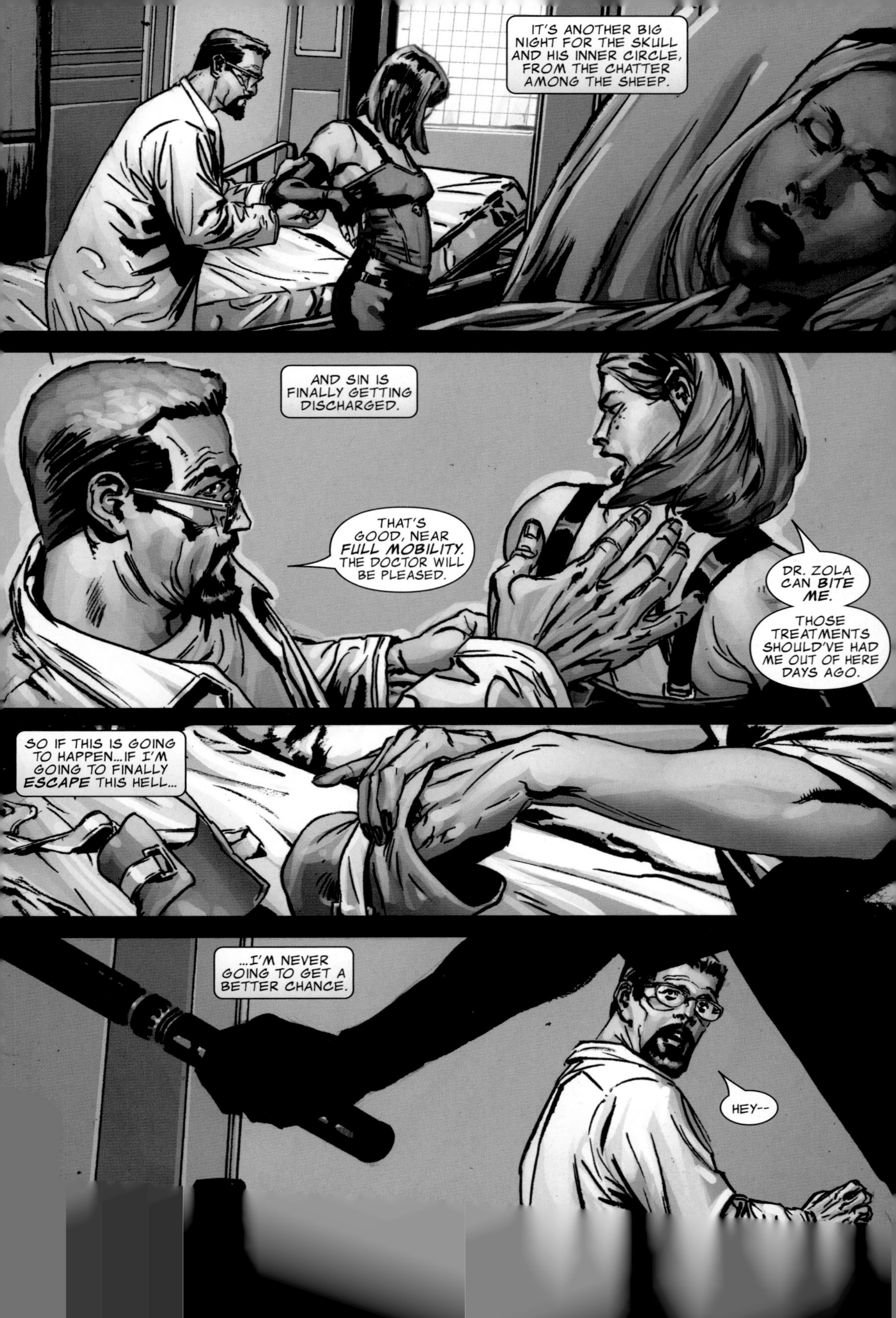
IT'S ANOTHER BIG NIGHT FOR THE SKULL AND HIS INNER CIRCLE, FROM THE CHATTER AMONG THE SHEEP.
AND SIN IS FINALLY GETTING DISCHARGED.
THAT'S GOOD, NEAR FULL MOBILITY. THE DOCTOR WILL BE PLEASED.
DR. ZOLA CAN BITE ME.
THOSE TREATMENTS SHOULD'VE HAD ME OUT OF HERE DAYS AGO.
SO IF THIS IS GOING TO HAPPEN...IF I'M GOING TO FINALLY ESCAPE THIS HELL...
...I'M NEVER GOING TO GET A BETTER CHANCE.
HEY--

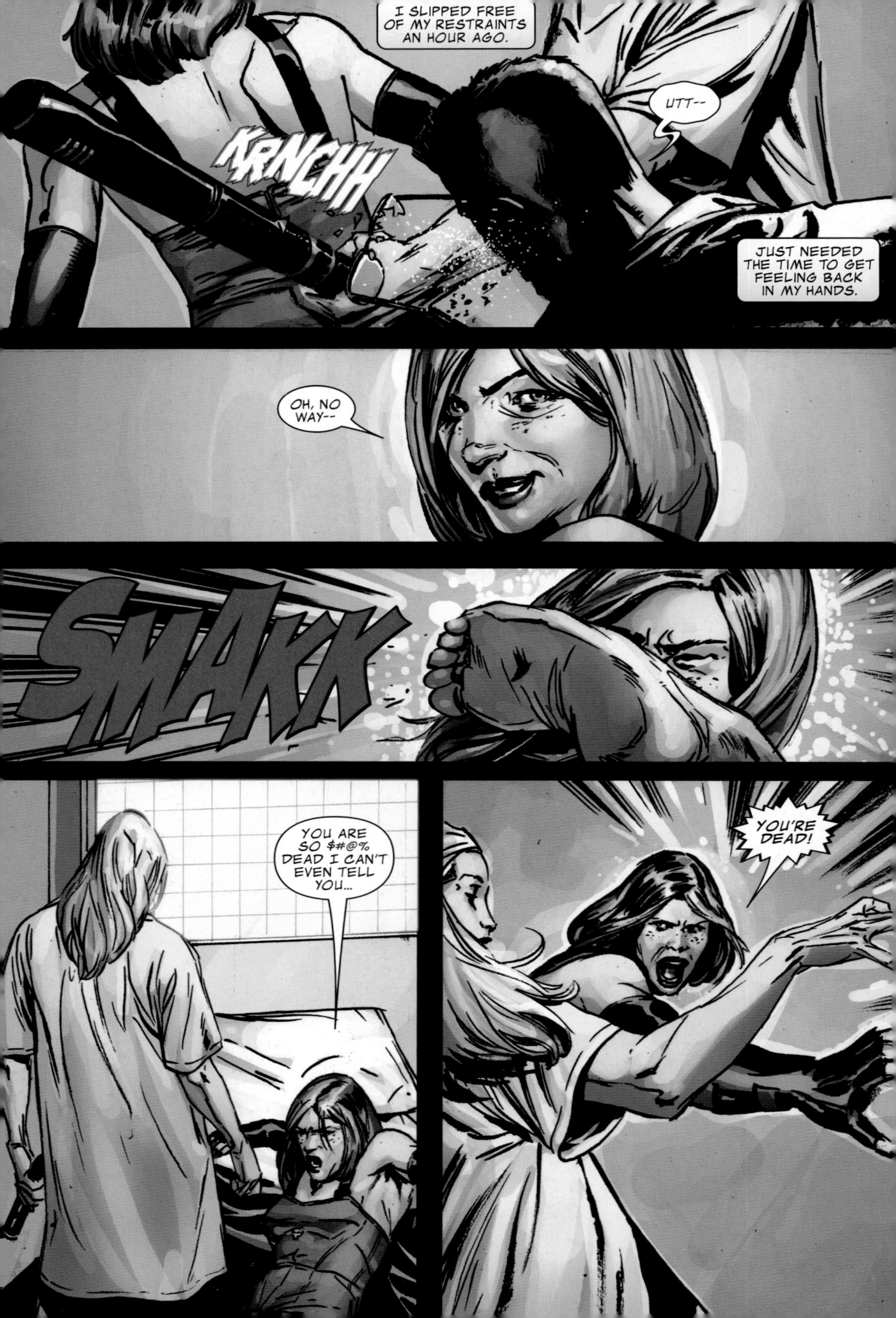
I SLIPPED FREE OF MY RESTRAINTS AN HOUR AGO.
KRNCHH
UTT--
JUST NEEDED THE TIME TO GET FEELING BACK IN MY HANDS.
OH, NO WAY--
SHAKK
YOU ARE SO $#@% DEAD I CAN'T EVEN TELL YOU...
YOU'RE DEAD!

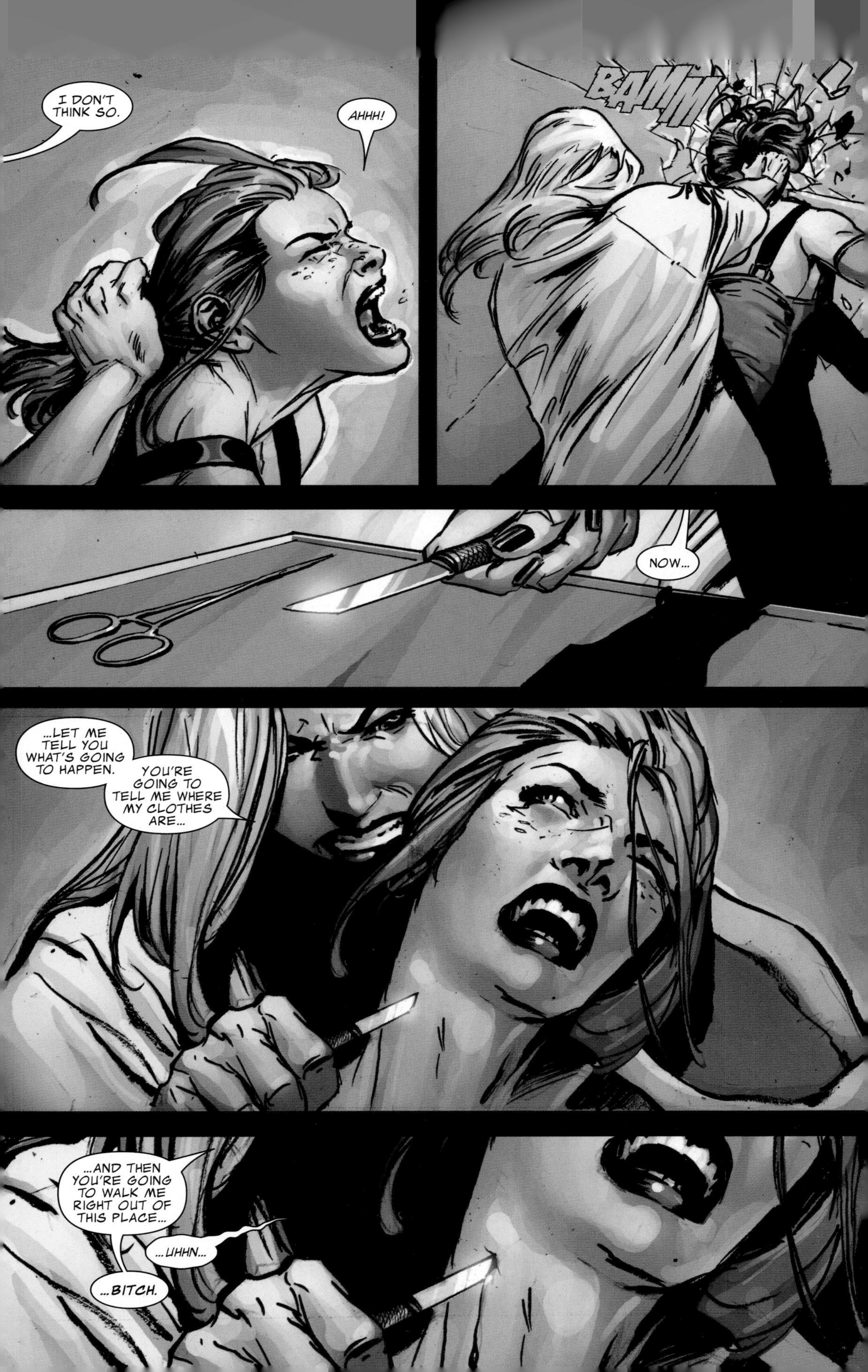
I DON'T THINK SO.
AHHH!
BAMM
NOW...
...LET ME TELL YOU WHAT'S GOING TO HAPPEN.
YOU'RE GOING TO TELL ME WHERE MY CLOTHES ARE...
...AND THEN YOU'RE GOING TO WALK ME RIGHT OUT OF THIS PLACE...
...UHHN...
...BITCH.

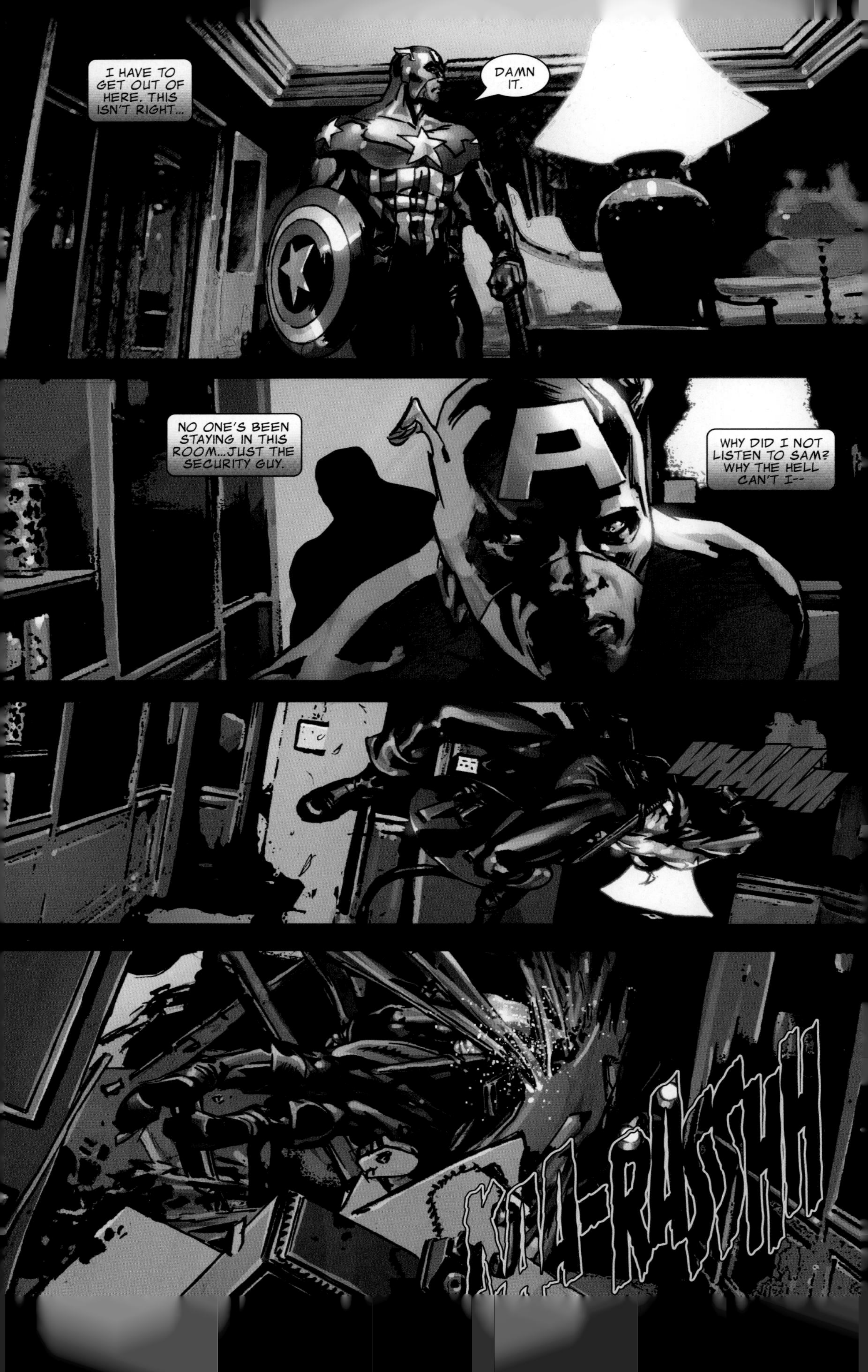
I HAVE TO GET OUT OF HERE. THIS ISN'T RIGHT...
DAMN IT.
NO ONE'S BEEN STAYING IN THIS ROOM...JUST THE SECURITY GUY.
WHY DID I NOT LISTEN TO SAM? WHY THE HELL CAN'T I--
WHANM
KRA-RASSHH

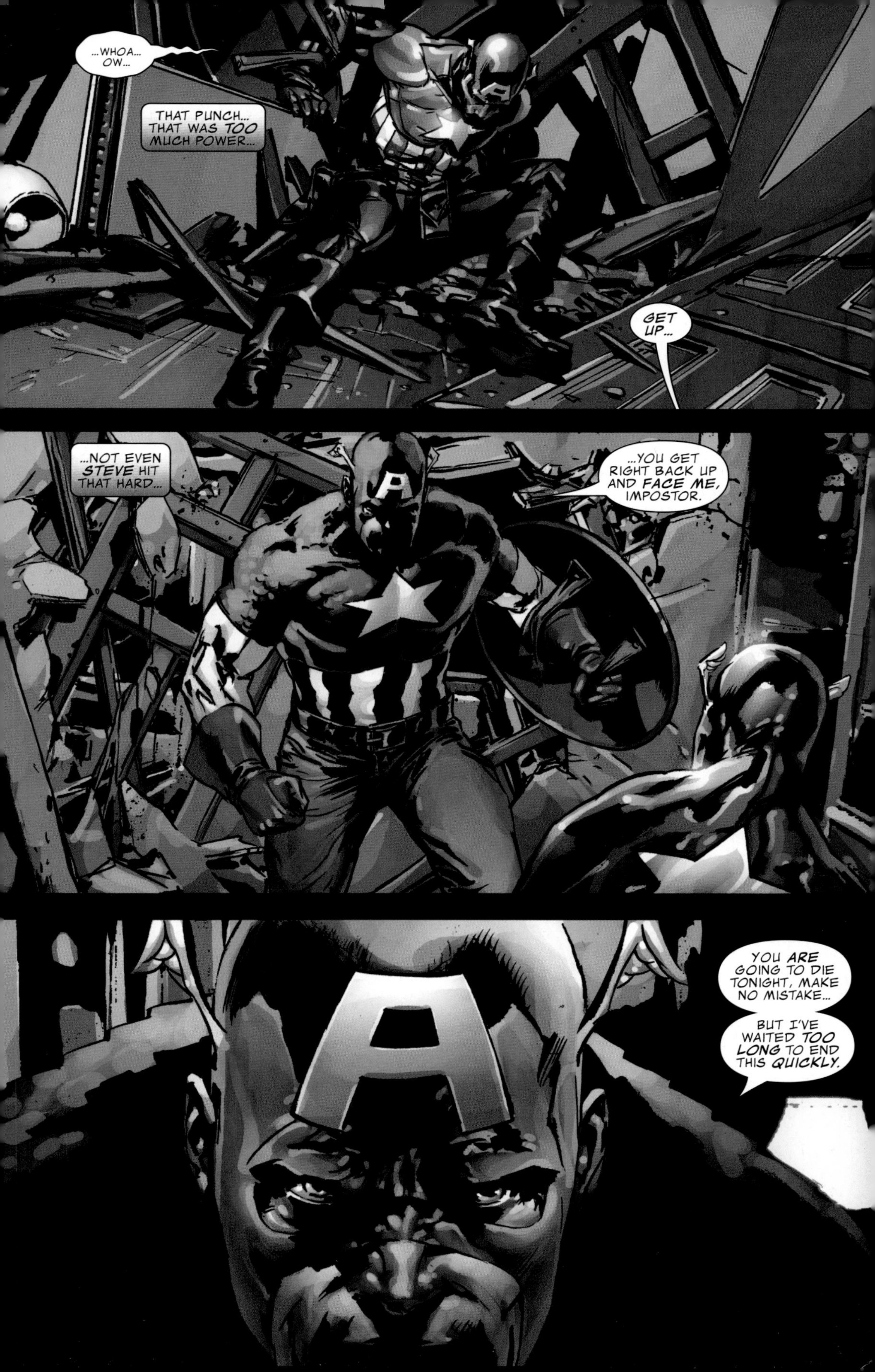
...WHOA... OW...
THAT PUNCH... THAT WAS TOO MUCH POWER...
GET UP...
...NOT EVEN STEVE HIT THAT HARD...
...YOU GET RIGHT BACK UP AND FACE ME, IMPOSTOR.
YOU ARE GOING TO DIE TONIGHT, MAKE NO MISTAKE...
BUT I'VE WAITED TOO LONG TO END THIS QUICKLY.

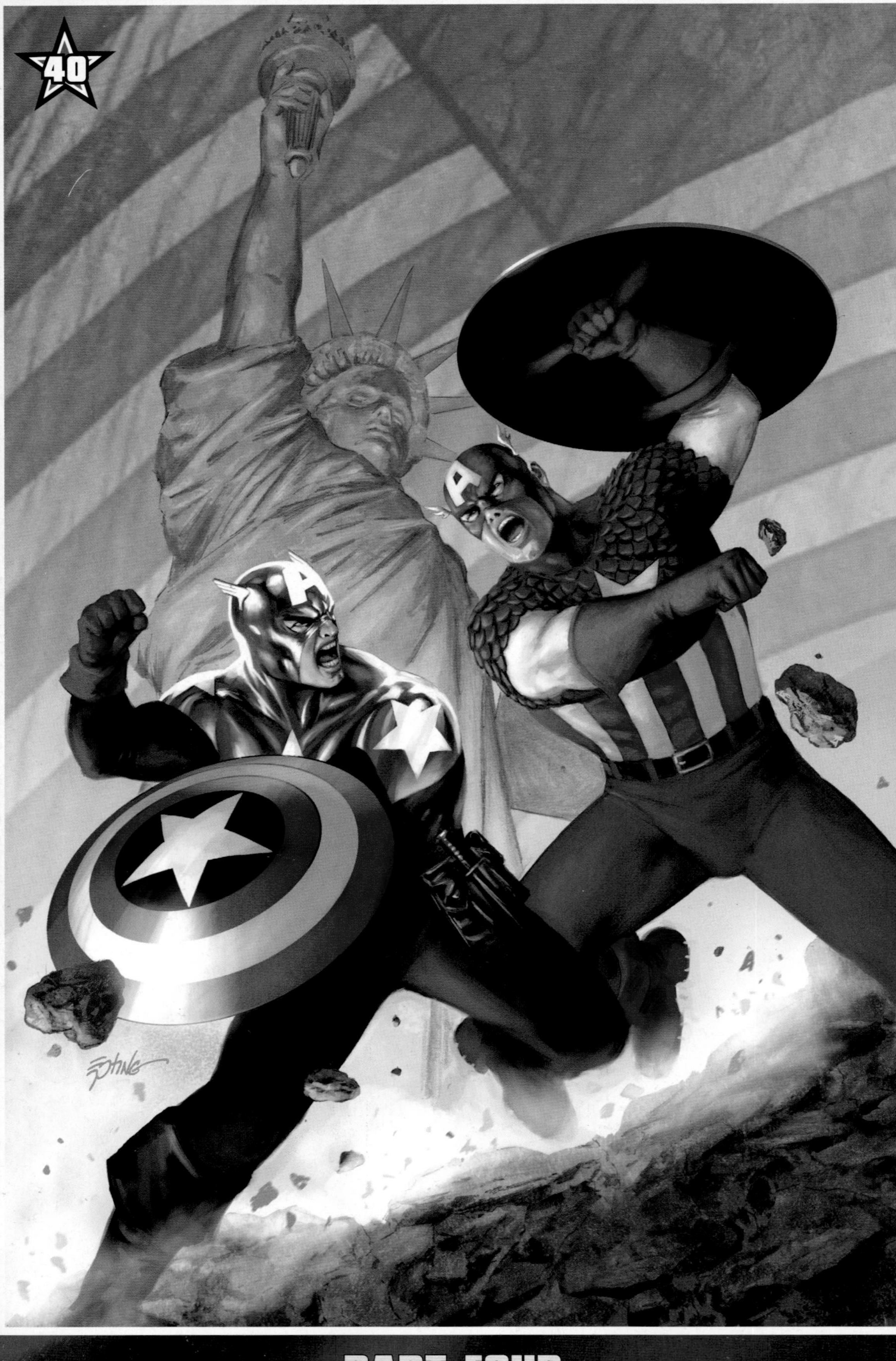
40

PART FOUR

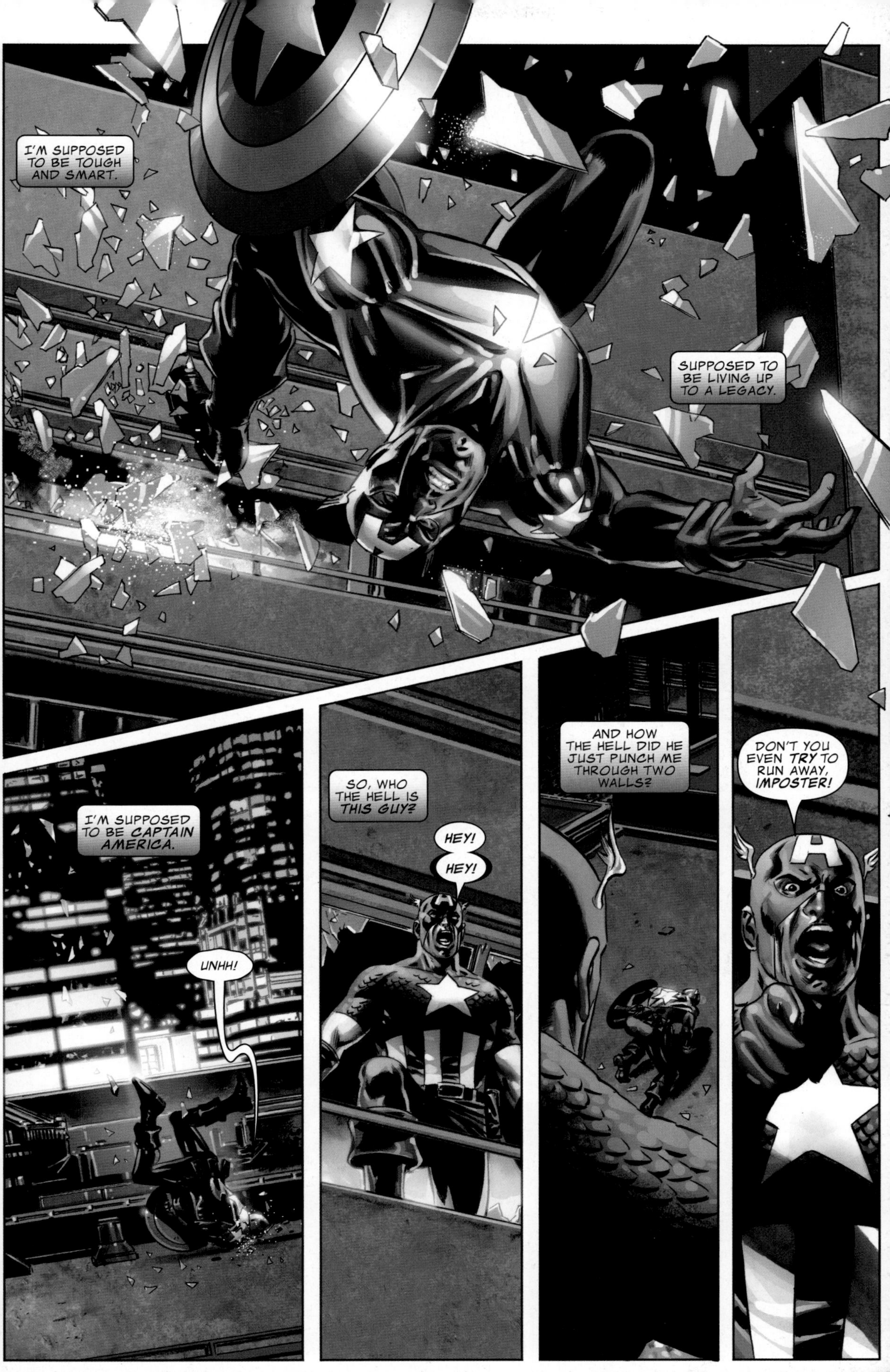
I'M SUPPOSED TO BE TOUGH AND SMART.
SUPPOSED TO BE LIVING UP TO A LEGACY.
I'M SUPPOSED TO BE CAPTAIN AMERICA.
UNHH!
SO, WHO THE HELL IS THIS GUY?
HEY!
HEY!
AND HOW THE HELL DID HE JUST PUNCH ME THROUGH TWO WALLS?
DON'T YOU EVEN TRY TO RUN AWAY, IMPOSTER!

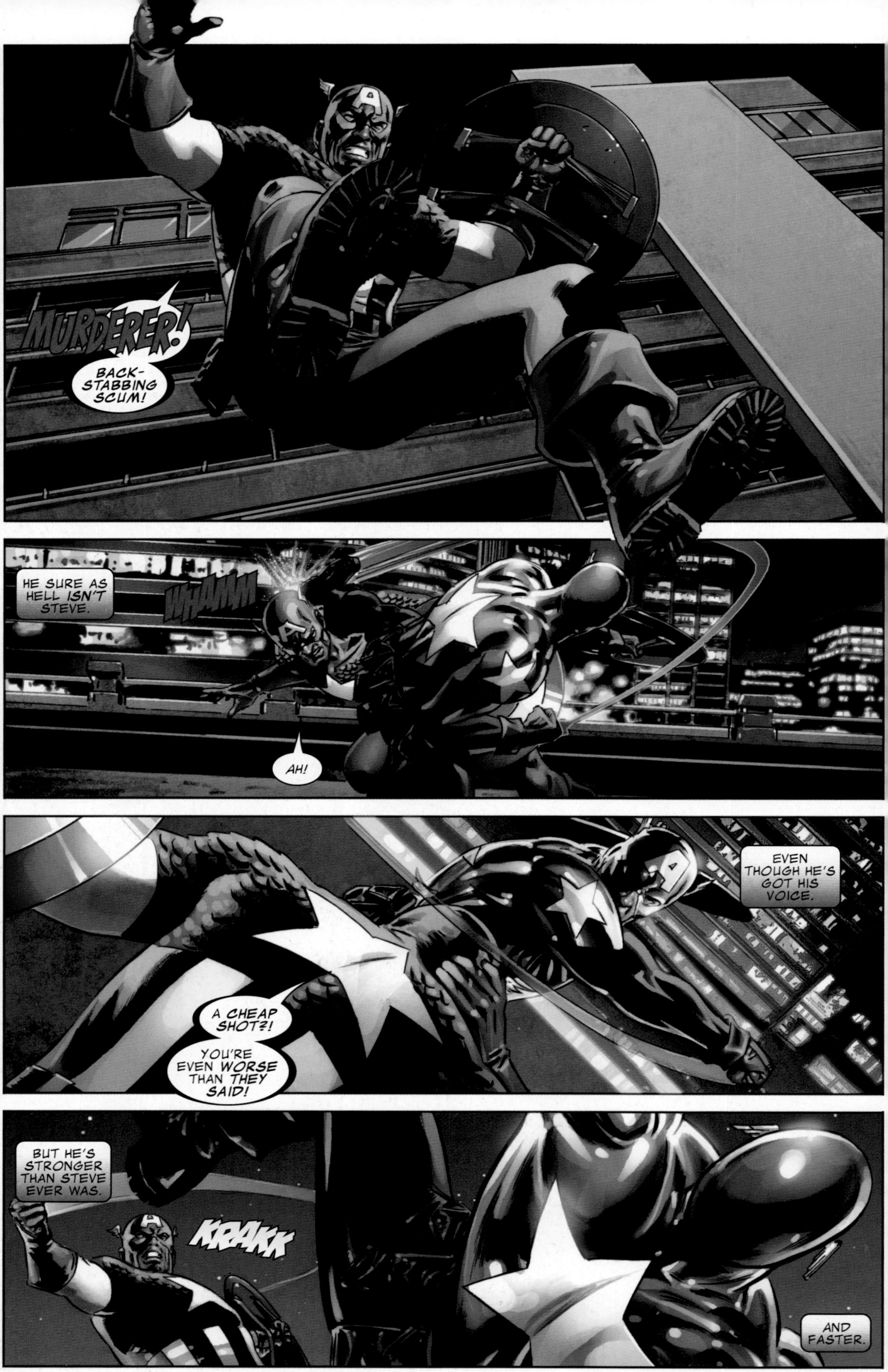
MURDERER!
BACK-STABBING SCUM!
HE SURE AS HELL ISN'T STEVE.
WHAMM
AH!
EVEN THOUGH HE'S GOT HIS VOICE.
A CHEAP SHOT?!
YOU'RE EVEN WORSE THAN THEY SAID!
BUT HE'S STRONGER THAN STEVE EVER WAS.
KRAKK
AND FASTER.

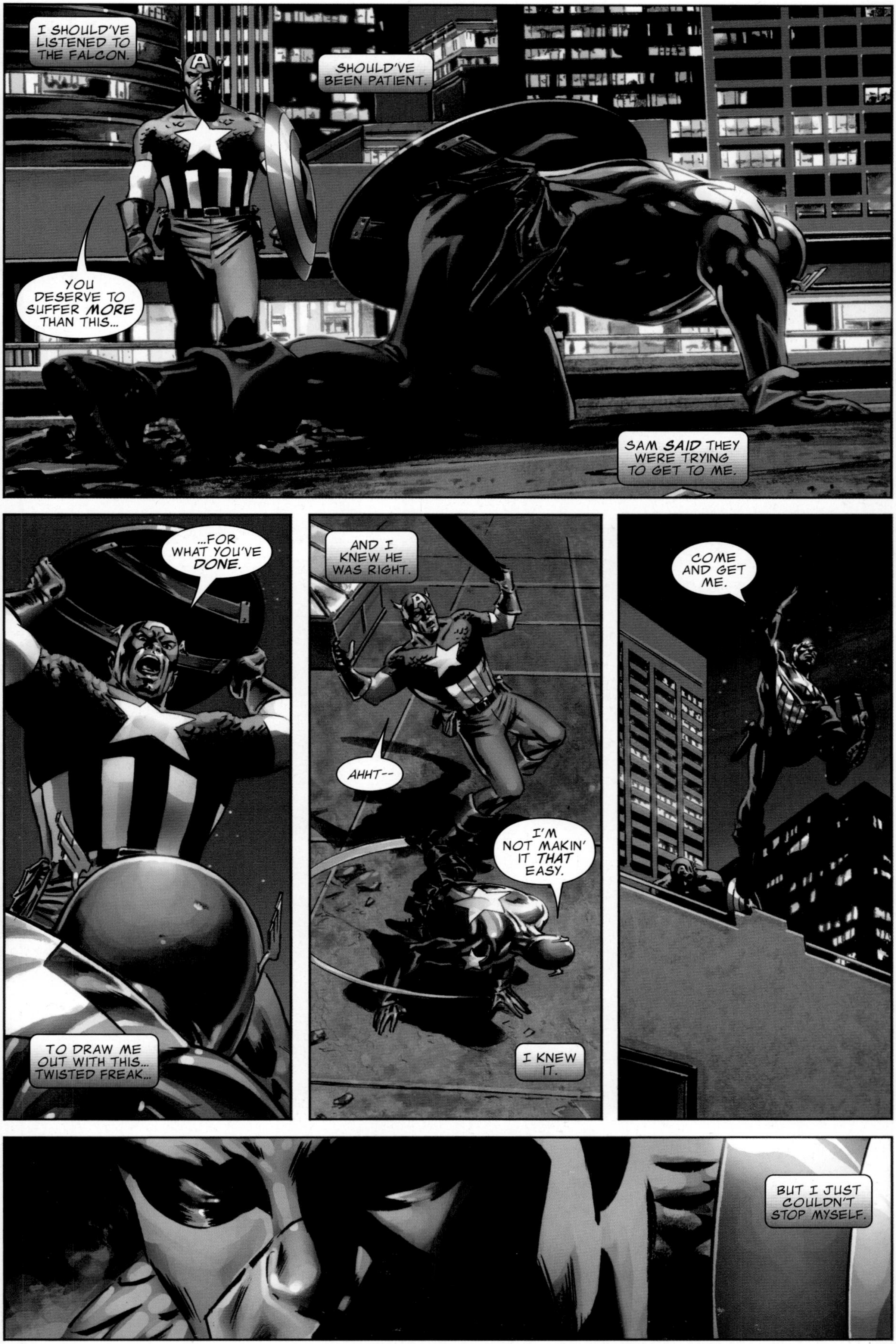
I SHOULD'VE LISTENED TO THE FALCON.
SHOULD'VE BEEN PATIENT.
YOU DESERVE TO SUFFER MORE THAN THIS...
SAM SAID THEY WERE TRYING TO GET TO ME.
...FOR WHAT YOU'VE DONE.
TO DRAW ME OUT WITH THIS... TWISTED FREAK...
AND I KNEW HE WAS RIGHT.
AHHT--
I'M NOT MAKIN' IT THAT EASY.
I KNEW IT.
COME AND GET ME.
BUT I JUST COULDN'T STOP MYSELF.

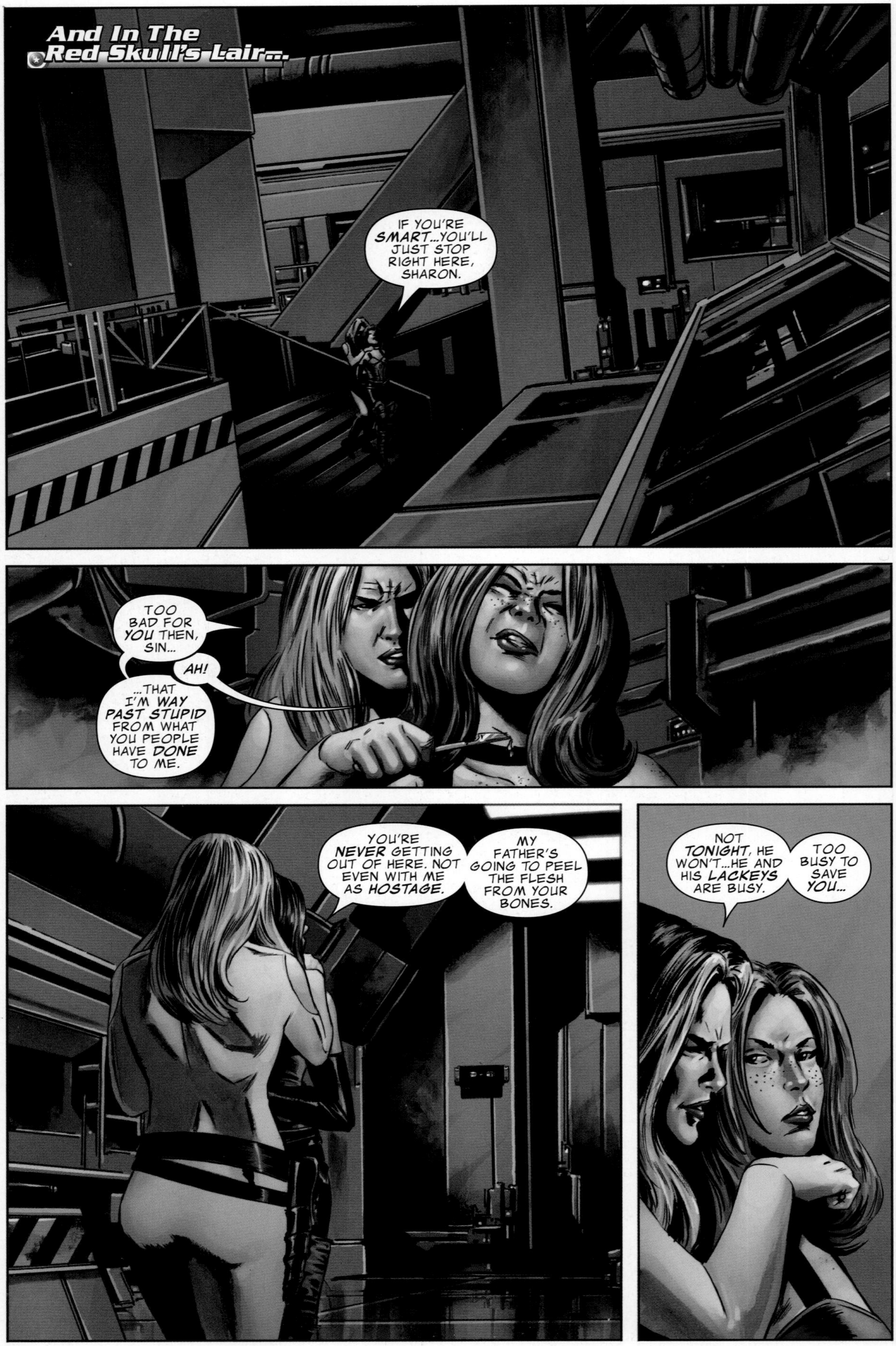
And In The Red Skull's Lair...
IF YOU'RE SMART...YOU'LL JUST STOP RIGHT HERE, SHARON.
TOO BAD FOR YOU THEN, SIN...
AH!
...THAT I'M WAY PAST STUPID FROM WHAT YOU PEOPLE HAVE DONE TO ME.
YOU'RE NEVER GETTING OUT OF HERE. NOT EVEN WITH ME AS HOSTAGE.
MY FATHER'S GOING TO PEEL THE FLESH FROM YOUR BONES.
NOT TONIGHT, HE WON'T...HE AND HIS LACKEYS ARE BUSY.
TOO BUSY TO SAVE YOU...

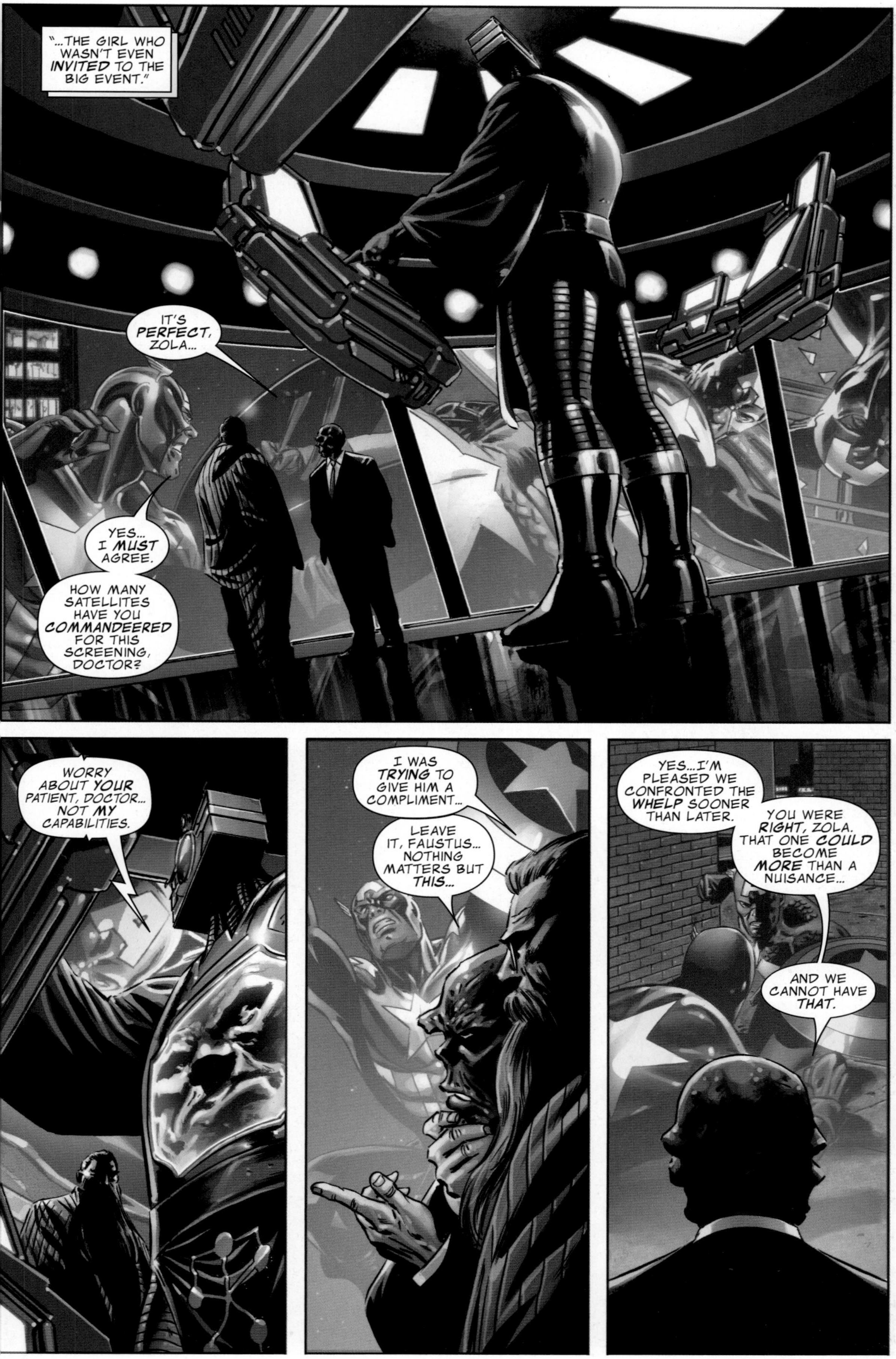
"...THE GIRL WHO WASN'T EVEN INVITED TO THE BIG EVENT."
IT'S PERFECT, ZOLA...
YES... I MUST AGREE.
HOW MANY SATELLITES HAVE YOU COMMANDEERED FOR THIS SCREENING, DOCTOR?
WORRY ABOUT YOUR PATIENT, DOCTOR... NOT MY CAPABILITIES.
I WAS TRYING TO GIVE HIM A COMPLIMENT...
LEAVE IT, FAUSTUS... NOTHING MATTERS BUT THIS...
YES...I'M PLEASED WE CONFRONTED THE WHELP SOONER THAN LATER.
YOU WERE RIGHT, ZOLA. THAT ONE COULD BECOME MORE THAN A NUISANCE...
AND WE CANNOT HAVE THAT.

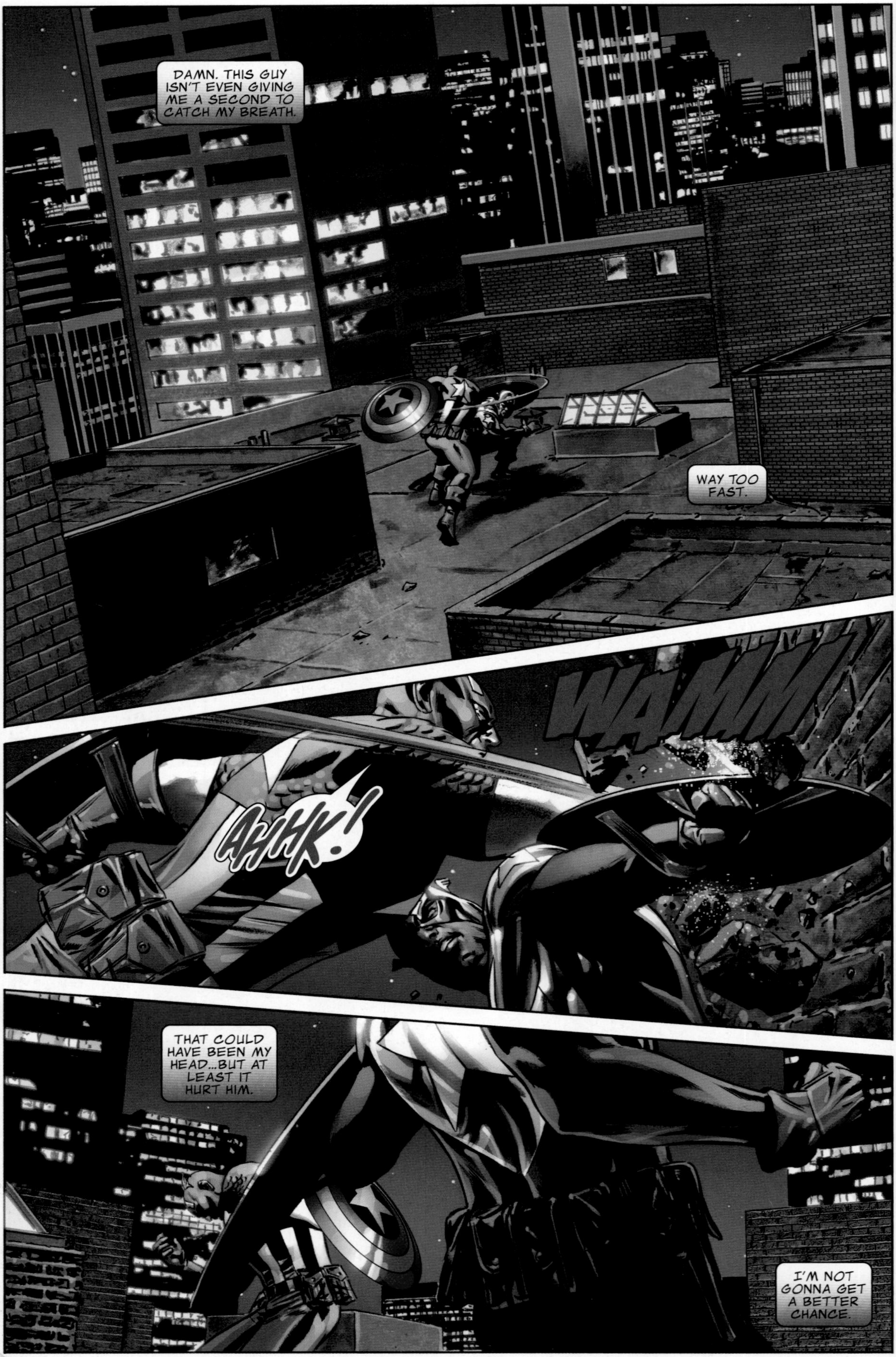
DAMN. THIS GUY ISN'T EVEN GIVING ME A SECOND TO CATCH MY BREATH.
WAY TOO FAST.
WAMM!
AHHK!
THAT COULD HAVE BEEN MY HEAD...BUT AT LEAST IT HURT HIM.
I'M NOT GONNA GET A BETTER CHANCE.

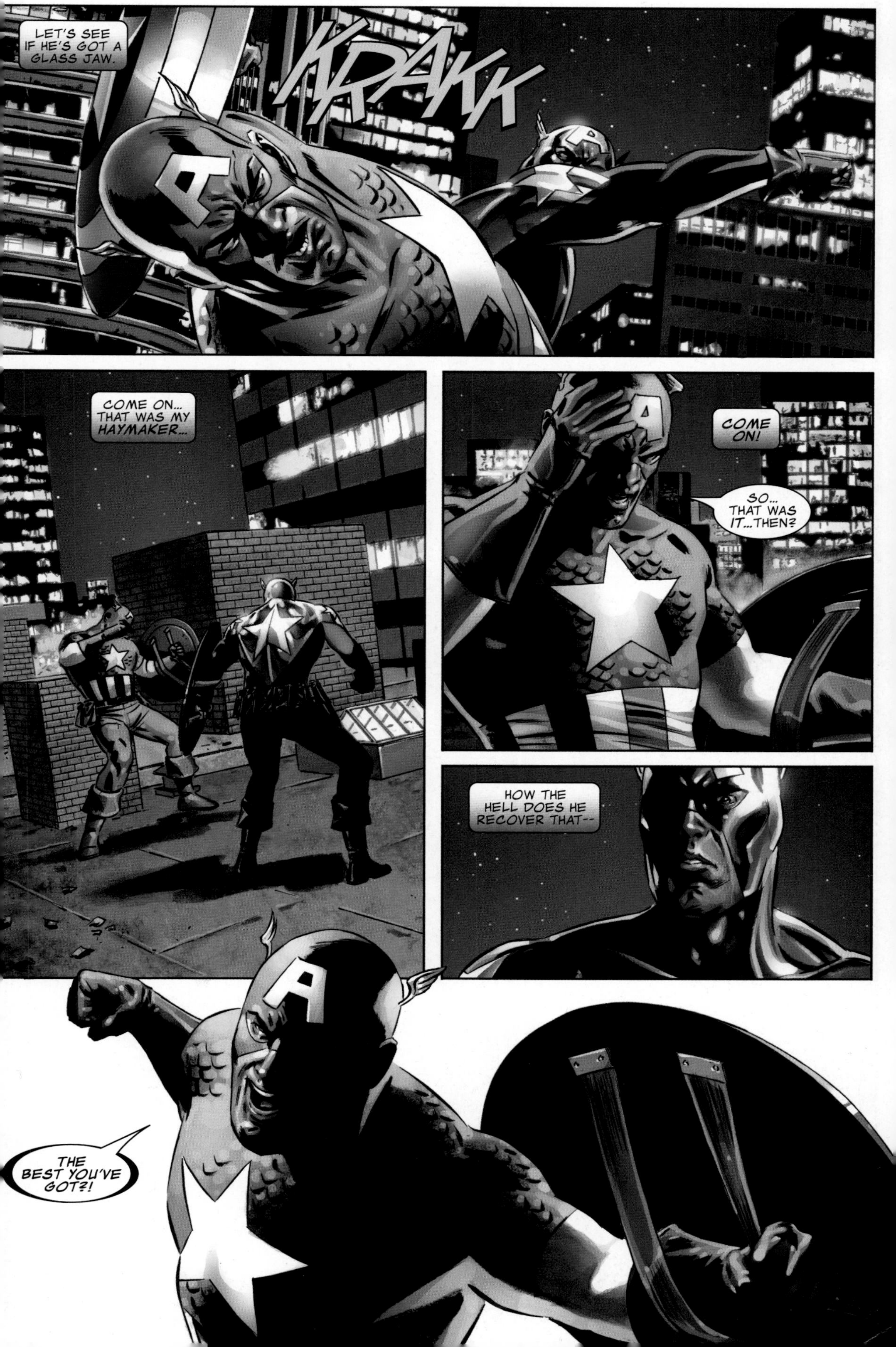
LET'S SEE IF HE'S GOT A GLASS JAW.
KRAKK
COME ON... THAT WAS MY HAYMAKER...
COME ON!
SO... THAT WAS IT...THEN?
HOW THE HELL DOES HE RECOVER THAT--
THE BEST YOU'VE GOT?!

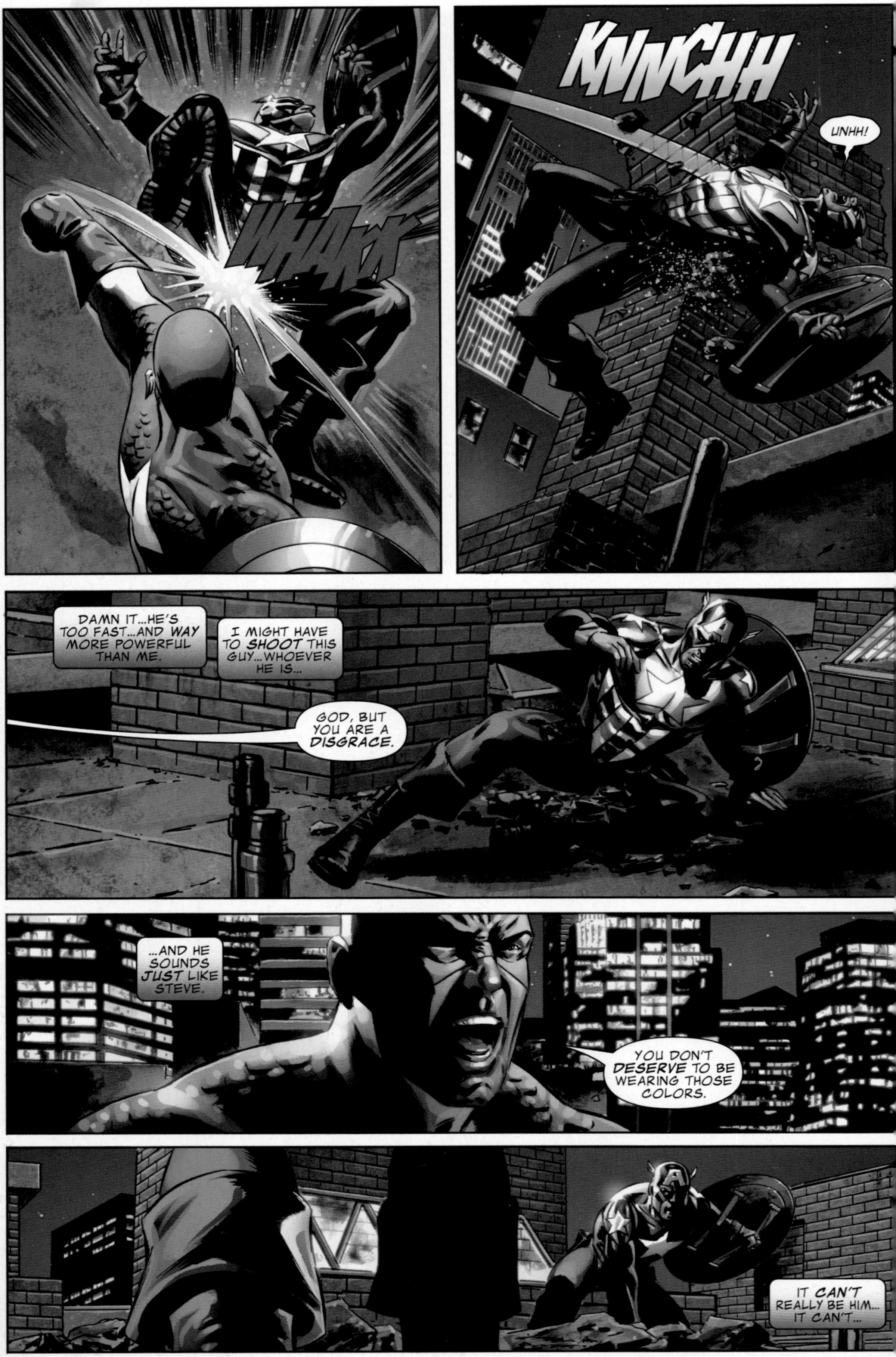
WHAKK
KNNCHH
UNHH!
DAMN IT...HE'S TOO FAST...AND WAY MORE POWERFUL THAN ME.
I MIGHT HAVE TO SHOOT THIS GUY...WHOEVER HE IS...
GOD, BUT YOU ARE A DISGRACE.
...AND HE SOUNDS JUST LIKE STEVE.
YOU DON'T DESERVE TO BE WEARING THOSE COLORS.
IT CAN'T REALLY BE HIM... IT CAN'T...

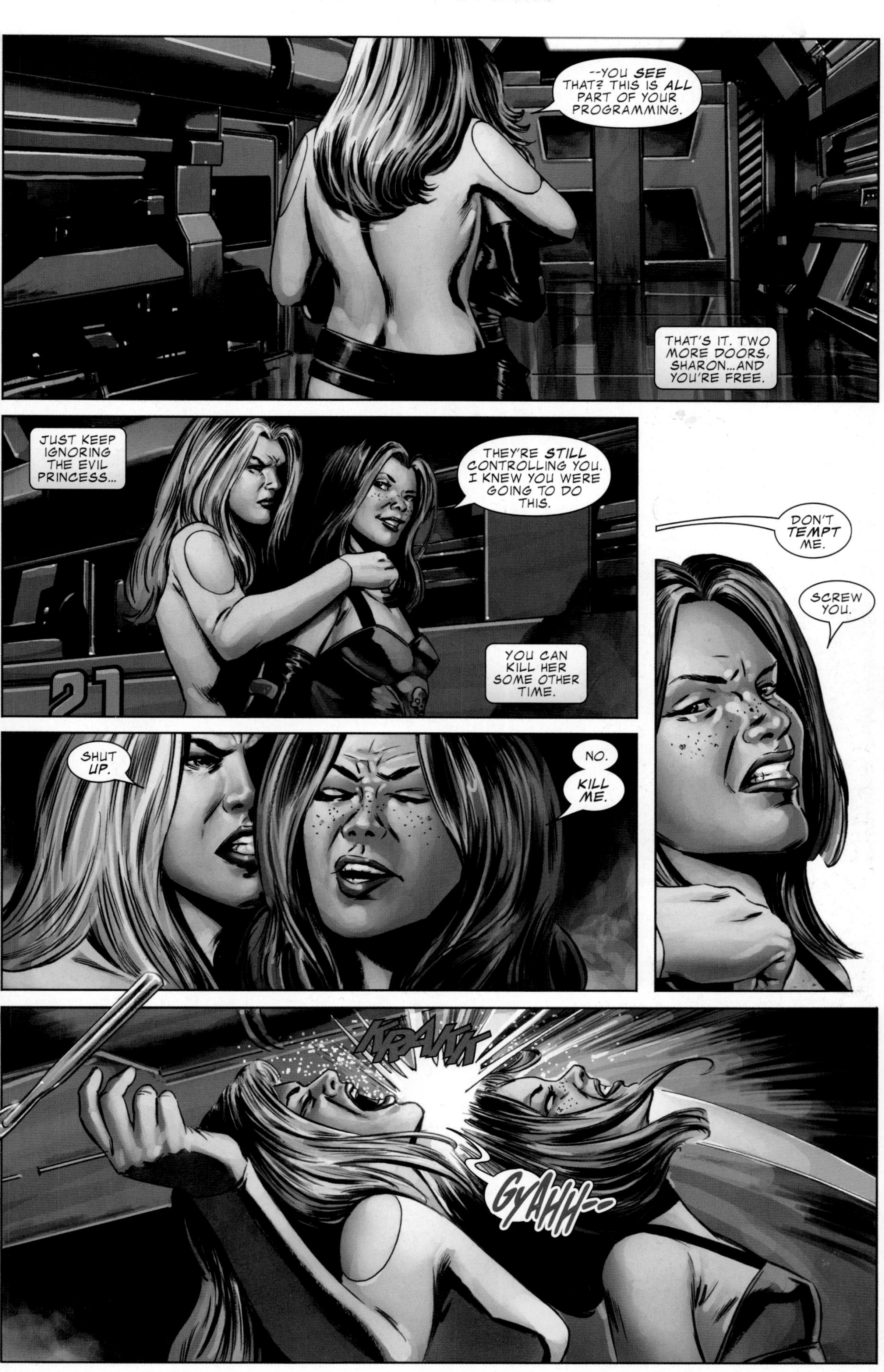
--YOU SEE THAT? THIS IS ALL PART OF YOUR PROGRAMMING.
THAT'S IT. TWO MORE DOORS, SHARON...AND YOU'RE FREE.
JUST KEEP IGNORING THE EVIL PRINCESS...
THEY'RE STILL CONTROLLING YOU. I KNEW YOU WERE GOING TO DO THIS.
YOU CAN KILL HER SOME OTHER TIME.
DON'T TEMPT ME.
SCREW YOU.
SHUT UP.
NO. KILL ME.
KRAKK
GYAHH--

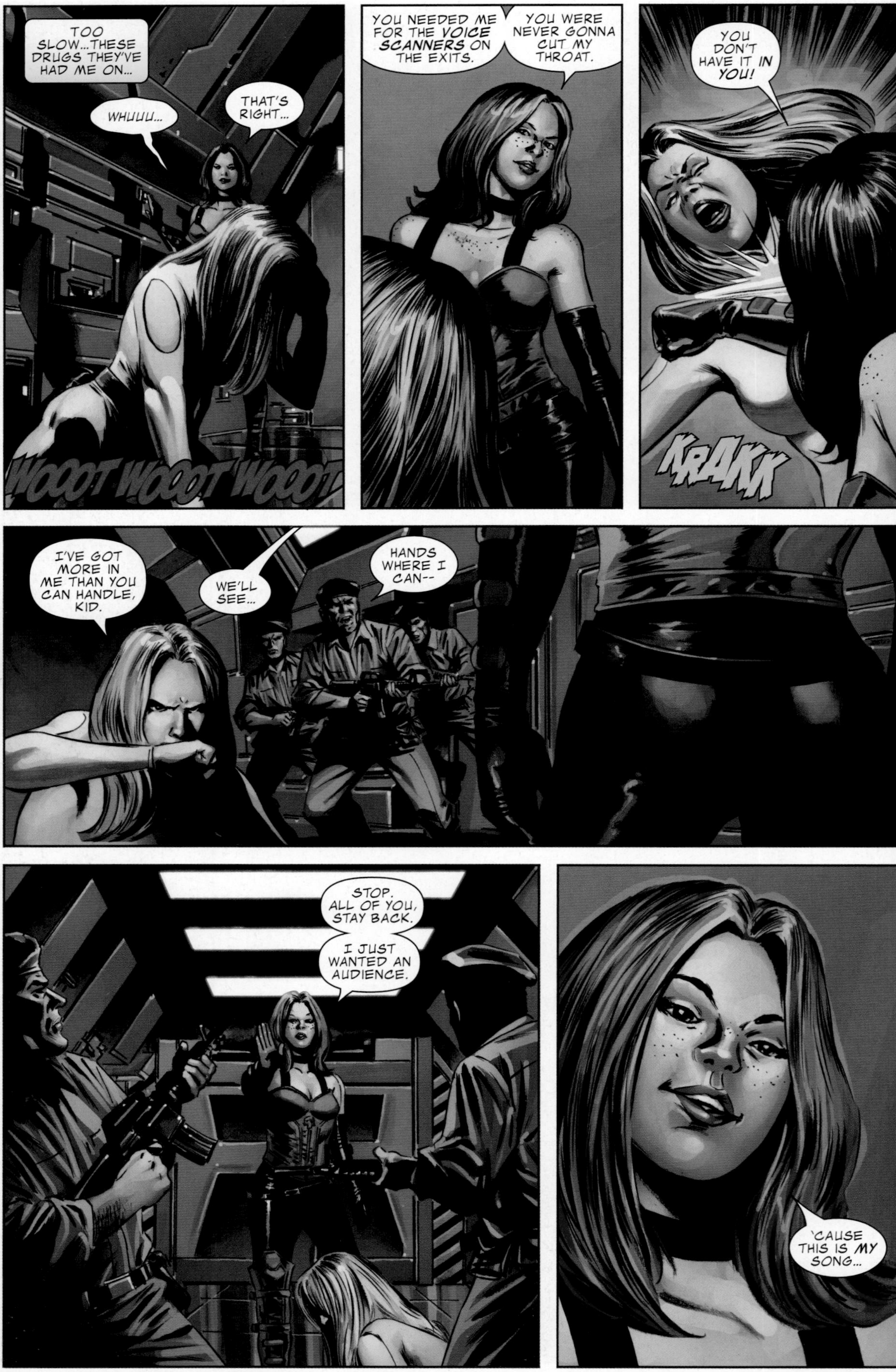
TOO SLOW...THESE DRUGS THEY'VE HAD ME ON...
WHUUU...
THAT'S RIGHT...
WOOOT WOOOT WOOOT
YOU NEEDED ME FOR THE VOICE SCANNERS ON THE EXITS.
YOU WERE NEVER GONNA CUT MY THROAT.
YOU DON'T HAVE IT IN YOU!
KRAKK
I'VE GOT MORE IN ME THAN YOU CAN HANDLE, KID.
WE'LL SEE...
HANDS WHERE I CAN--
STOP. ALL OF YOU, STAY BACK.
I JUST WANTED AN AUDIENCE.
'CAUSE THIS IS MY SONG...

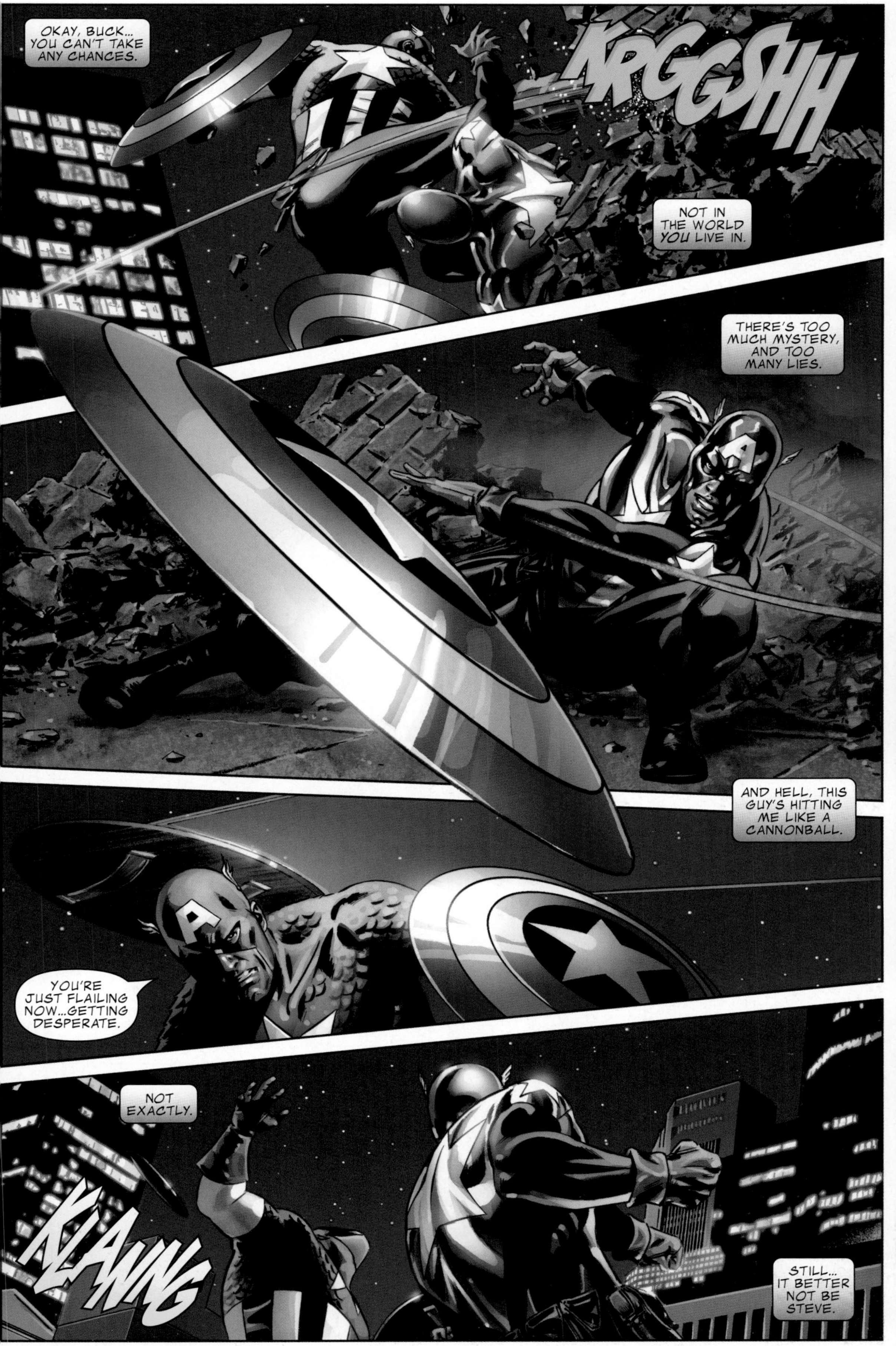
OKAY, BUCK... YOU CAN'T TAKE ANY CHANCES.
KRGGSHH
NOT IN THE WORLD YOU LIVE IN.
THERE'S TOO MUCH MYSTERY, AND TOO MANY LIES.
AND HELL, THIS GUY'S HITTING ME LIKE A CANNONBALL.
YOU'RE JUST FLAILING NOW...GETTING DESPERATE.
NOT EXACTLY.
KLANNG
STILL... IT BETTER NOT BE STEVE.

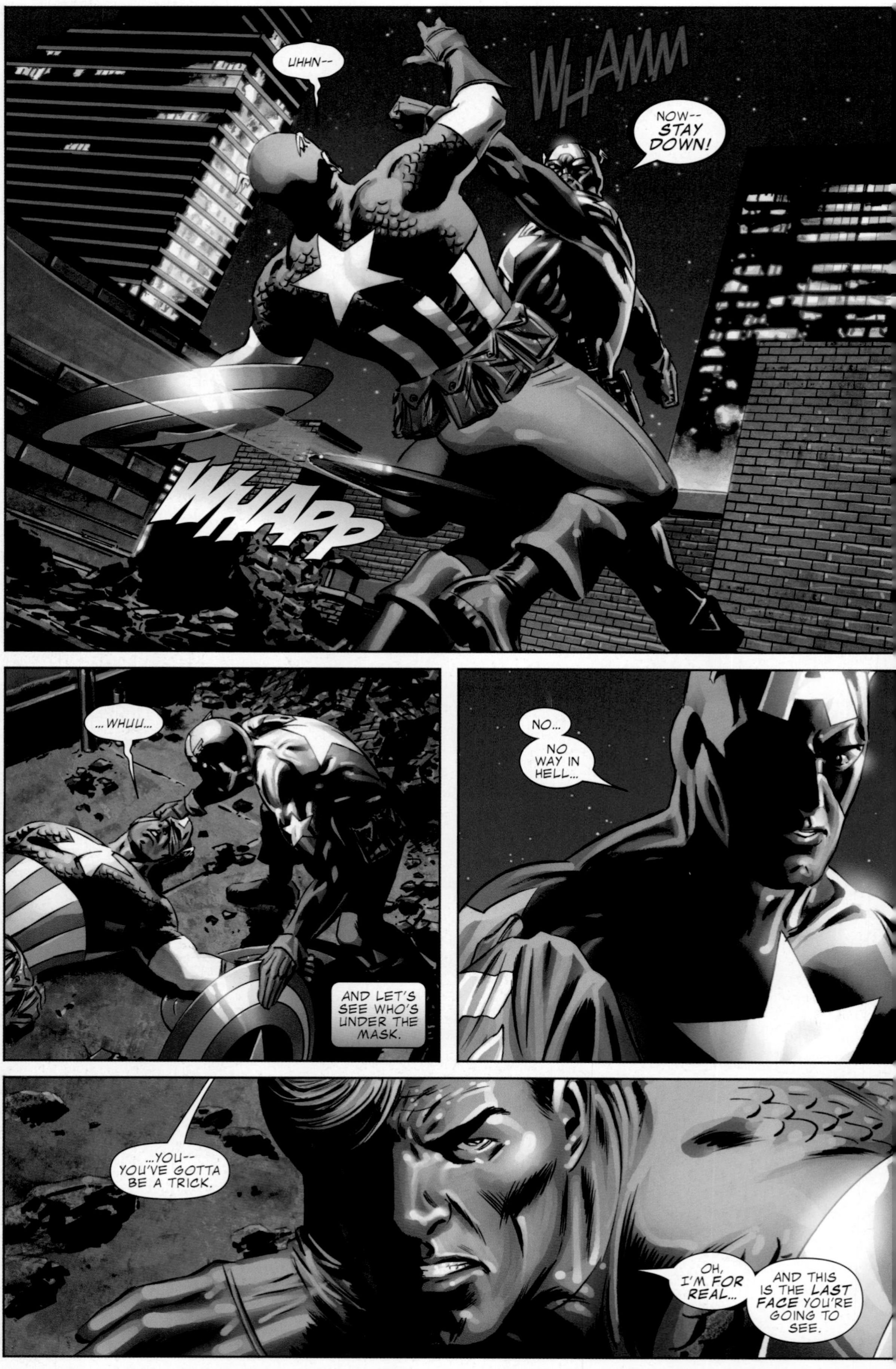
UHHN--
WHAMM
NOW-- STAY DOWN!
WHAPP
...WHUU...
AND LET'S SEE WHO'S UNDER THE MASK.
NO...
NO WAY IN HELL...
...YOU-- YOU'VE GOTTA BE A TRICK.
OH, I'M FOR REAL...
AND THIS IS THE LAST FACE YOU'RE GOING TO SEE.

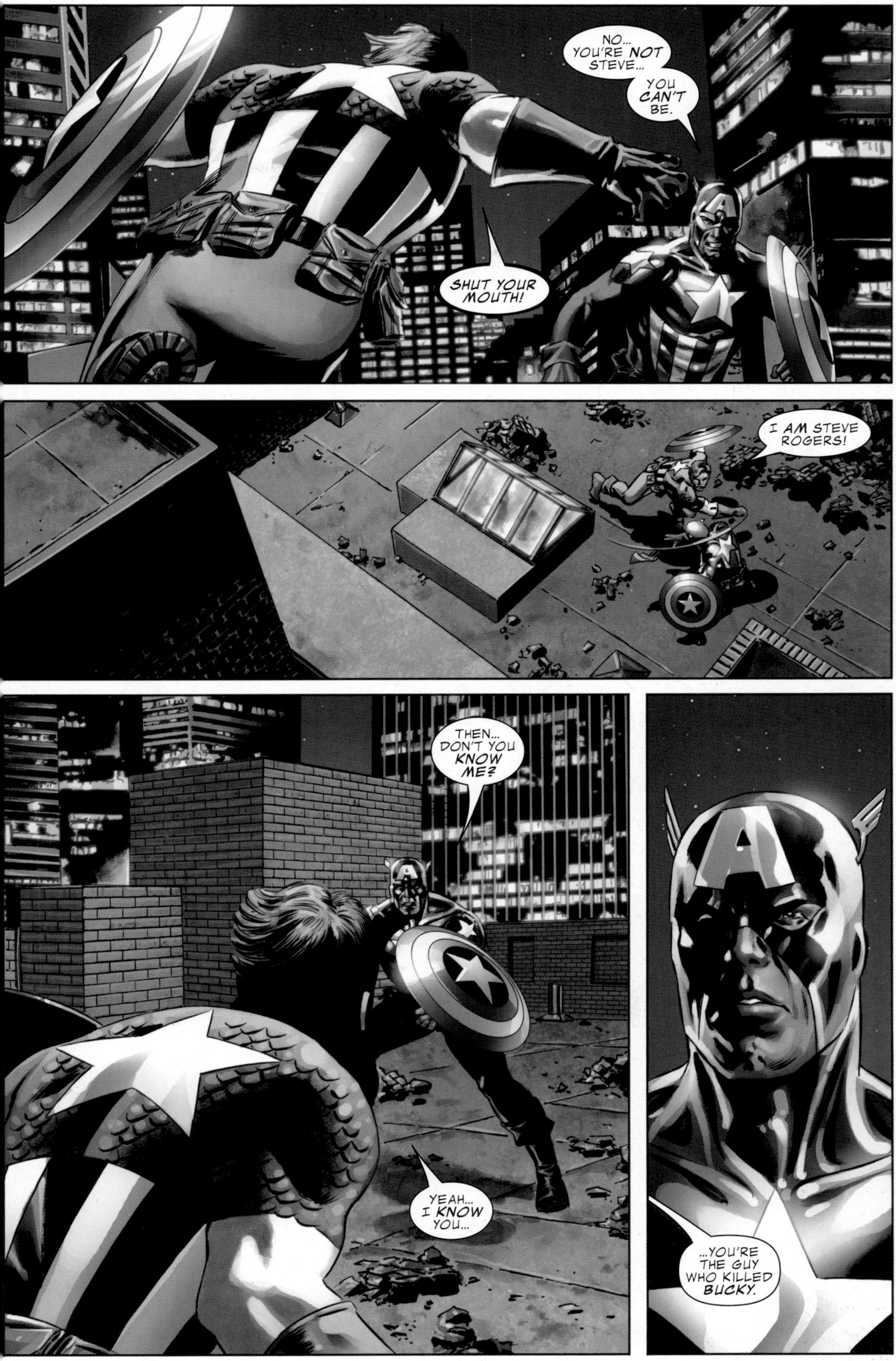
NO... YOU'RE NOT STEVE...
YOU CAN'T BE.
SHUT YOUR MOUTH!
I AM STEVE ROGERS!
THEN... DON'T YOU KNOW ME?
YEAH... I KNOW YOU...
...YOU'RE THE GUY WHO KILLED BUCKY.

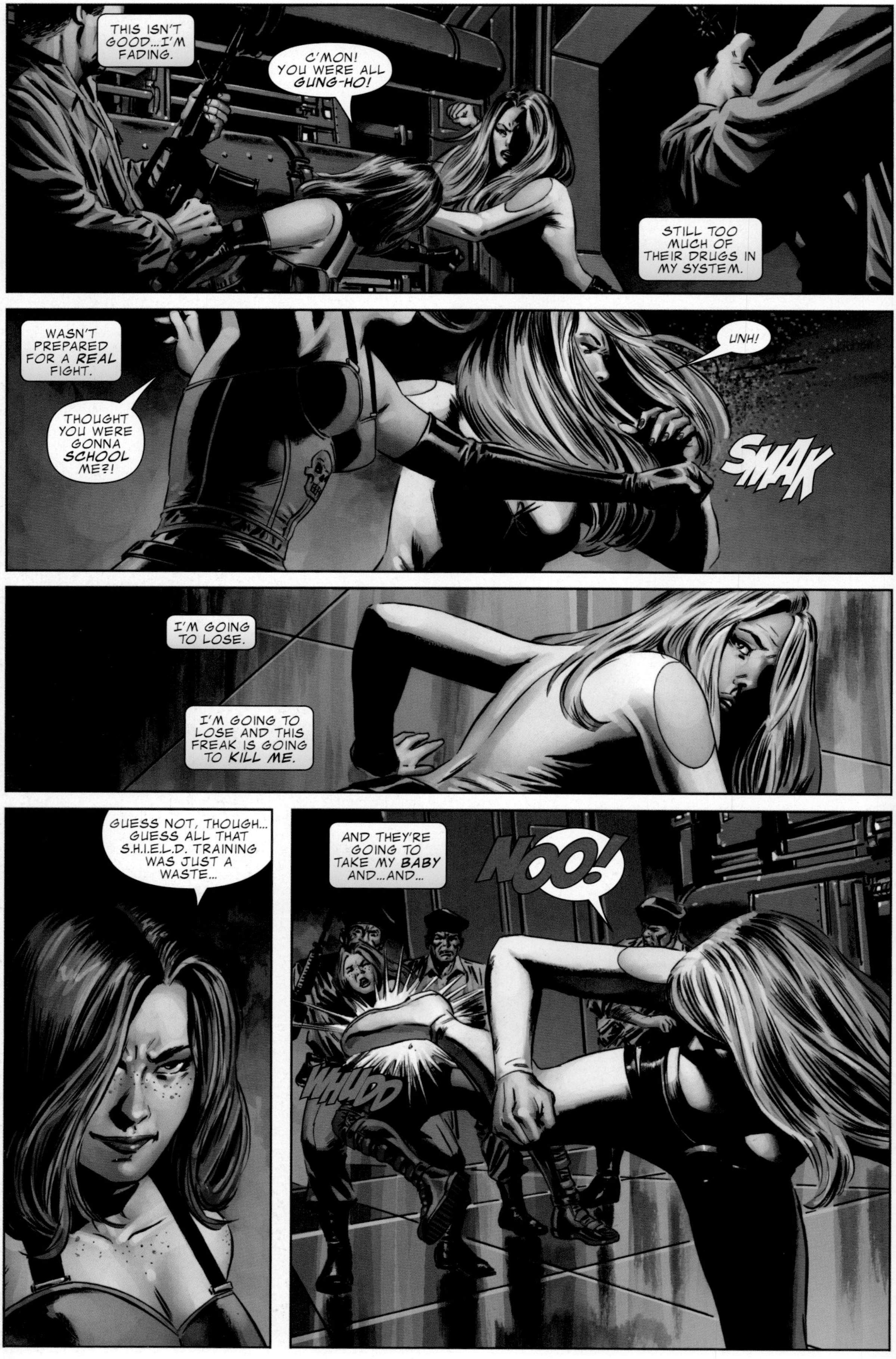
THIS ISN'T GOOD...I'M FADING.
C'MON! YOU WERE ALL GUNG-HO!
STILL TOO MUCH OF THEIR DRUGS IN MY SYSTEM.
WASN'T PREPARED FOR A REAL FIGHT.
THOUGHT YOU WERE GONNA SCHOOL ME?!
UNH!
SMAK
I'M GOING TO LOSE.
I'M GOING TO LOSE AND THIS FREAK IS GOING TO KILL ME.
GUESS NOT, THOUGH... GUESS ALL THAT S.H.I.E.L.D. TRAINING WAS JUST A WASTE...
AND THEY'RE GOING TO TAKE MY BABY AND...AND...
NOO!
WHUDD

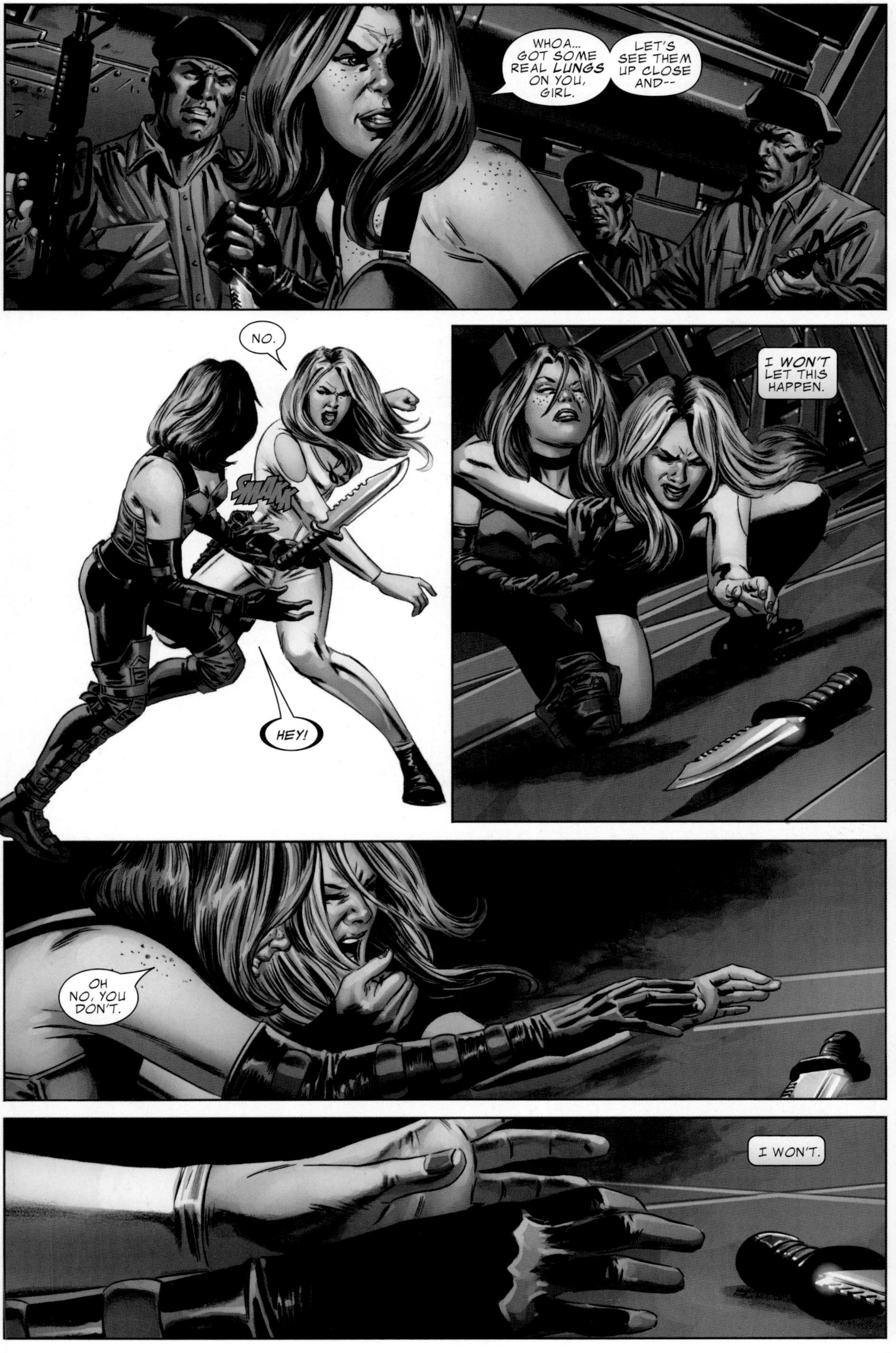
WHOA... GOT SOME REAL LUNGS ON YOU, GIRL.
LET'S SEE THEM UP CLOSE AND--
NO.
SHAKK
HEY!
I WON'T LET THIS HAPPEN.
OH NO, YOU DON'T.
I WON'T.

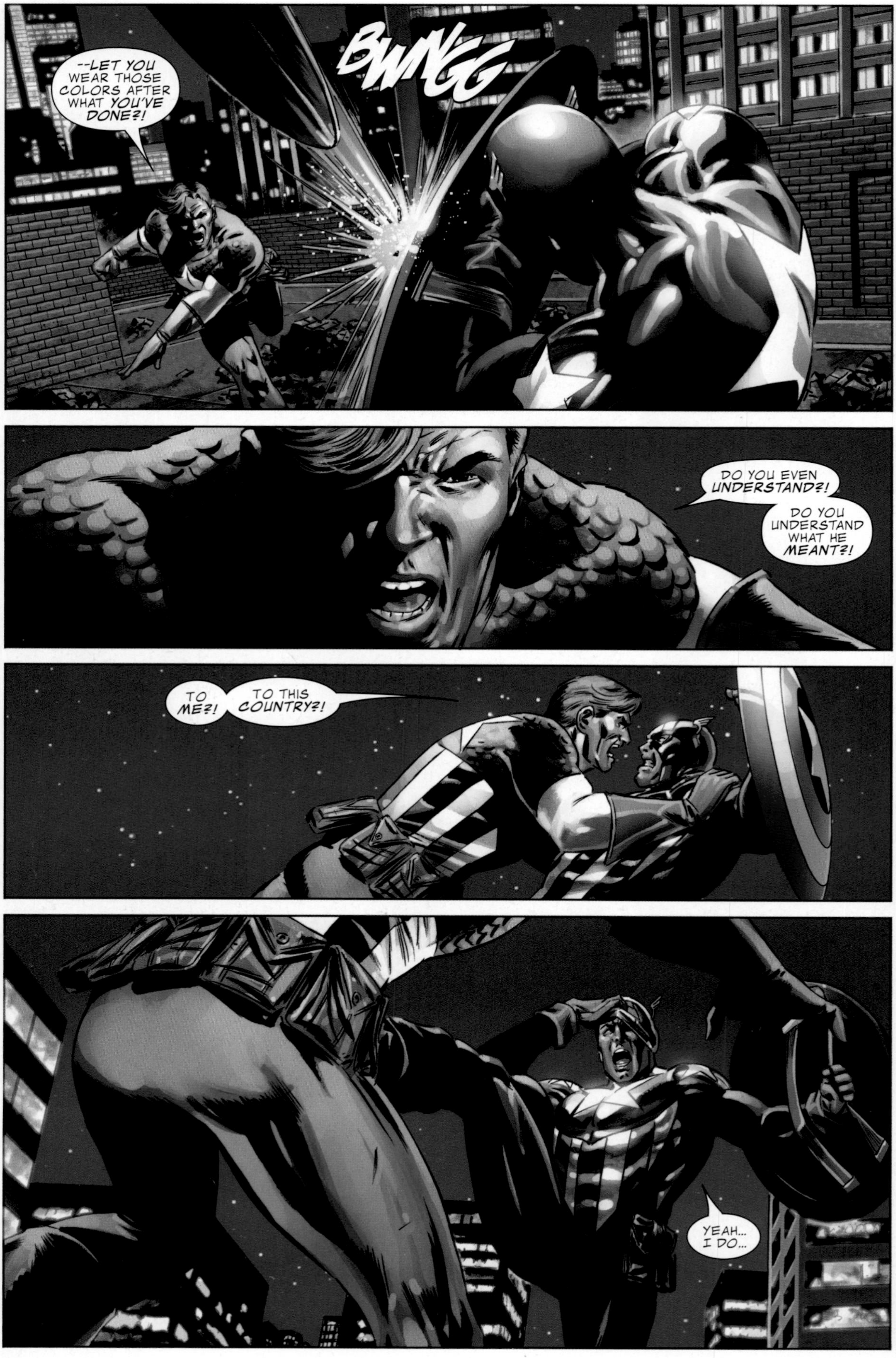
--LET YOU WEAR THOSE COLORS AFTER WHAT YOU'VE DONE?!
BWNGG
DO YOU EVEN UNDERSTAND?!
DO YOU UNDERSTAND WHAT HE MEANT?!
TO ME?!
TO THIS COUNTRY?!
YEAH... I DO...

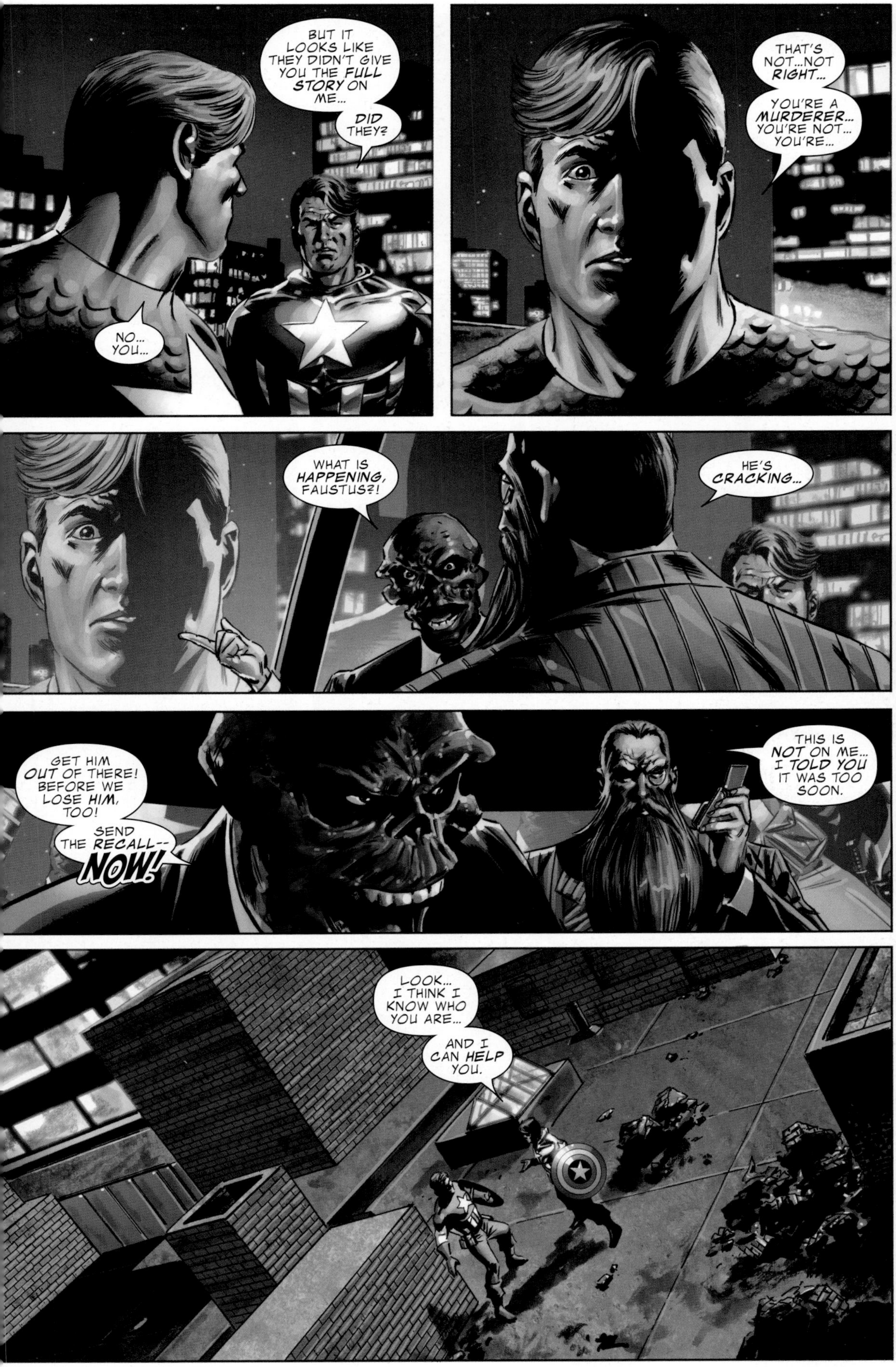
BUT IT LOOKS LIKE THEY DIDN'T GIVE YOU THE FULL STORY ON ME...
DID THEY?
NO... YOU...
THAT'S NOT...NOT RIGHT...
YOU'RE A MURDERER... YOU'RE NOT... YOU'RE...
WHAT IS HAPPENING, FAUSTUS?!
HE'S CRACKING...
GET HIM OUT OF THERE! BEFORE WE LOSE HIM, TOO!
SEND THE RECALL-- NOW!
THIS IS NOT ON ME... I TOLD YOU IT WAS TOO SOON.
LOOK... I THINK I KNOW WHO YOU ARE...
AND I CAN HELP YOU.

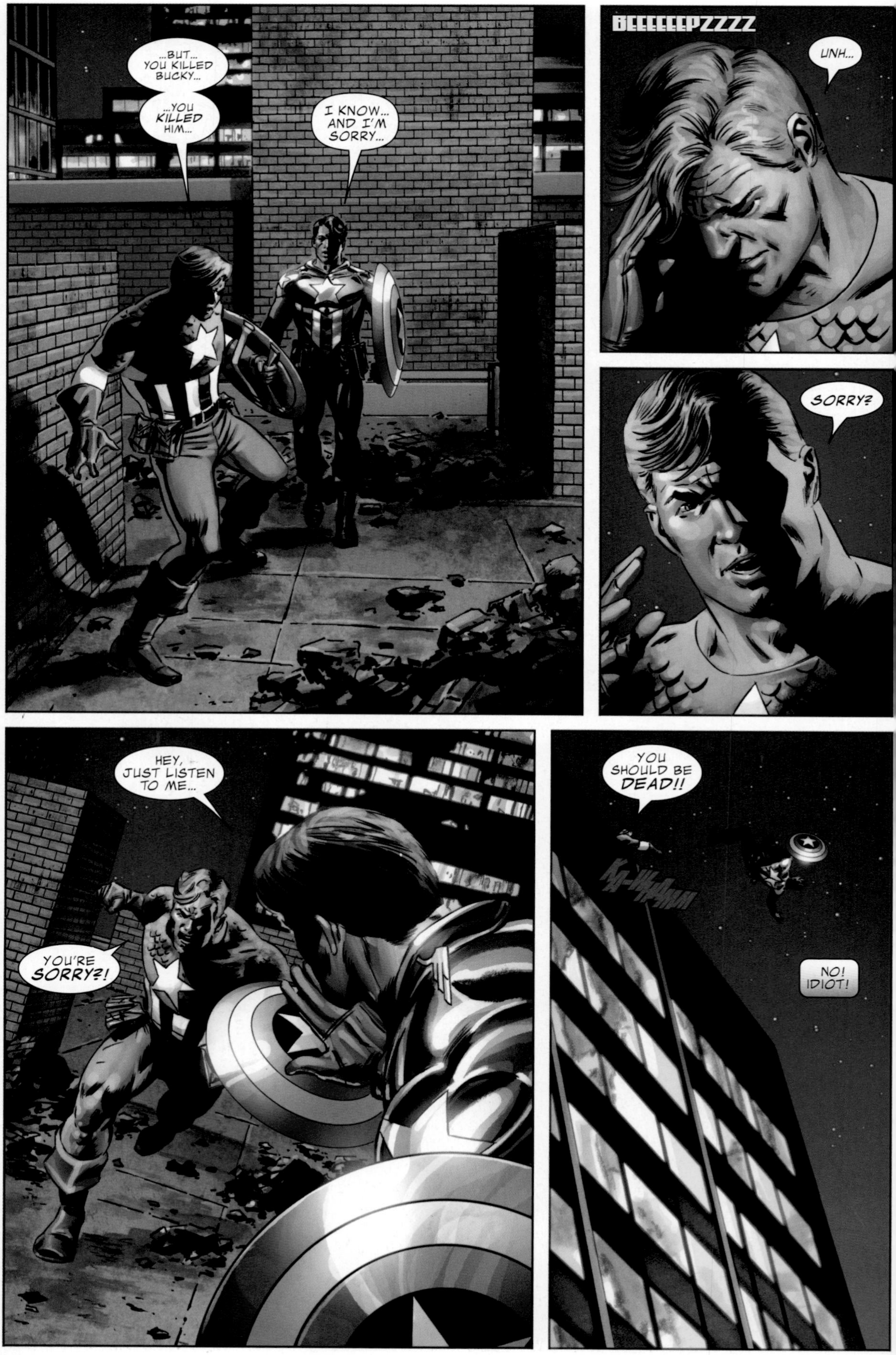
...BUT... YOU KILLED BUCKY...
...YOU KILLED HIM...
I KNOW... AND I'M SORRY...
BEEEEEEPZZZZ
UNH...
SORRY?
HEY, JUST LISTEN TO ME...
YOU'RE SORRY?!
YOU SHOULD BE DEAD!!
NO! IDIOT!

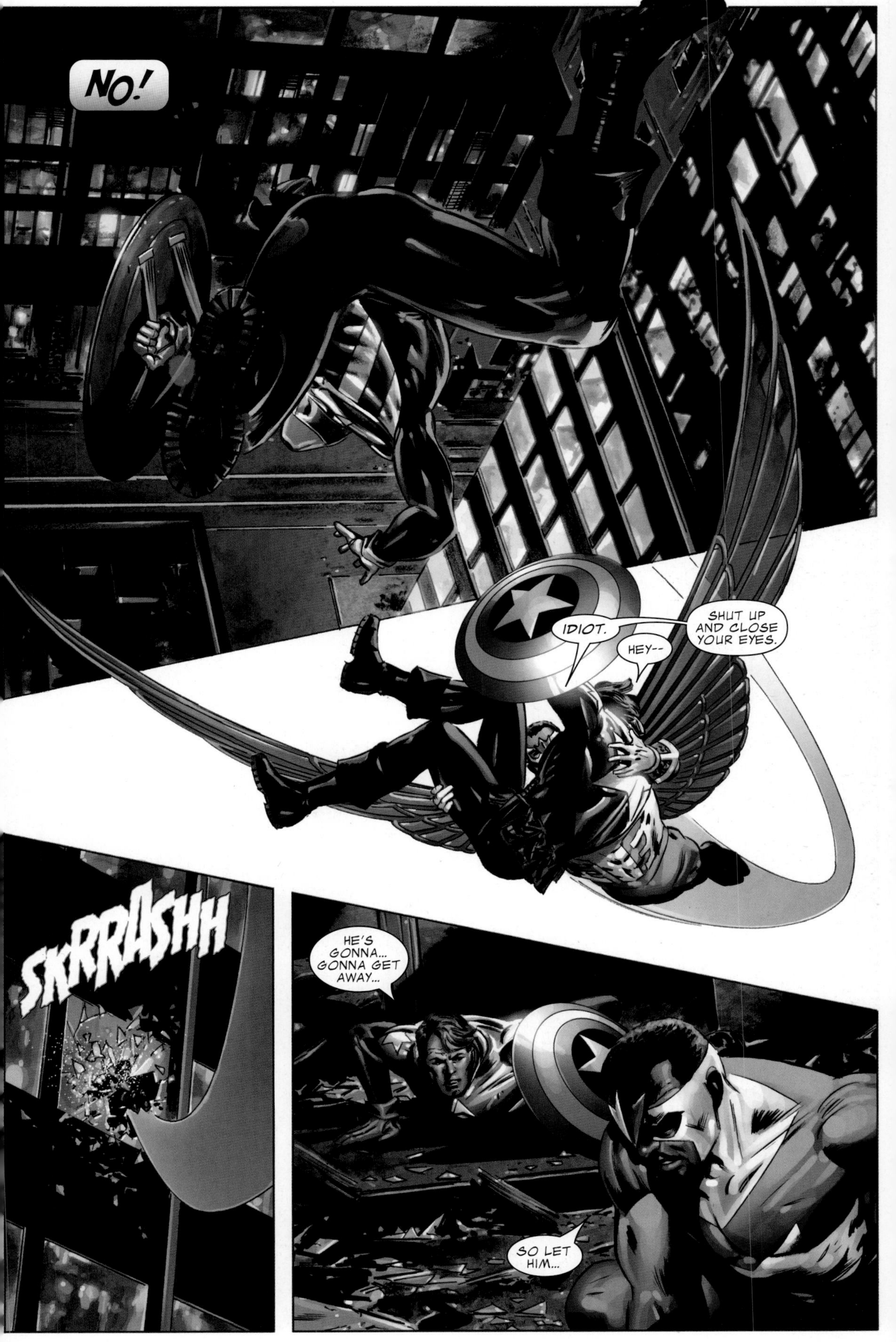
NO!
IDIOT.
HEY--
SHUT UP AND CLOSE YOUR EYES.
SKRRASHH
HE'S GONNA... GONNA GET AWAY...
SO LET HIM...

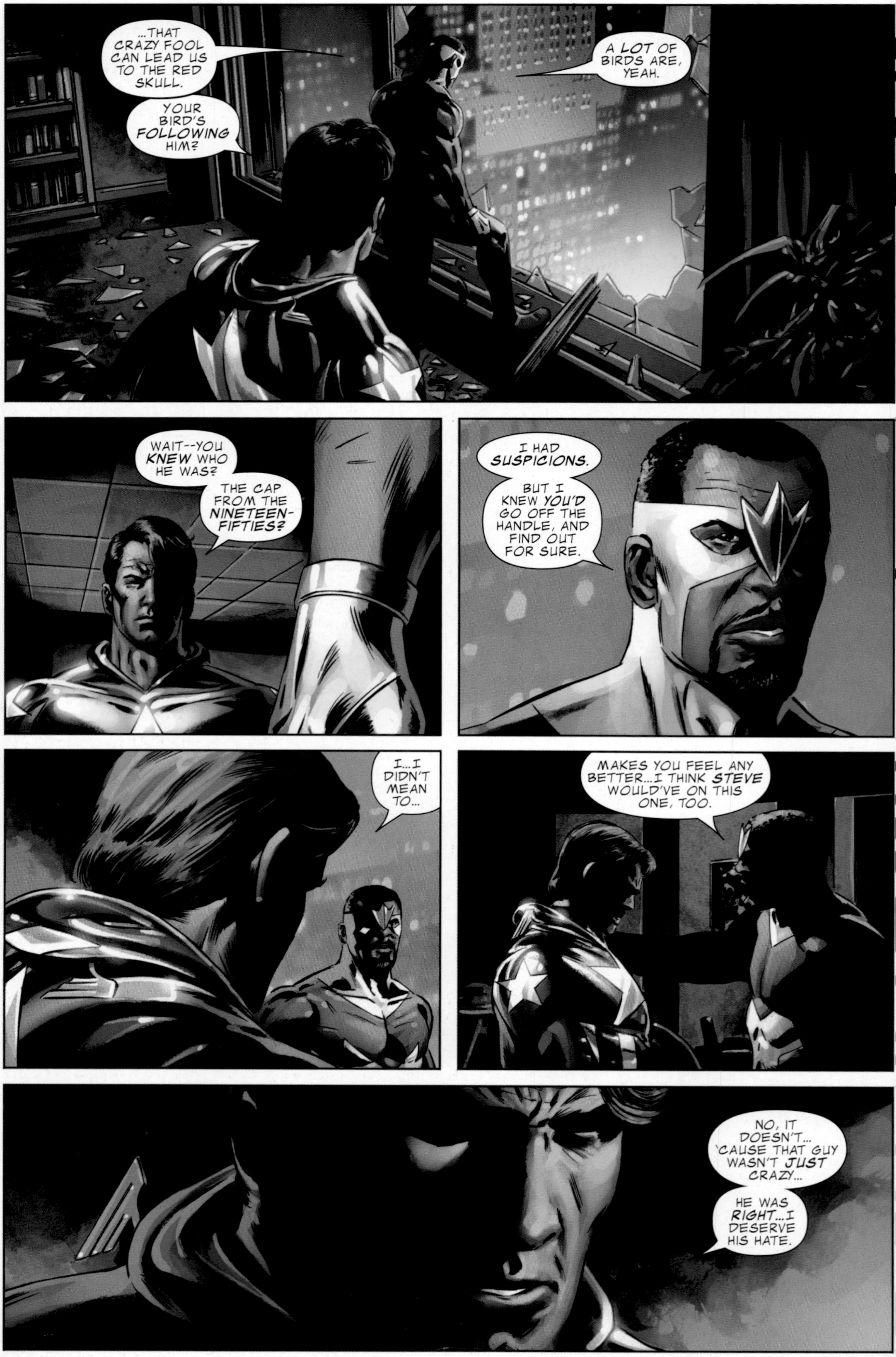
...THAT CRAZY FOOL CAN LEAD US TO THE RED SKULL.
YOUR BIRD'S FOLLOWING HIM?
A LOT OF BIRDS ARE, YEAH.
WAIT--YOU KNEW WHO HE WAS?
THE CAP FROM THE NINETEEN-FIFTIES?
I HAD SUSPICIONS.
BUT I KNEW YOU'D GO OFF THE HANDLE, AND FIND OUT FOR SURE.
I...I DIDN'T MEAN TO...
MAKES YOU FEEL ANY BETTER...I THINK STEVE WOULD'VE ON THIS ONE, TOO.
NO, IT DOESN'T... 'CAUSE THAT GUY WASN'T JUST CRAZY...
HE WAS RIGHT...I DESERVE HIS HATE.

--YOU'VE EARNED MORE THAN *THAT,* FAUSTUS!

YOU *INCOMPETENT,* OVERBLOWN--

YOU WERE THE ONE--YOU AND YOUR *ROBOT* HERE!

DO NOT POINT AT ME, DOCTOR.

IT'S ALL GONE ACCORDING TO *YOUR* SCHEDULE!

AND *THIS FOOL* HASN'T EVEN CRACKED VON DOOM'S DEVICE YET!

YOU DON'T EVEN *KNOW* IF YOU CAN MAKE THE RE--

SIR?!

WHAT?! WHAT IS THE *MEANING* OF THIS INTERRUPTION?

IT'S...UM... THERE'S A PROBLEM, SIR...

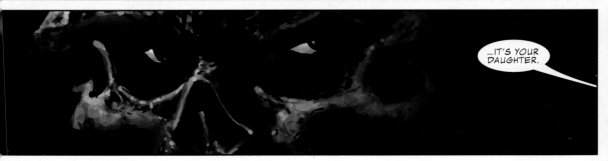

...IT'S YOUR DAUGHTER.

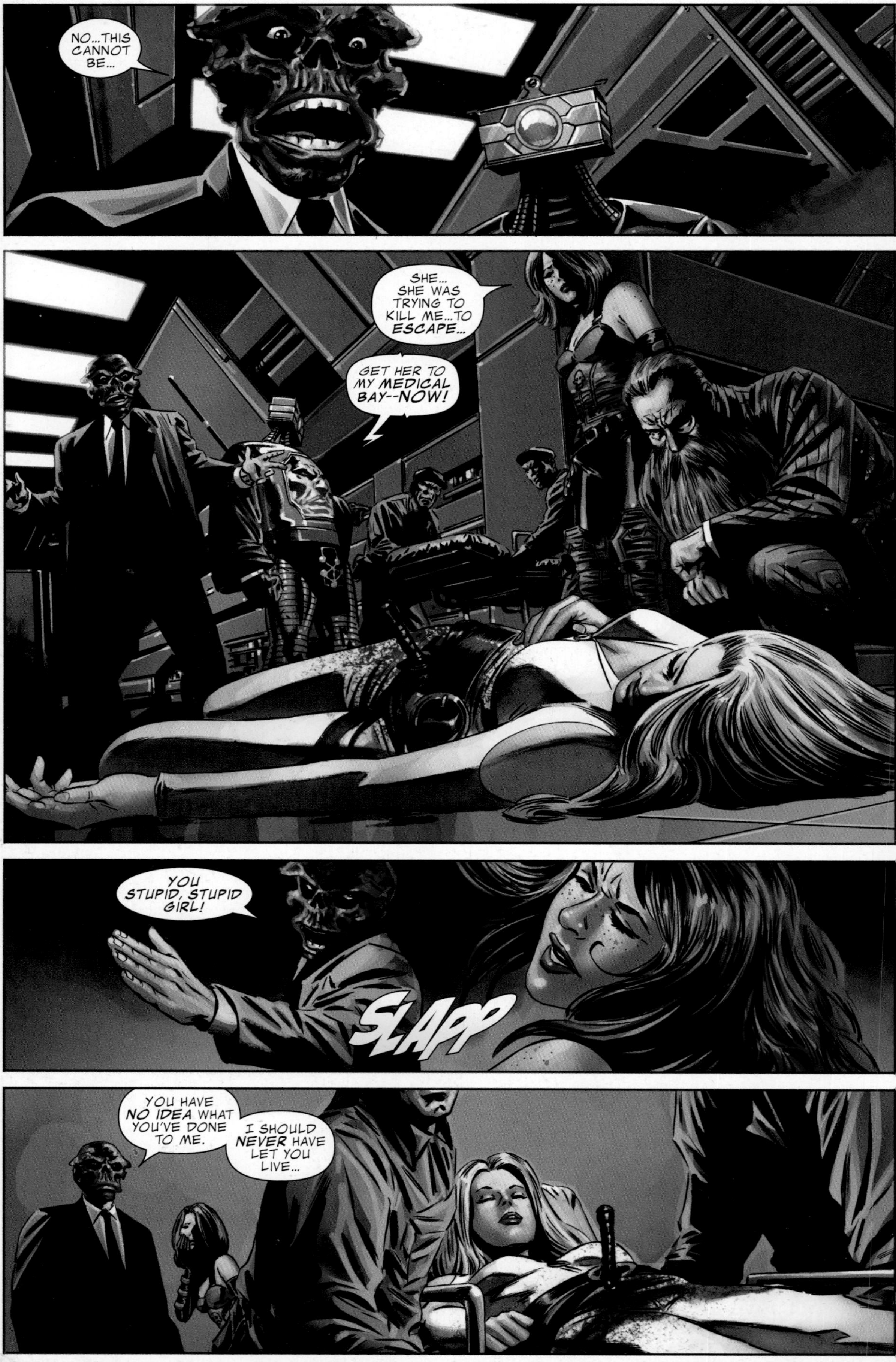
NO...THIS CANNOT BE...
SHE... SHE WAS TRYING TO KILL ME...TO ESCAPE...
GET HER TO MY MEDICAL BAY--NOW!
YOU STUPID, STUPID GIRL!
SLAPP
YOU HAVE NO IDEA WHAT YOU'VE DONE TO ME.
I SHOULD NEVER HAVE LET YOU LIVE...

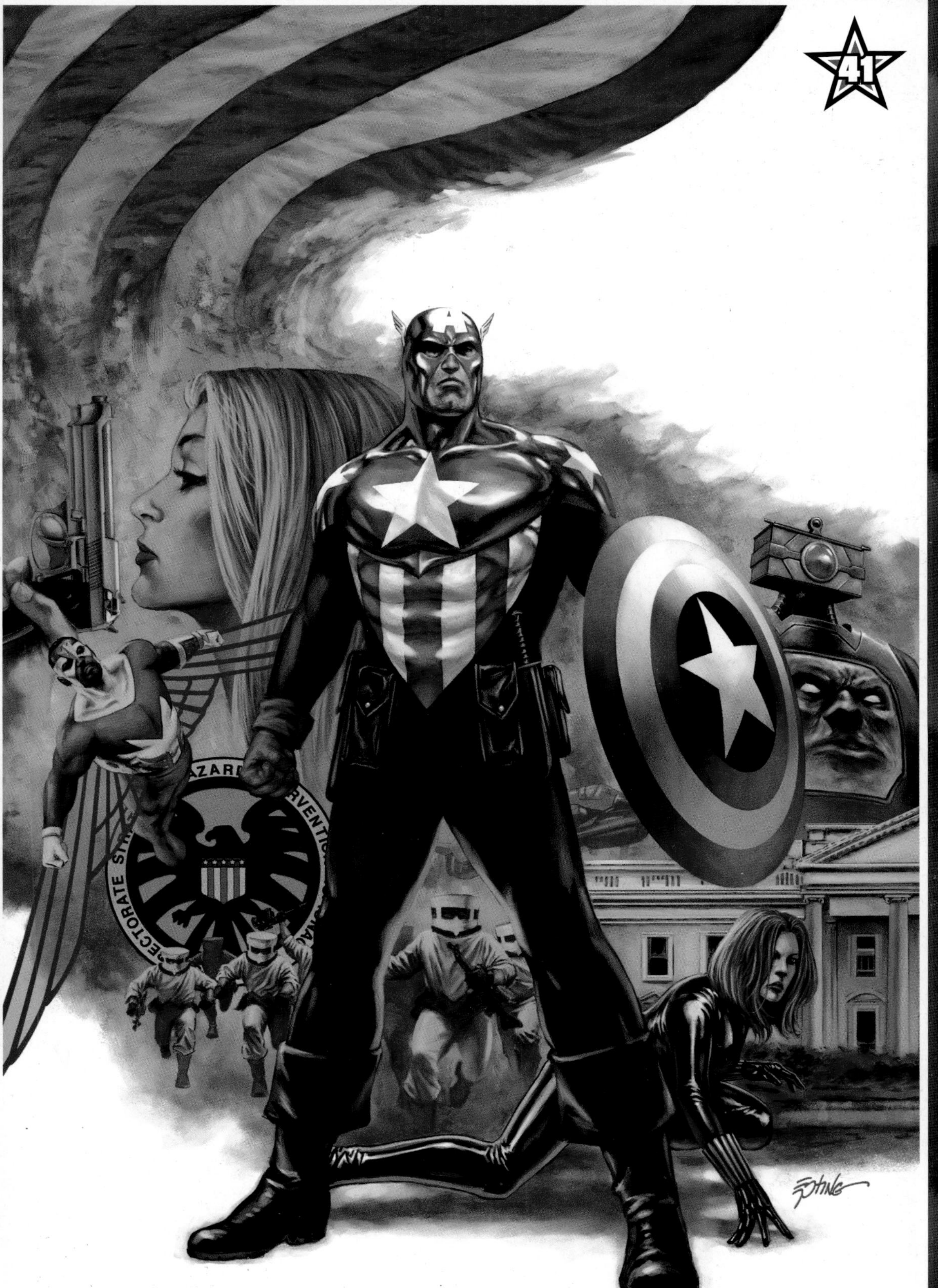
41

PART FIVE

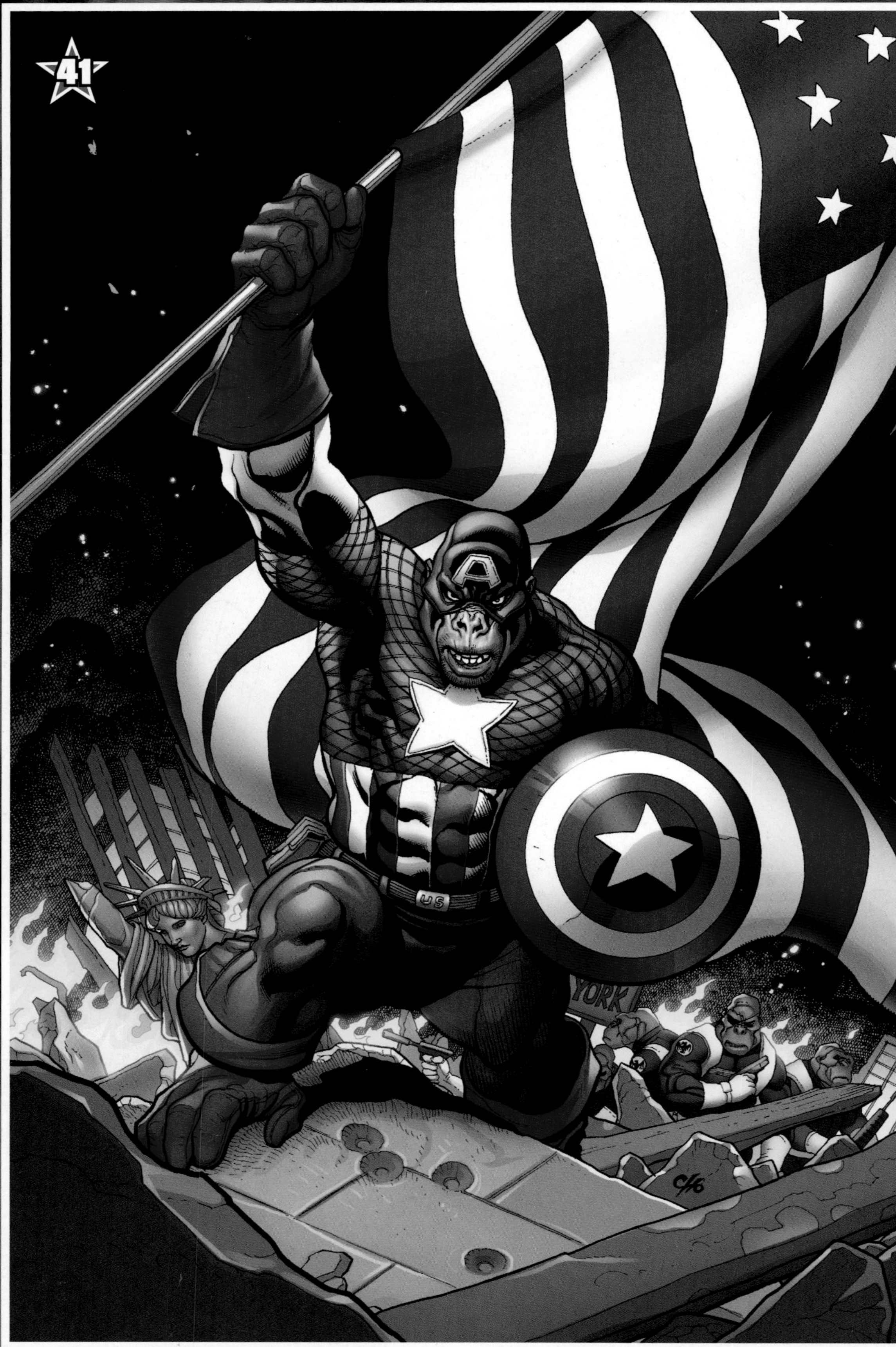
41
US
YORK

APES VARIANT BY FRANK CHO

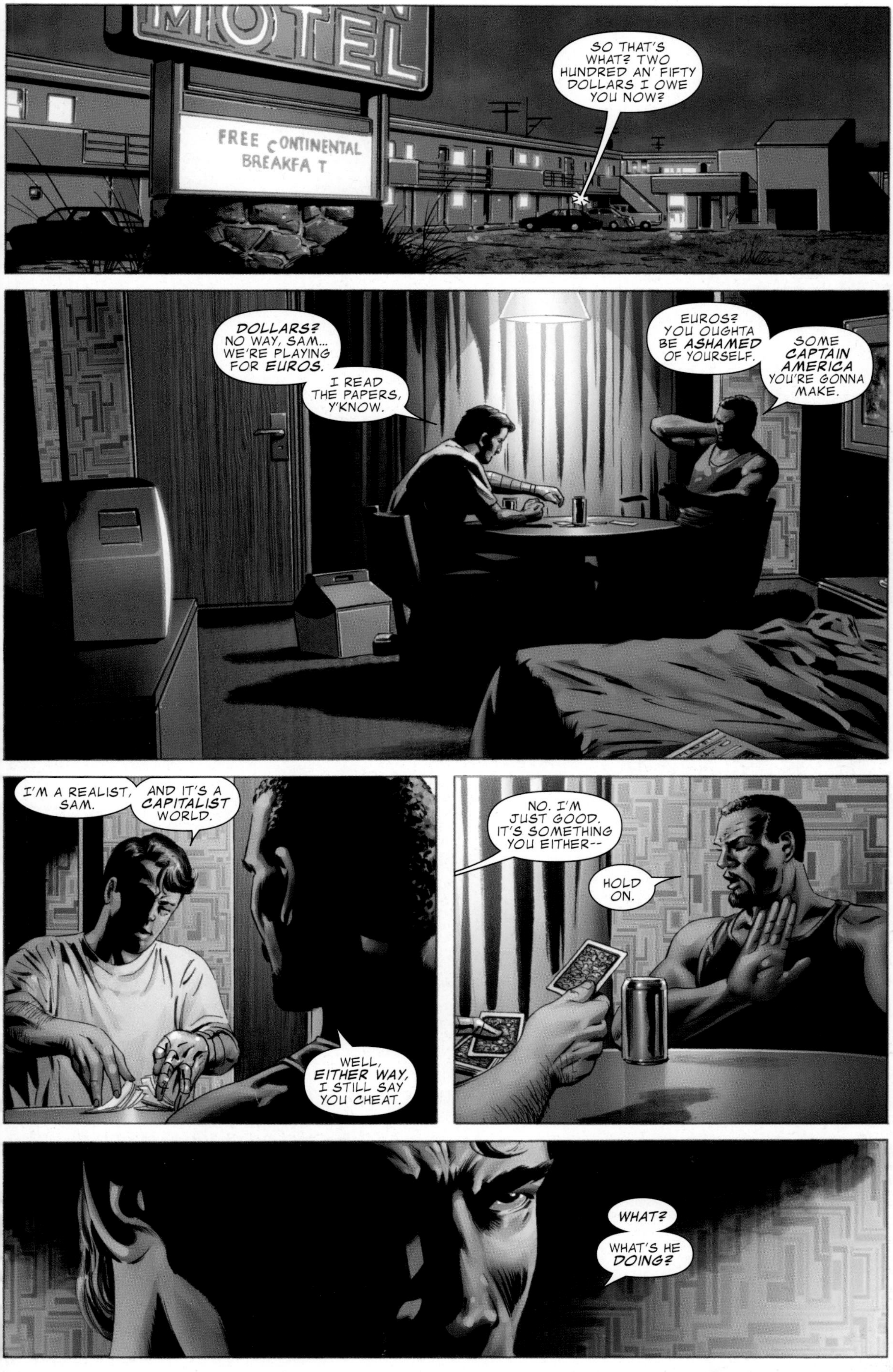
MOTEL
FREE CONTINENTAL BREAKFA T
SO THAT'S WHAT? TWO HUNDRED AN' FIFTY DOLLARS I OWE YOU NOW?
DOLLARS? NO WAY, SAM... WE'RE PLAYING FOR EUROS.
I READ THE PAPERS, Y'KNOW.
EUROS? YOU OUGHTA BE ASHAMED OF YOURSELF.
SOME CAPTAIN AMERICA YOU'RE GONNA MAKE.
I'M A REALIST, SAM.
AND IT'S A CAPITALIST WORLD.
WELL, EITHER WAY, I STILL SAY YOU CHEAT.
NO. I'M JUST GOOD. IT'S SOMETHING YOU EITHER--
HOLD ON.
WHAT?
WHAT'S HE DOING?

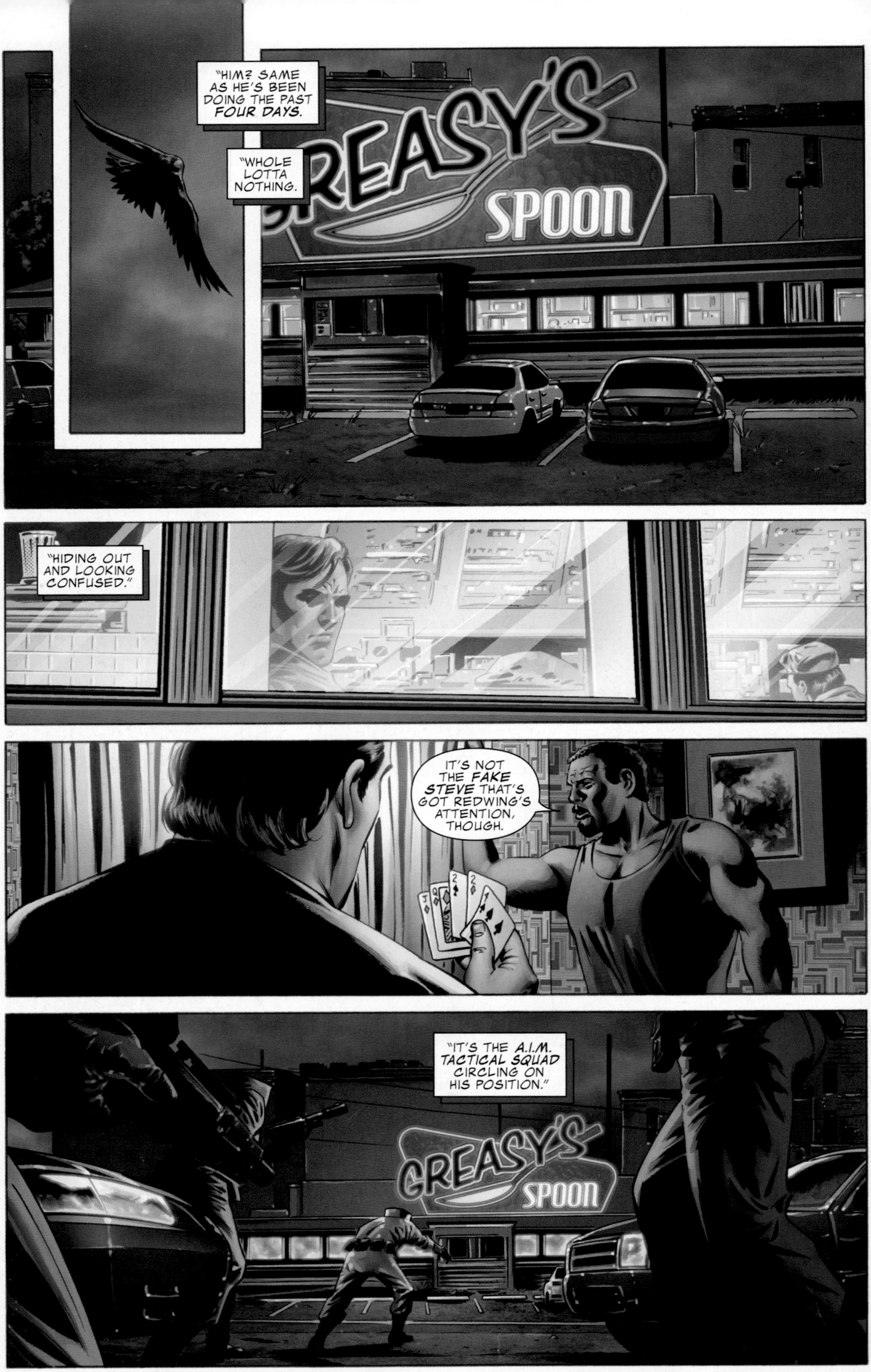
"HIM? SAME AS HE'S BEEN DOING THE PAST FOUR DAYS.
"WHOLE LOTTA NOTHING.
GREASY'S SPOON
"HIDING OUT AND LOOKING CONFUSED."
IT'S NOT THE FAKE STEVE THAT'S GOT REDWING'S ATTENTION, THOUGH.
"IT'S THE A.I.M. TACTICAL SQUAD CIRCLING ON HIS POSITION."
GREASY'S SPOON

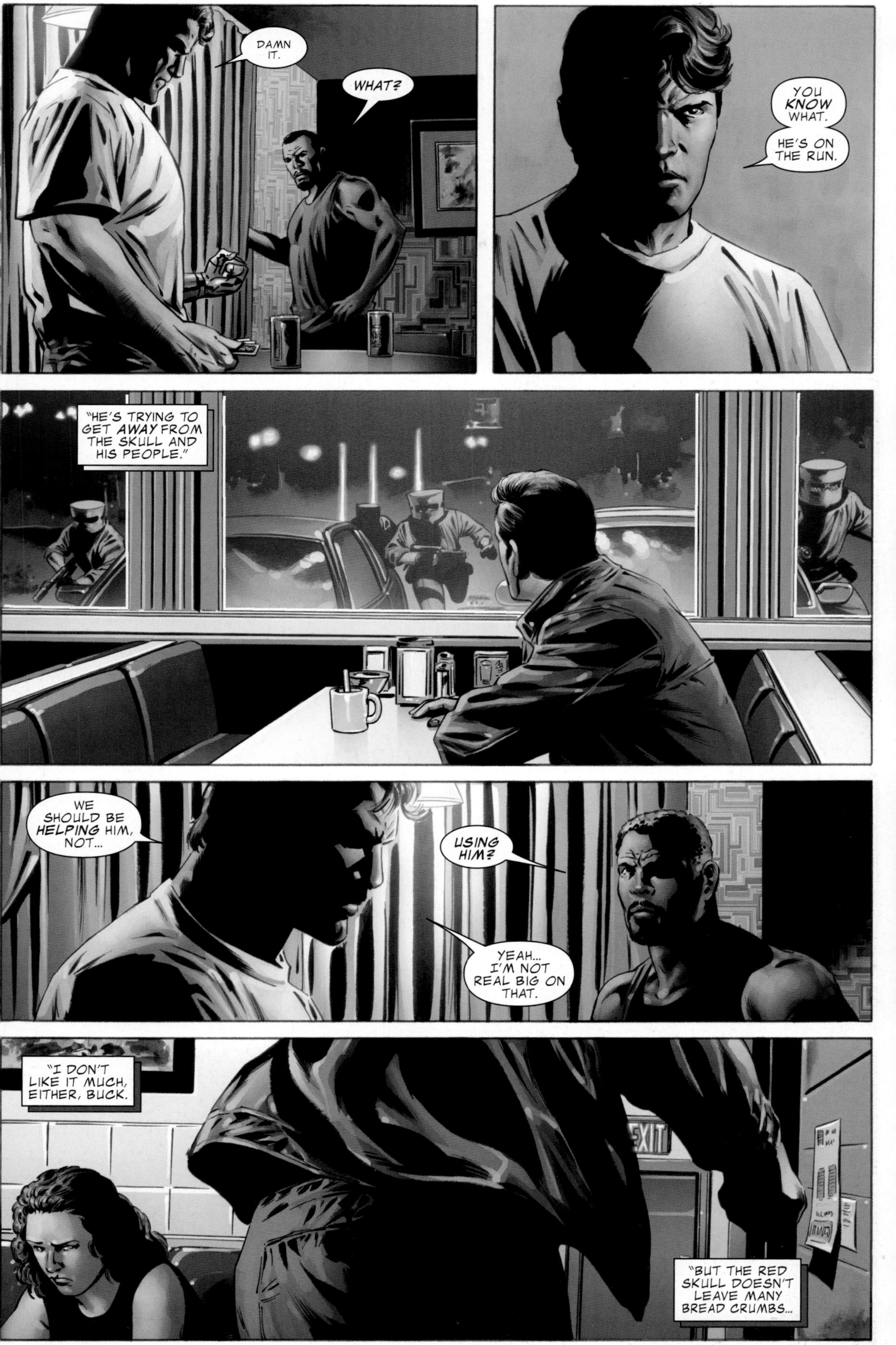
DAMN IT.
WHAT?
YOU KNOW WHAT.
HE'S ON THE RUN.
"HE'S TRYING TO GET AWAY FROM THE SKULL AND HIS PEOPLE."
WE SHOULD BE HELPING HIM, NOT...
USING HIM?
YEAH... I'M NOT REAL BIG ON THAT.
"I DON'T LIKE IT MUCH, EITHER, BUCK.
EXIT
"BUT THE RED SKULL DOESN'T LEAVE MANY BREAD CRUMBS...

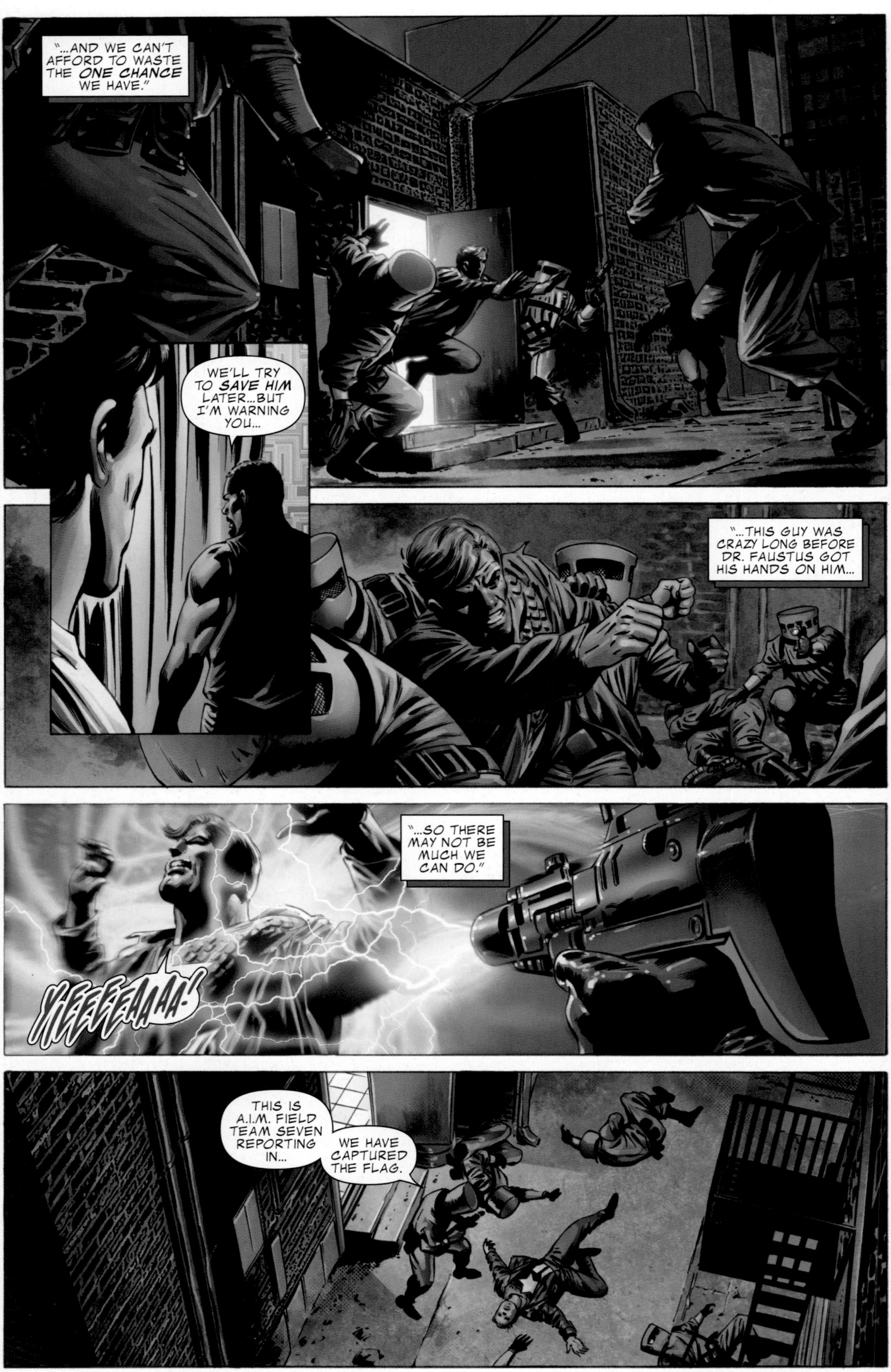
"...AND WE CAN'T AFFORD TO WASTE THE ONE CHANCE WE HAVE."
WE'LL TRY TO SAVE HIM LATER...BUT I'M WARNING YOU...
"...THIS GUY WAS CRAZY LONG BEFORE DR. FAUSTUS GOT HIS HANDS ON HIM...
"...SO THERE MAY NOT BE MUCH WE CAN DO."
YIEEEEAAAA!
THIS IS A.I.M. FIELD TEAM SEVEN REPORTING IN...
WE HAVE CAPTURED THE FLAG.

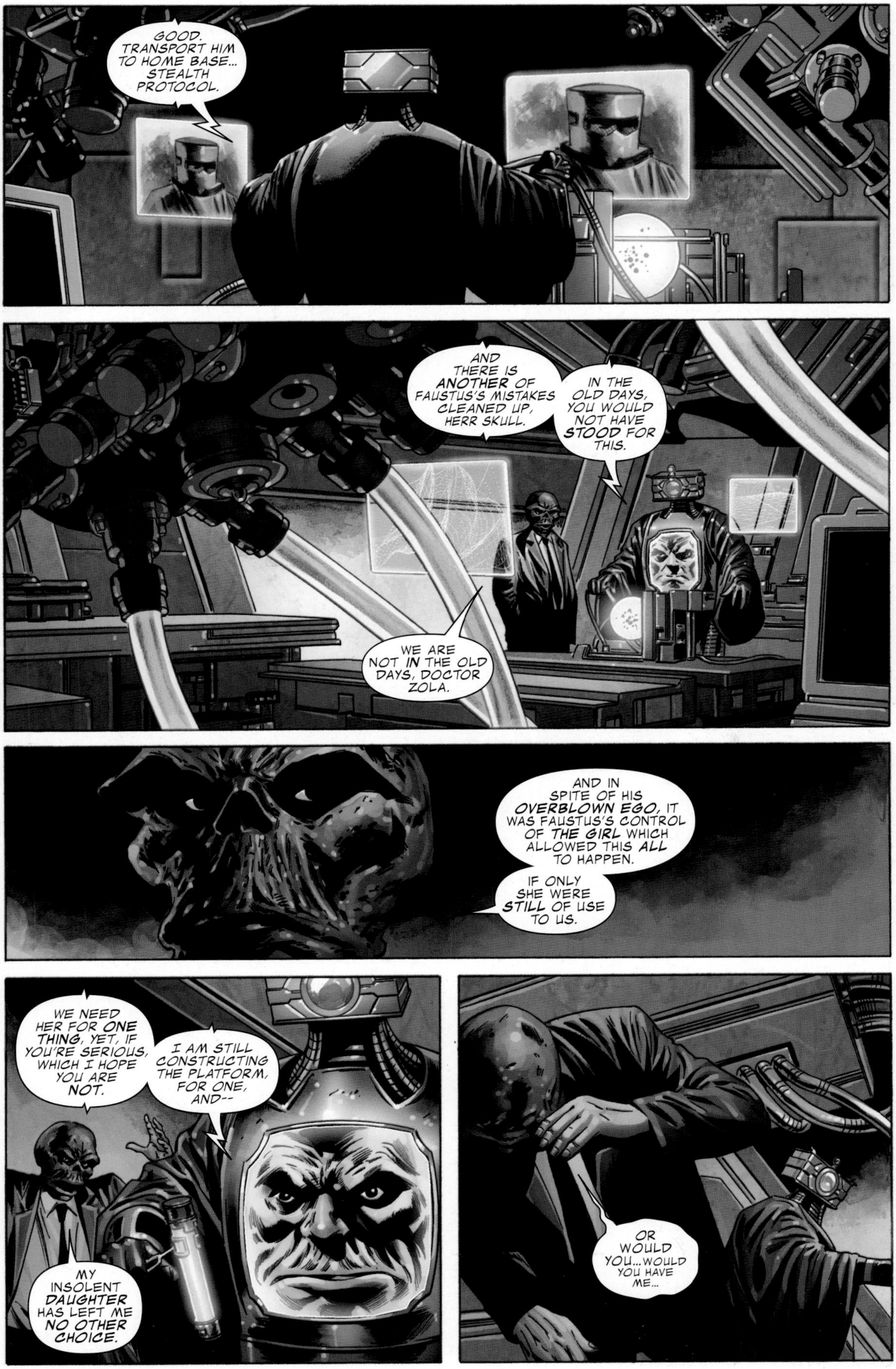
GOOD. TRANSPORT HIM TO HOME BASE... STEALTH PROTOCOL.
AND THERE IS ANOTHER OF FAUSTUS'S MISTAKES CLEANED UP, HERR SKULL.
IN THE OLD DAYS, YOU WOULD NOT HAVE STOOD FOR THIS.
WE ARE NOT IN THE OLD DAYS, DOCTOR ZOLA.
AND IN SPITE OF HIS OVERBLOWN EGO, IT WAS FAUSTUS'S CONTROL OF THE GIRL WHICH ALLOWED THIS ALL TO HAPPEN.
IF ONLY SHE WERE STILL OF USE TO US.
WE NEED HER FOR ONE THING, YET, IF YOU'RE SERIOUS, WHICH I HOPE YOU ARE NOT.
I AM STILL CONSTRUCTING THE PLATFORM, FOR ONE, AND--
MY INSOLENT DAUGHTER HAS LEFT ME NO OTHER CHOICE.
OR WOULD YOU...WOULD YOU HAVE ME...

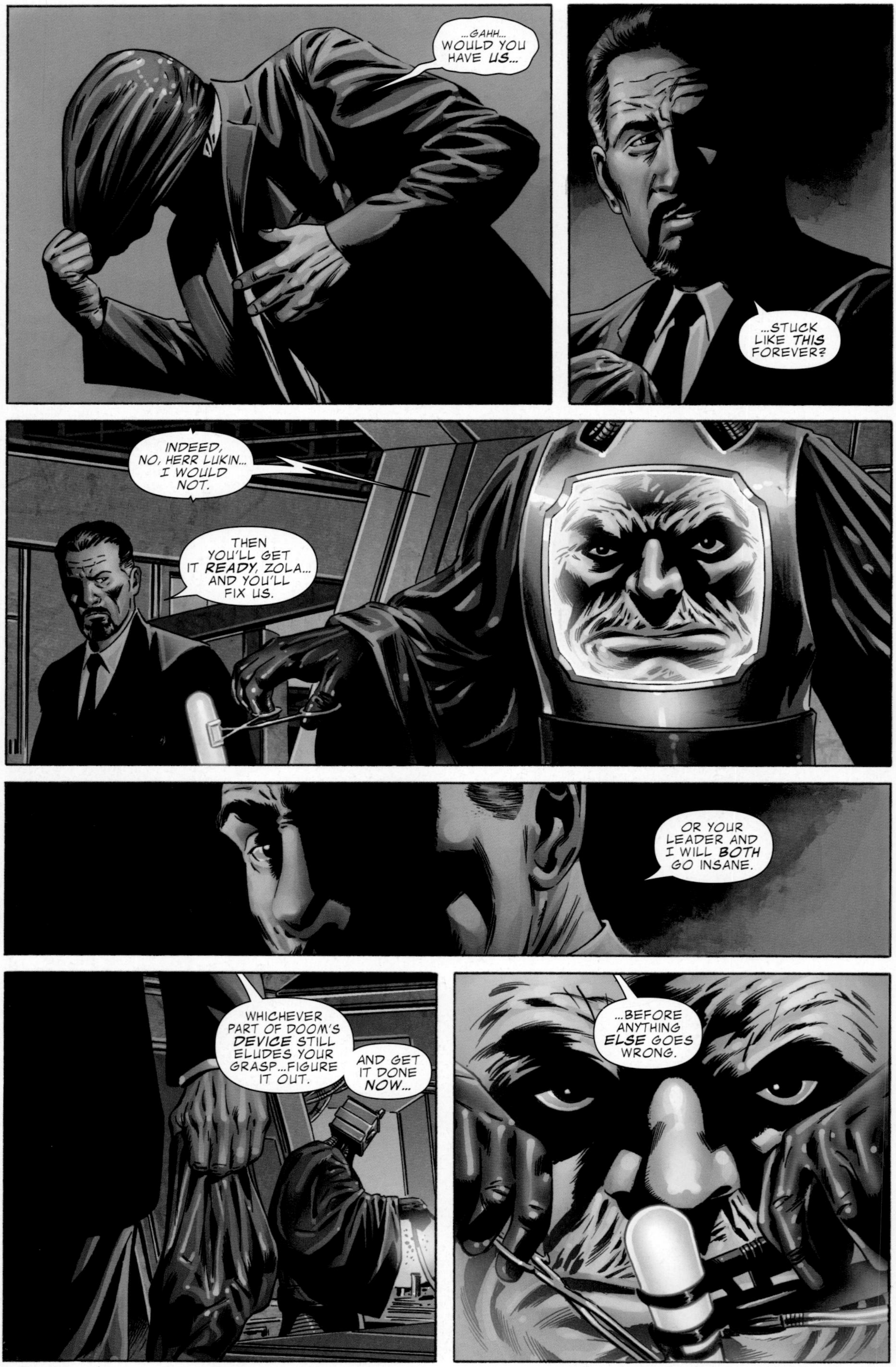
...GAHH... WOULD YOU HAVE US...
...STUCK LIKE THIS FOREVER?
INDEED, NO, HERR LUKIN... I WOULD NOT.
THEN YOU'LL GET IT READY, ZOLA... AND YOU'LL FIX US.
OR YOUR LEADER AND I WILL BOTH GO INSANE.
WHICHEVER PART OF DOOM'S DEVICE STILL ELUDES YOUR GRASP...FIGURE IT OUT.
AND GET IT DONE NOW...
...BEFORE ANYTHING ELSE GOES WRONG.

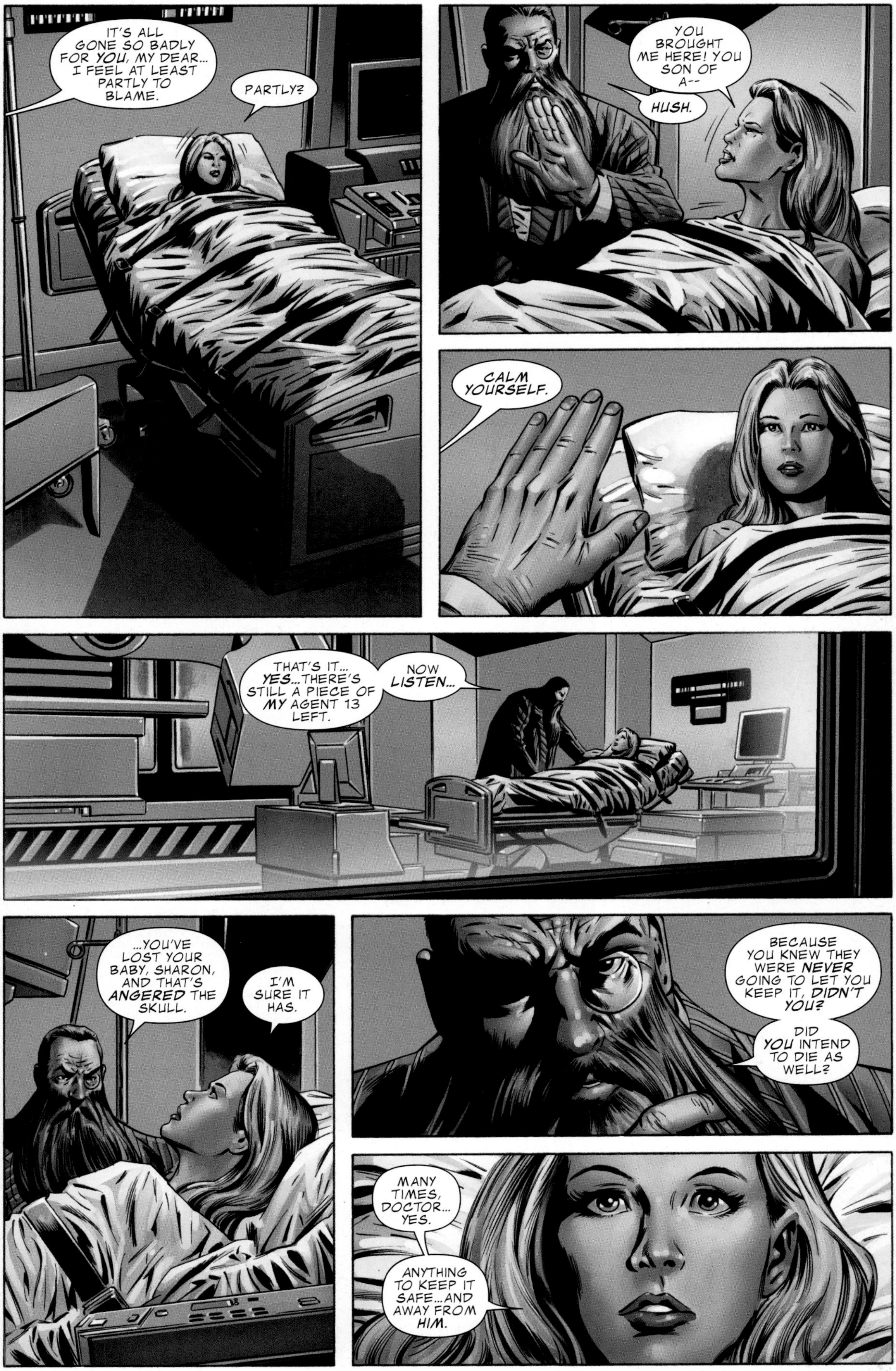
IT'S ALL GONE SO BADLY FOR YOU, MY DEAR... I FEEL AT LEAST PARTLY TO BLAME.
PARTLY?
YOU BROUGHT ME HERE! YOU SON OF A--
HUSH.
CALM YOURSELF.
THAT'S IT... YES... THERE'S STILL A PIECE OF MY AGENT 13 LEFT.
NOW LISTEN...
...YOU'VE LOST YOUR BABY, SHARON, AND THAT'S ANGERED THE SKULL.
I'M SURE IT HAS.
BECAUSE YOU KNEW THEY WERE NEVER GOING TO LET YOU KEEP IT, DIDN'T YOU?
DID YOU INTEND TO DIE AS WELL?
MANY TIMES, DOCTOR... YES.
ANYTHING TO KEEP IT SAFE...AND AWAY FROM HIM.

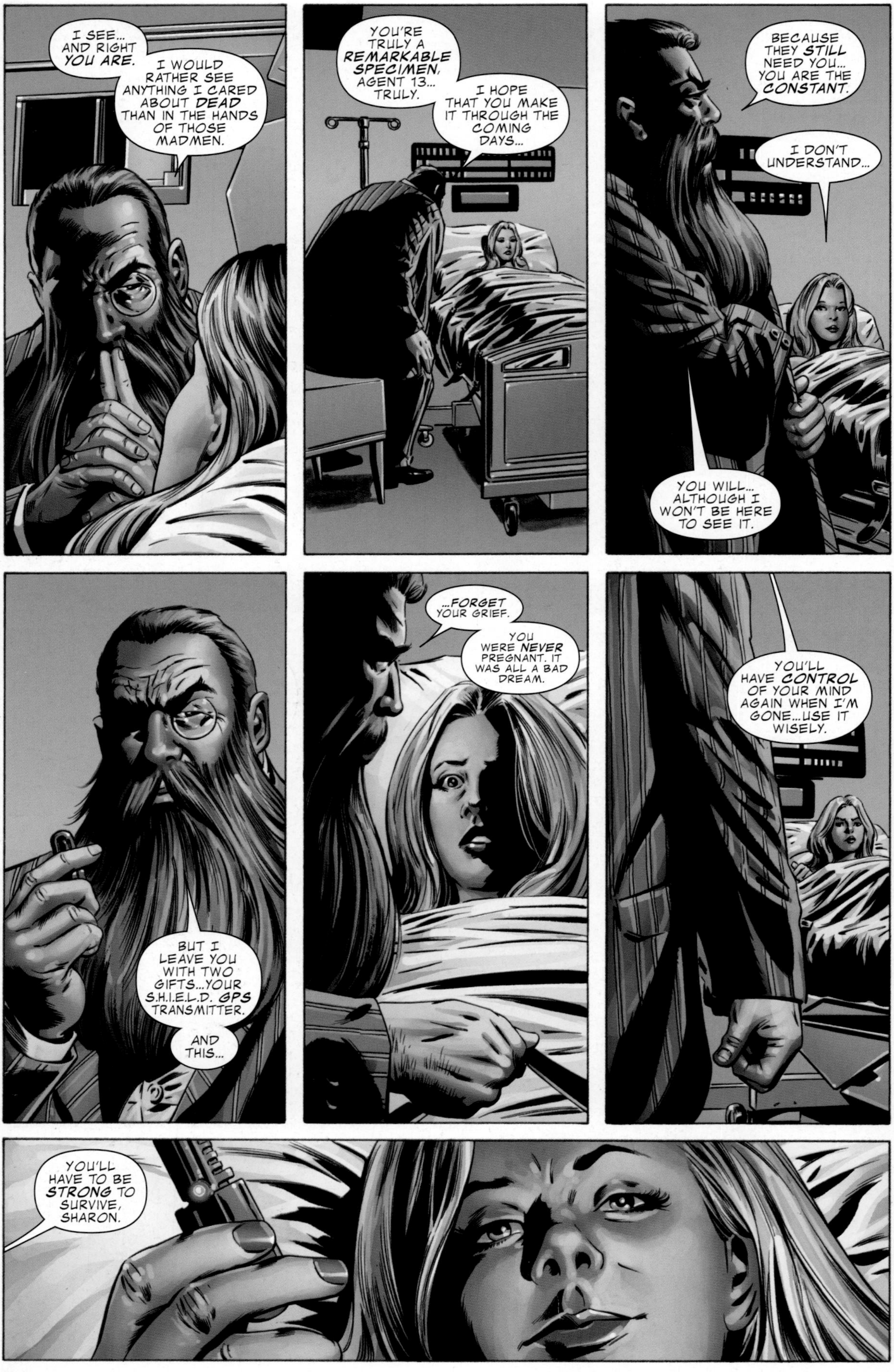
I SEE... AND RIGHT YOU ARE.
I WOULD RATHER SEE ANYTHING I CARED ABOUT DEAD THAN IN THE HANDS OF THOSE MADMEN.
YOU'RE TRULY A REMARKABLE SPECIMEN, AGENT 13... TRULY.
I HOPE THAT YOU MAKE IT THROUGH THE COMING DAYS...
BECAUSE THEY STILL NEED YOU... YOU ARE THE CONSTANT.
I DON'T UNDERSTAND...
YOU WILL... ALTHOUGH I WON'T BE HERE TO SEE IT.
BUT I LEAVE YOU WITH TWO GIFTS...YOUR S.H.I.E.L.D. GPS TRANSMITTER.
AND THIS...
...FORGET YOUR GRIEF.
YOU WERE NEVER PREGNANT. IT WAS ALL A BAD DREAM.
YOU'LL HAVE CONTROL OF YOUR MIND AGAIN WHEN I'M GONE...USE IT WISELY.
YOU'LL HAVE TO BE STRONG TO SURVIVE, SHARON.

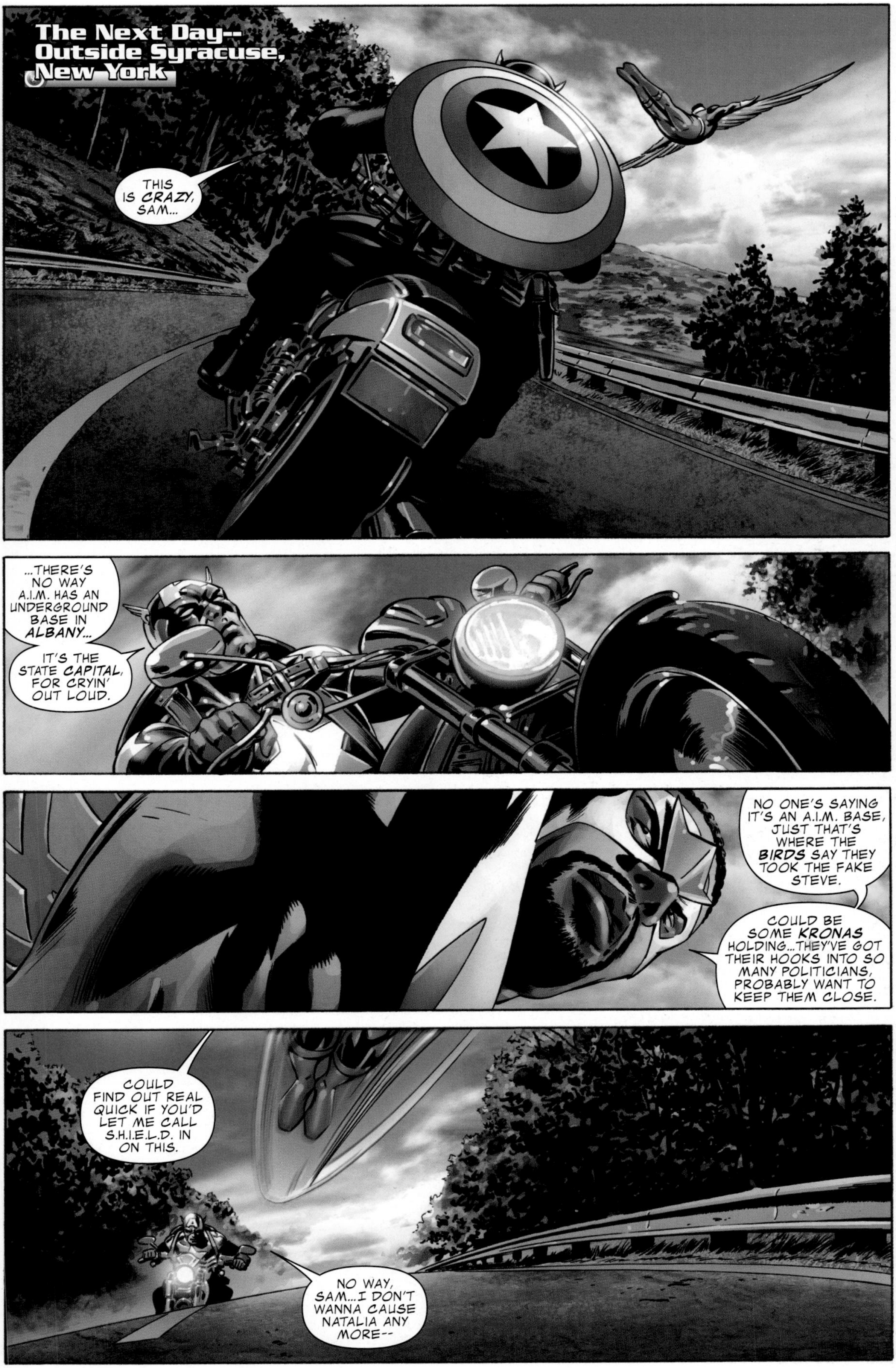
The Next Day--
Outside Syracuse, New York
THIS IS CRAZY, SAM...
...THERE'S NO WAY A.I.M. HAS AN UNDERGROUND BASE IN ALBANY...
IT'S THE STATE CAPITAL, FOR CRYIN' OUT LOUD.
NO ONE'S SAYING IT'S AN A.I.M. BASE, JUST THAT'S WHERE THE BIRDS SAY THEY TOOK THE FAKE STEVE.
COULD BE SOME KRONAS HOLDING...THEY'VE GOT THEIR HOOKS INTO SO MANY POLITICIANS, PROBABLY WANT TO KEEP THEM CLOSE.
COULD FIND OUT REAL QUICK IF YOU'D LET ME CALL S.H.I.E.L.D. IN ON THIS.
NO WAY, SAM...I DON'T WANNA CAUSE NATALIA ANY MORE--

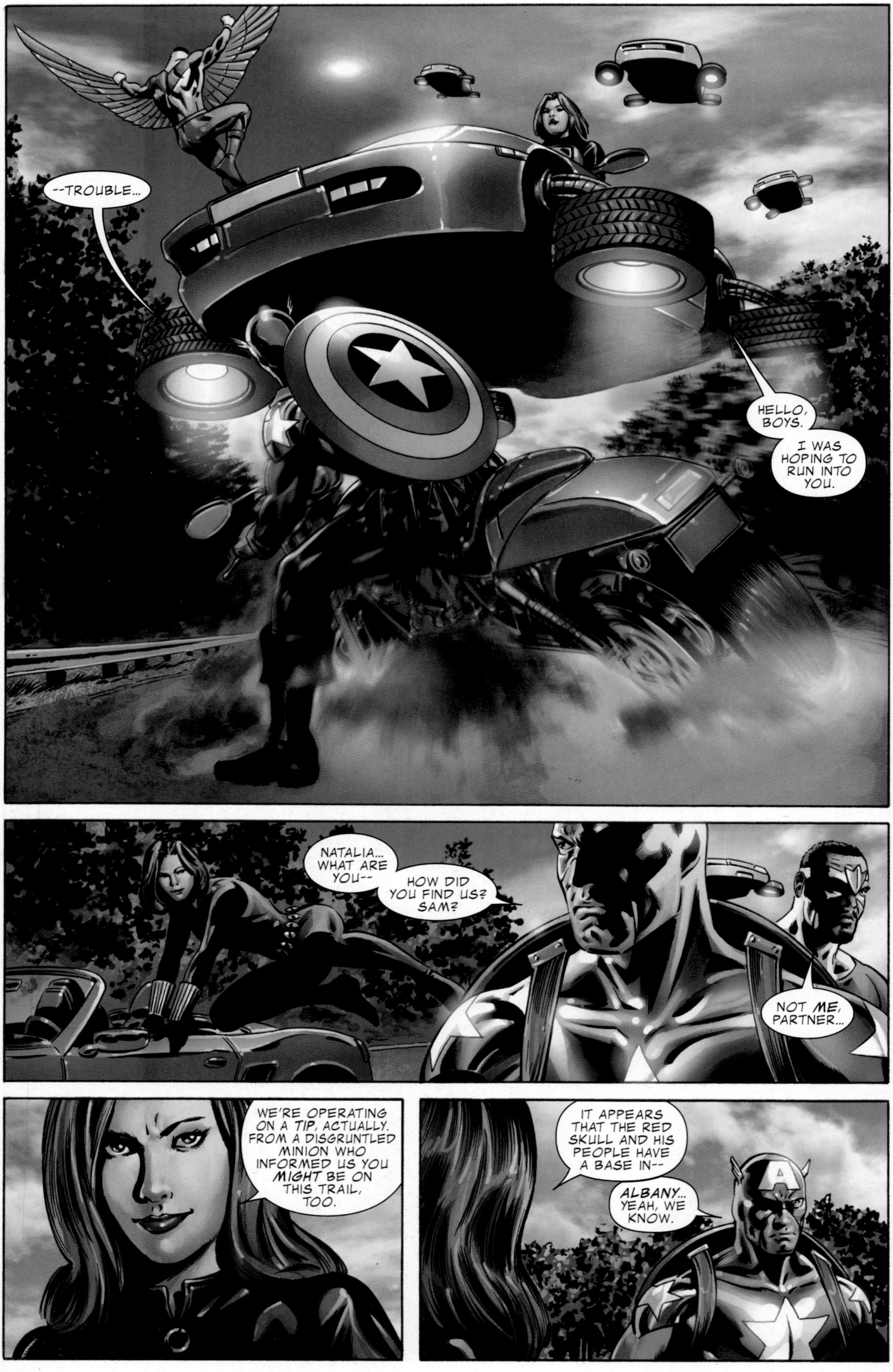
--TROUBLE...
HELLO, BOYS.
I WAS HOPING TO RUN INTO YOU.
NATALIA... WHAT ARE YOU--
HOW DID YOU FIND US? SAM?
NOT *ME*, PARTNER...
WE'RE OPERATING ON A *TIP*, ACTUALLY. FROM A DISGRUNTLED MINION WHO INFORMED US YOU *MIGHT* BE ON THIS TRAIL, TOO.
IT APPEARS THAT THE RED SKULL AND HIS PEOPLE HAVE A BASE IN--
ALBANY... YEAH, WE KNOW.

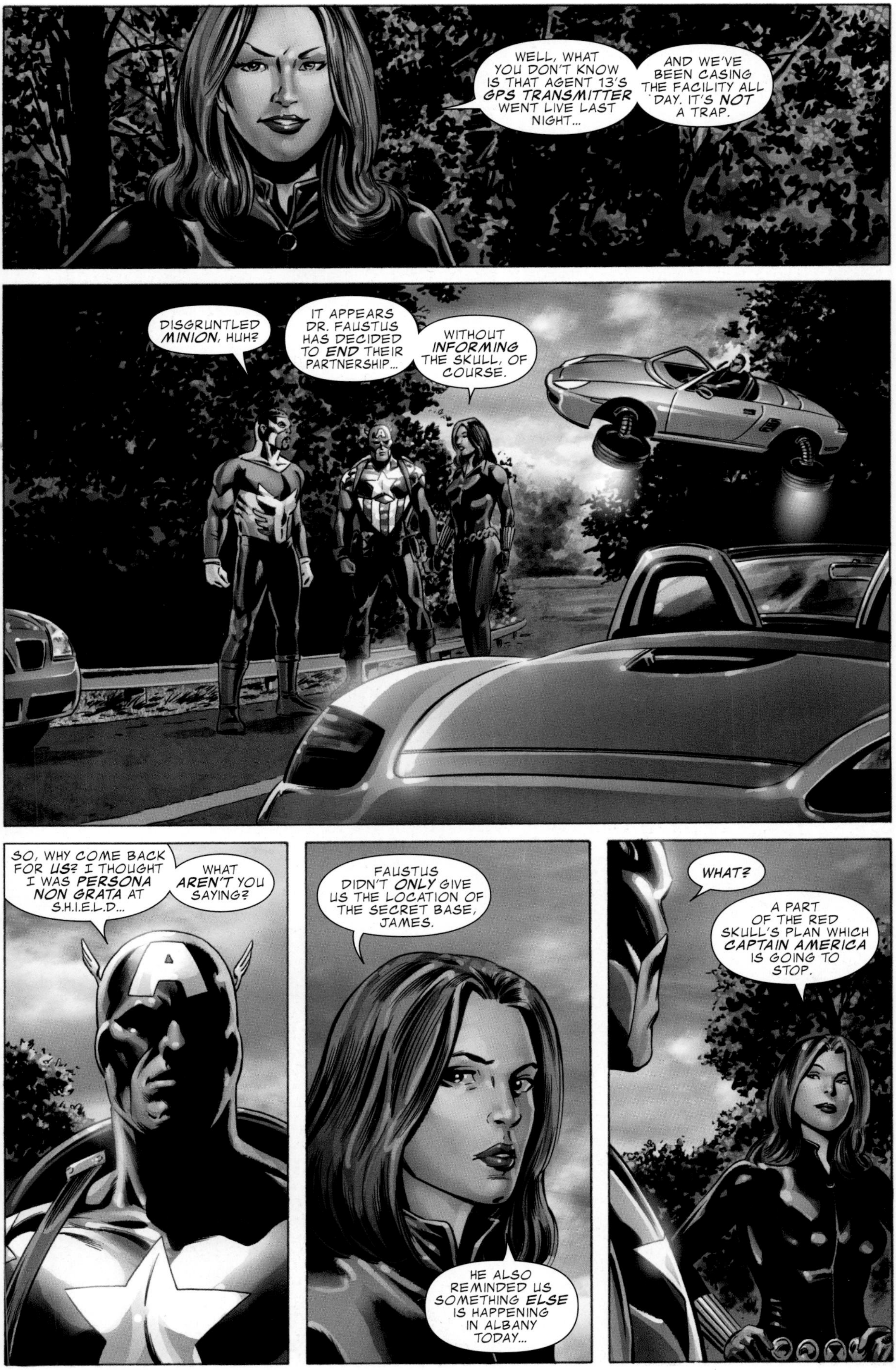

WELL, WHAT YOU DON'T KNOW IS THAT AGENT 13'S GPS TRANSMITTER WENT LIVE LAST NIGHT...
AND WE'VE BEEN CASING THE FACILITY ALL DAY. IT'S NOT A TRAP.
DISGRUNTLED MINION, HUH?
IT APPEARS DR. FAUSTUS HAS DECIDED TO END THEIR PARTNERSHIP...
WITHOUT INFORMING THE SKULL, OF COURSE.
SO, WHY COME BACK FOR US? I THOUGHT I WAS PERSONA NON GRATA AT S.H.I.E.L.D...
WHAT AREN'T YOU SAYING?
FAUSTUS DIDN'T ONLY GIVE US THE LOCATION OF THE SECRET BASE, JAMES.
HE ALSO REMINDED US SOMETHING ELSE IS HAPPENING IN ALBANY TODAY...
WHAT?
A PART OF THE RED SKULL'S PLAN WHICH CAPTAIN AMERICA IS GOING TO STOP.

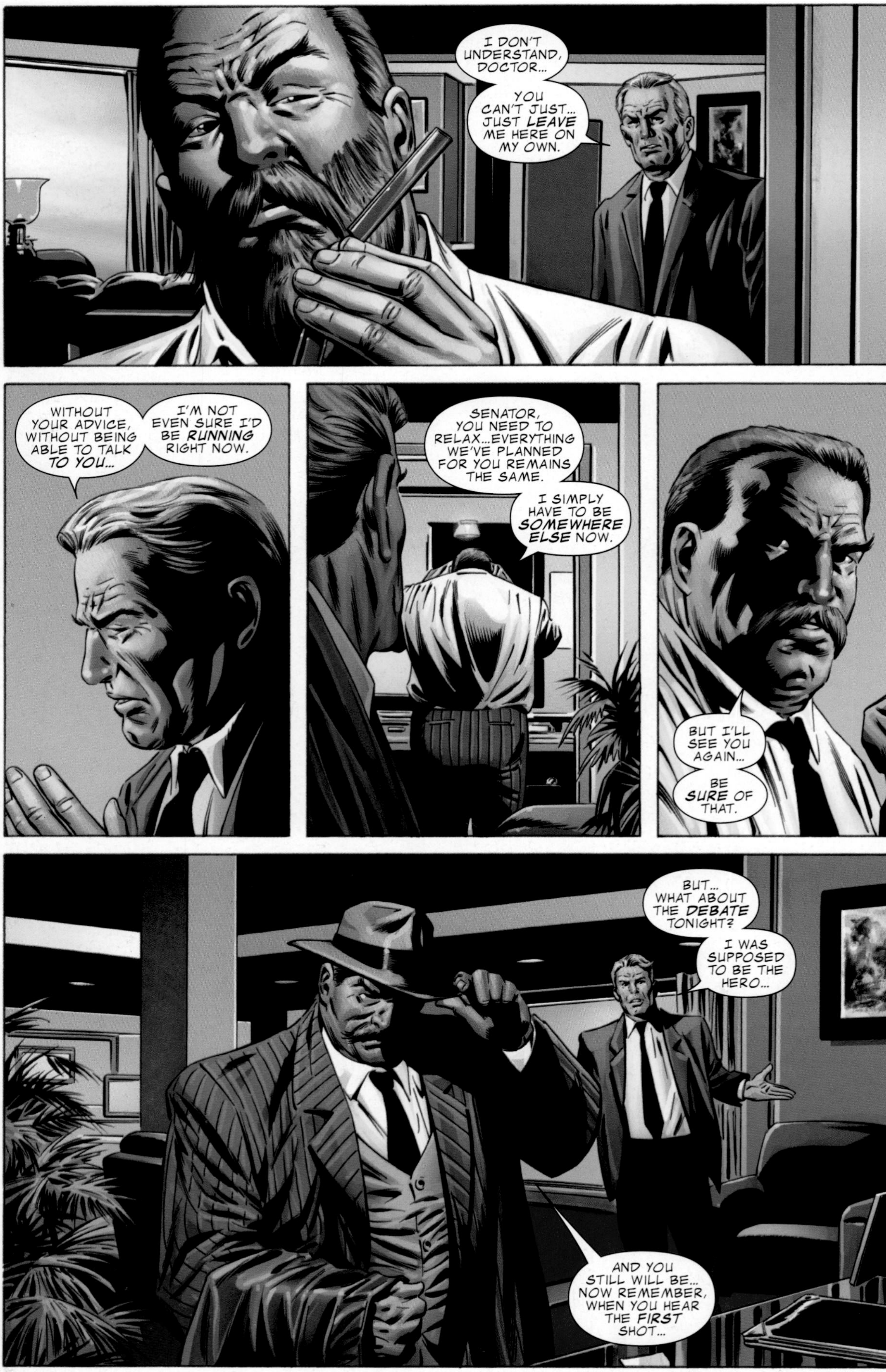
I DON'T UNDERSTAND, DOCTOR...
YOU CAN'T JUST... JUST LEAVE ME HERE ON MY OWN.
WITHOUT YOUR ADVICE, WITHOUT BEING ABLE TO TALK TO YOU...
I'M NOT EVEN SURE I'D BE RUNNING RIGHT NOW.
SENATOR, YOU NEED TO RELAX...EVERYTHING WE'VE PLANNED FOR YOU REMAINS THE SAME.
I SIMPLY HAVE TO BE SOMEWHERE ELSE NOW.
BUT I'LL SEE YOU AGAIN...
BE SURE OF THAT.
BUT... WHAT ABOUT THE DEBATE TONIGHT?
I WAS SUPPOSED TO BE THE HERO...
AND YOU STILL WILL BE... NOW REMEMBER, WHEN YOU HEAR THE FIRST SHOT...

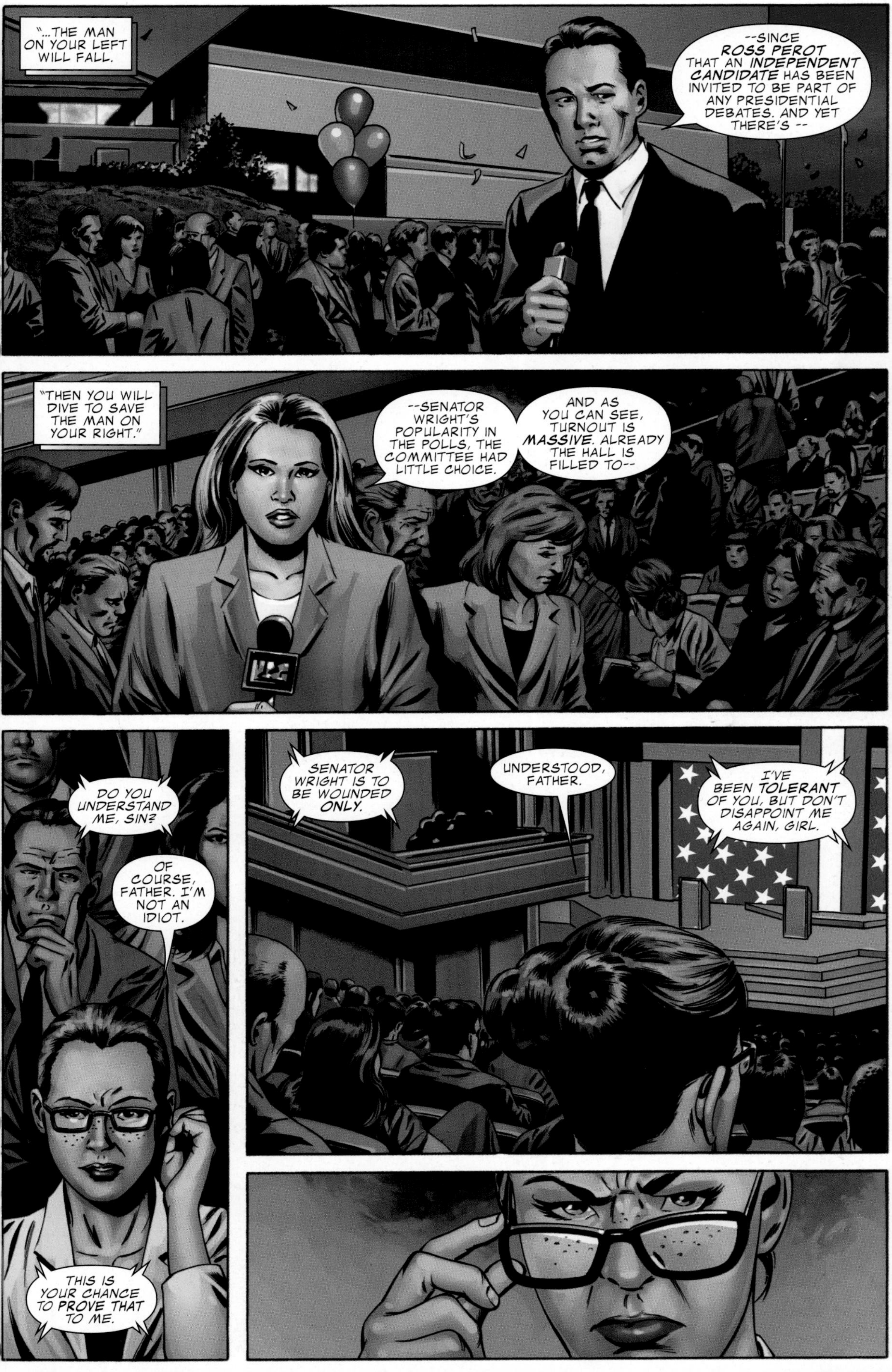
"...THE MAN ON YOUR LEFT WILL FALL.
--SINCE ROSS PEROT THAT AN INDEPENDENT CANDIDATE HAS BEEN INVITED TO BE PART OF ANY PRESIDENTIAL DEBATES. AND YET THERE'S --
"THEN YOU WILL DIVE TO SAVE THE MAN ON YOUR RIGHT."
--SENATOR WRIGHT'S POPULARITY IN THE POLLS, THE COMMITTEE HAD LITTLE CHOICE.
AND AS YOU CAN SEE, TURNOUT IS MASSIVE. ALREADY THE HALL IS FILLED TO--
DO YOU UNDERSTAND ME, SIN?
OF COURSE, FATHER. I'M NOT AN IDIOT.
THIS IS YOUR CHANCE TO PROVE THAT TO ME.
SENATOR WRIGHT IS TO BE WOUNDED ONLY.
UNDERSTOOD, FATHER.
I'VE BEEN TOLERANT OF YOU, BUT DON'T DISAPPOINT ME AGAIN, GIRL.

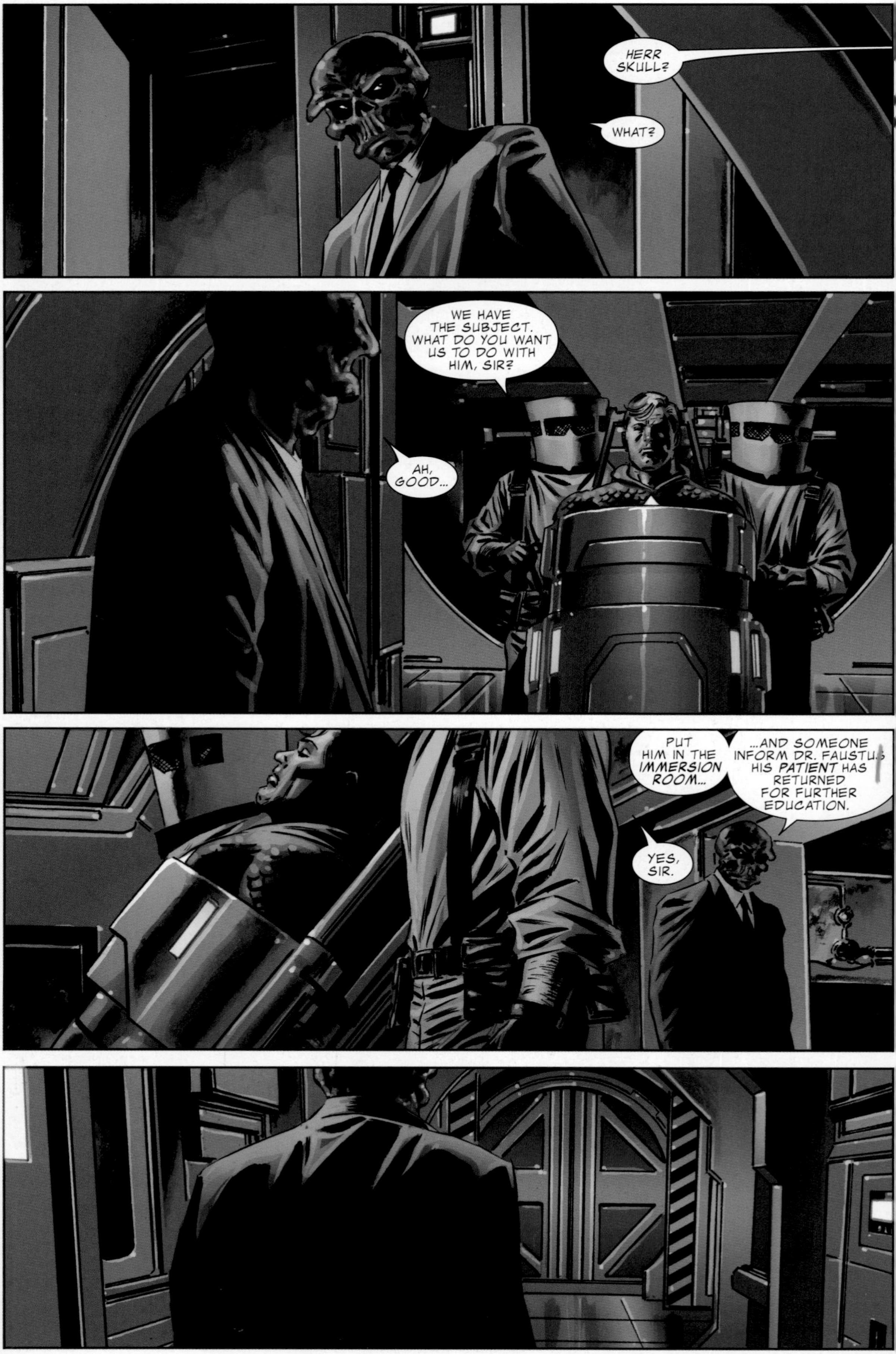
HERR SKULL?
WHAT?
WE HAVE THE SUBJECT. WHAT DO YOU WANT US TO DO WITH HIM, SIR?
AH, GOOD...
PUT HIM IN THE *IMMERSION ROOM*...
...AND SOMEONE INFORM DR. FAUSTUS HIS *PATIENT* HAS RETURNED FOR FURTHER EDUCATION.
YES, SIR.

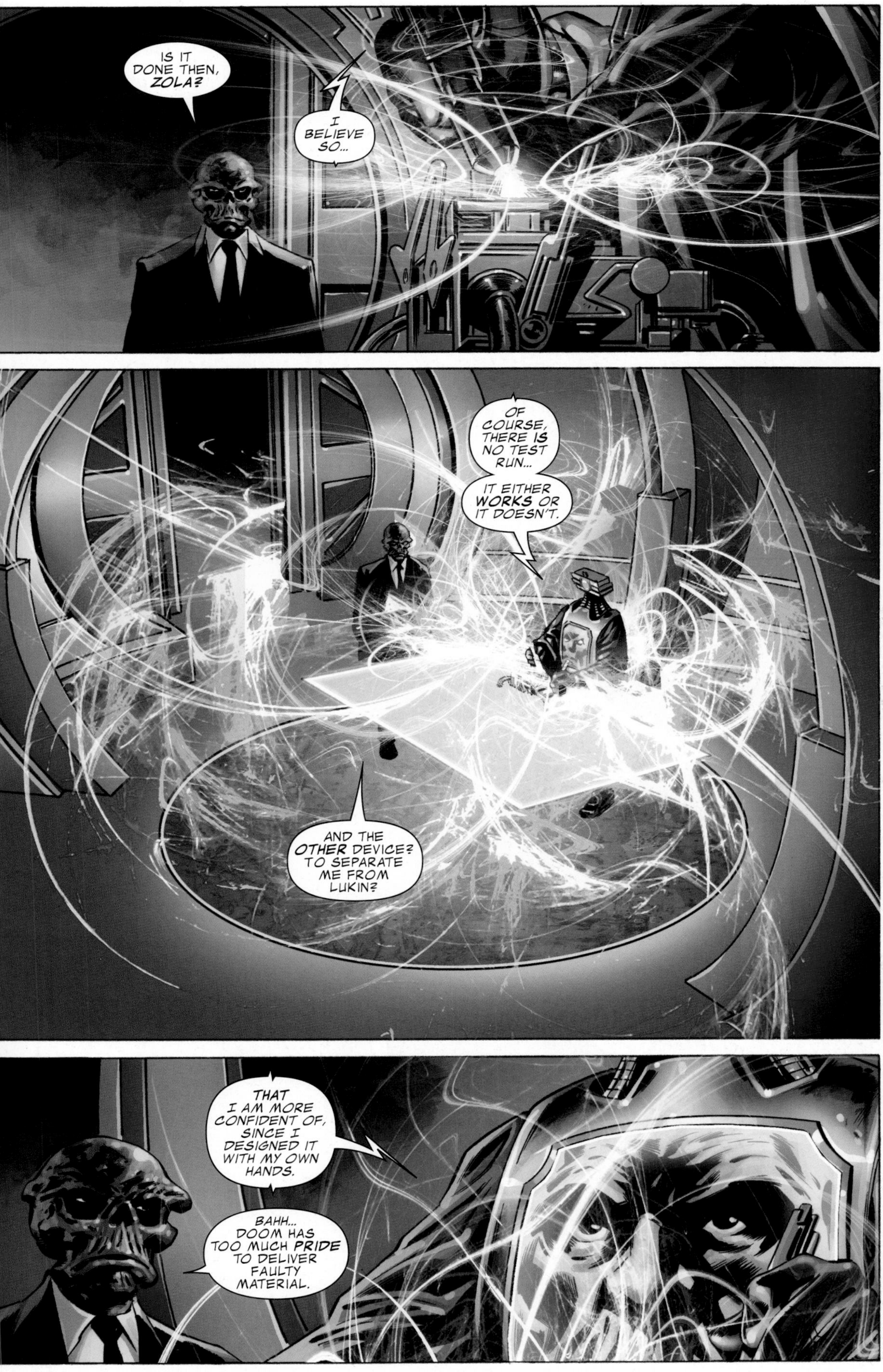
IS IT DONE THEN, ZOLA?
I BELIEVE SO...
OF COURSE, THERE IS NO TEST RUN...
IT EITHER WORKS OR IT DOESN'T.
AND THE OTHER DEVICE? TO SEPARATE ME FROM LUKIN?
THAT I AM MORE CONFIDENT OF, SINCE I DESIGNED IT WITH MY OWN HANDS.
BAHH... DOOM HAS TOO MUCH PRIDE TO DELIVER FAULTY MATERIAL.

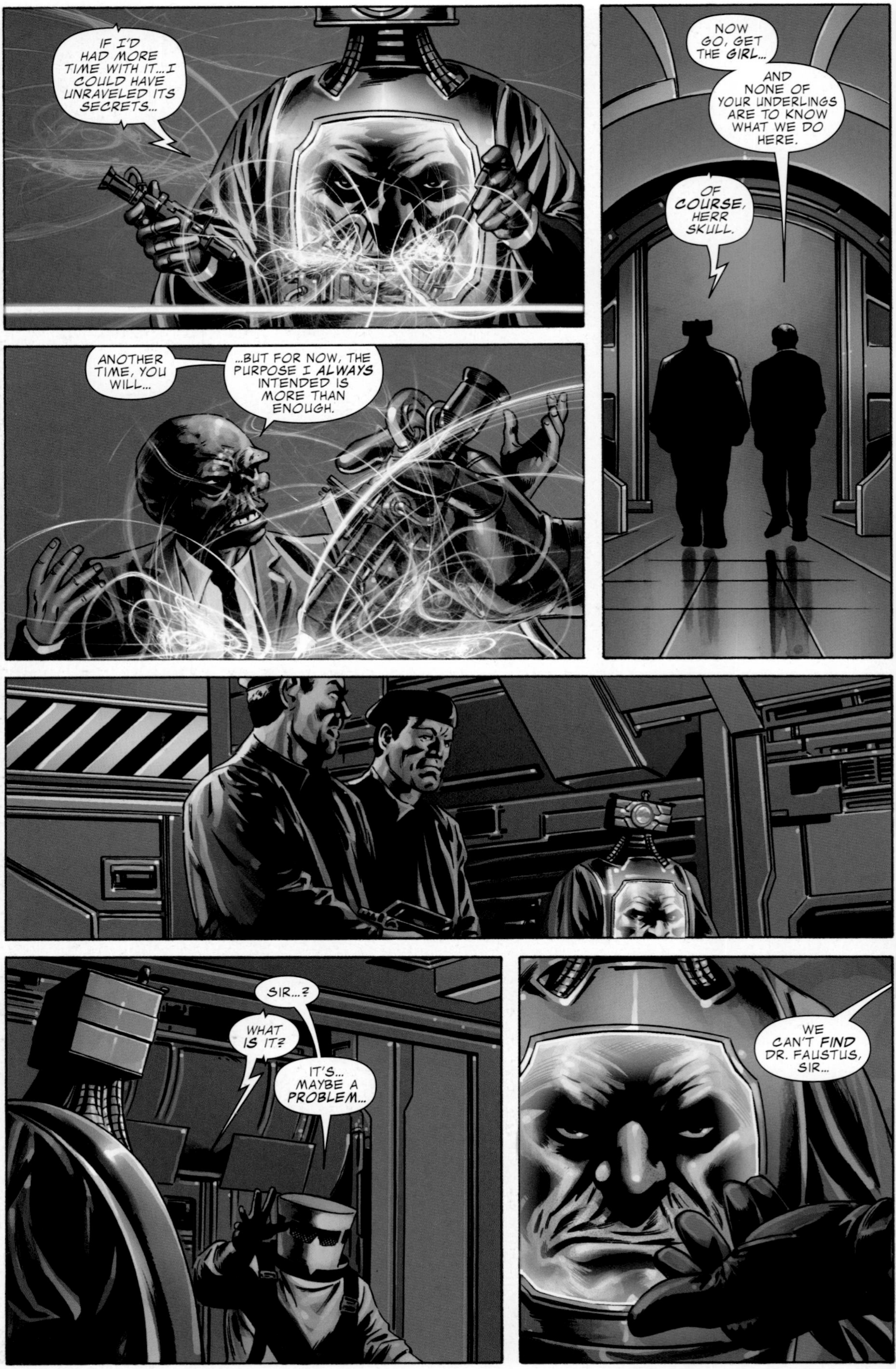
IF I'D HAD MORE TIME WITH IT...I COULD HAVE UNRAVELED ITS SECRETS...
ANOTHER TIME, YOU WILL...
...BUT FOR NOW, THE PURPOSE I ALWAYS INTENDED IS MORE THAN ENOUGH.
NOW GO, GET THE GIRL...
AND NONE OF YOUR UNDERLINGS ARE TO KNOW WHAT WE DO HERE.
OF COURSE, HERR SKULL.
SIR...?
WHAT IS IT?
IT'S... MAYBE A PROBLEM...
WE CAN'T FIND DR. FAUSTUS, SIR...

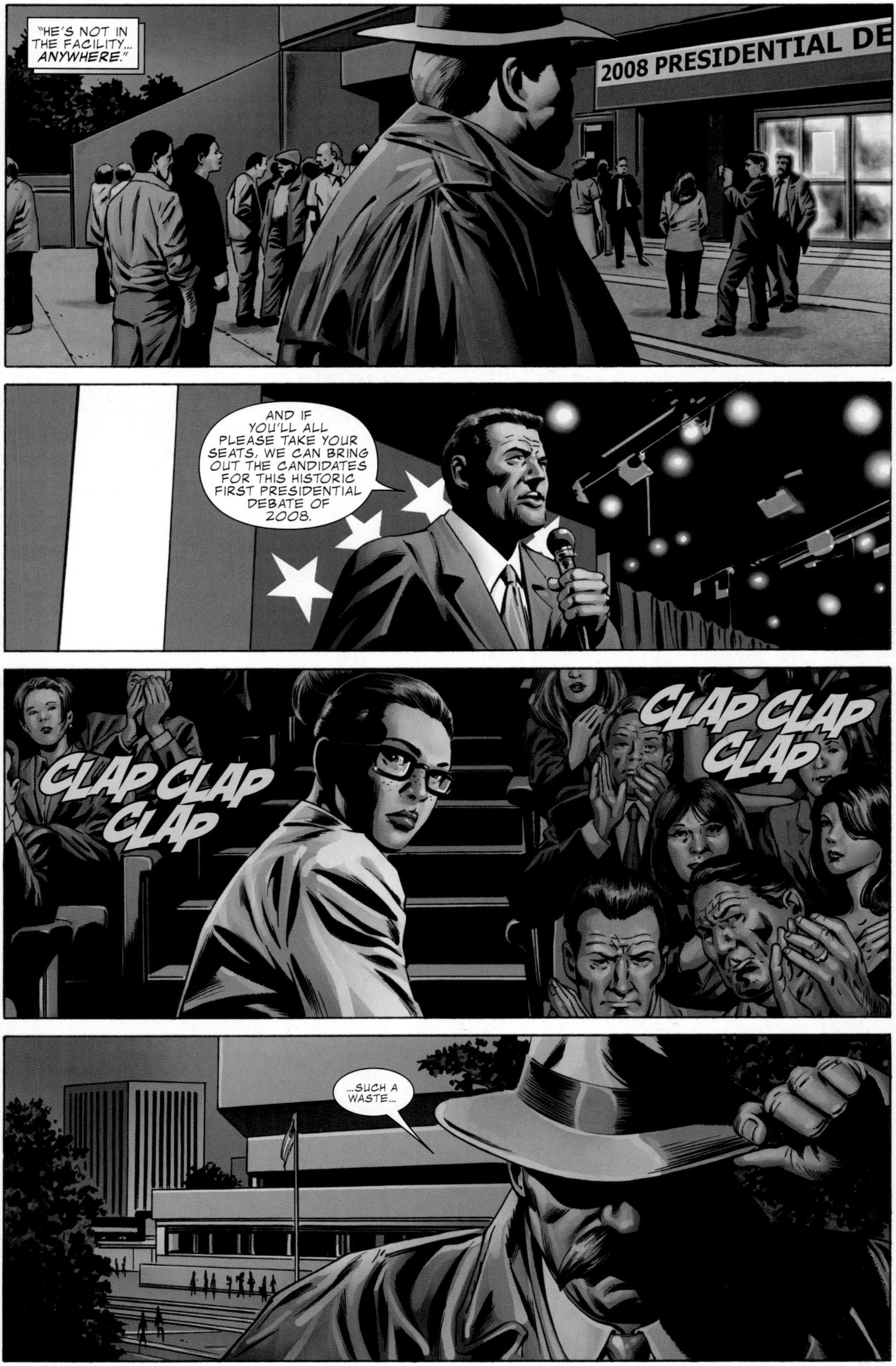
"HE'S NOT IN THE FACILITY... *ANYWHERE.*"
2008 PRESIDENTIAL DE
AND IF YOU'LL ALL PLEASE TAKE YOUR SEATS, WE CAN BRING OUT THE CANDIDATES FOR THIS HISTORIC FIRST PRESIDENTIAL DEBATE OF 2008.
CLAP CLAP CLAP
CLAP CLAP CLAP
...SUCH A WASTE...

AND WHAT OF YOU? HAVE YOU SEEN FAUSTUS, GIRL?

NO, WHY?

NEVER MIND, YOU. JUST MOVE.

WE HAVE NEED OF YOUR PATHETIC FRAME AGAIN.

OW--STOP PULLING.

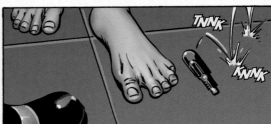

TNNK

KNNK

WHAT IN THE NAME OF--

BOOOM

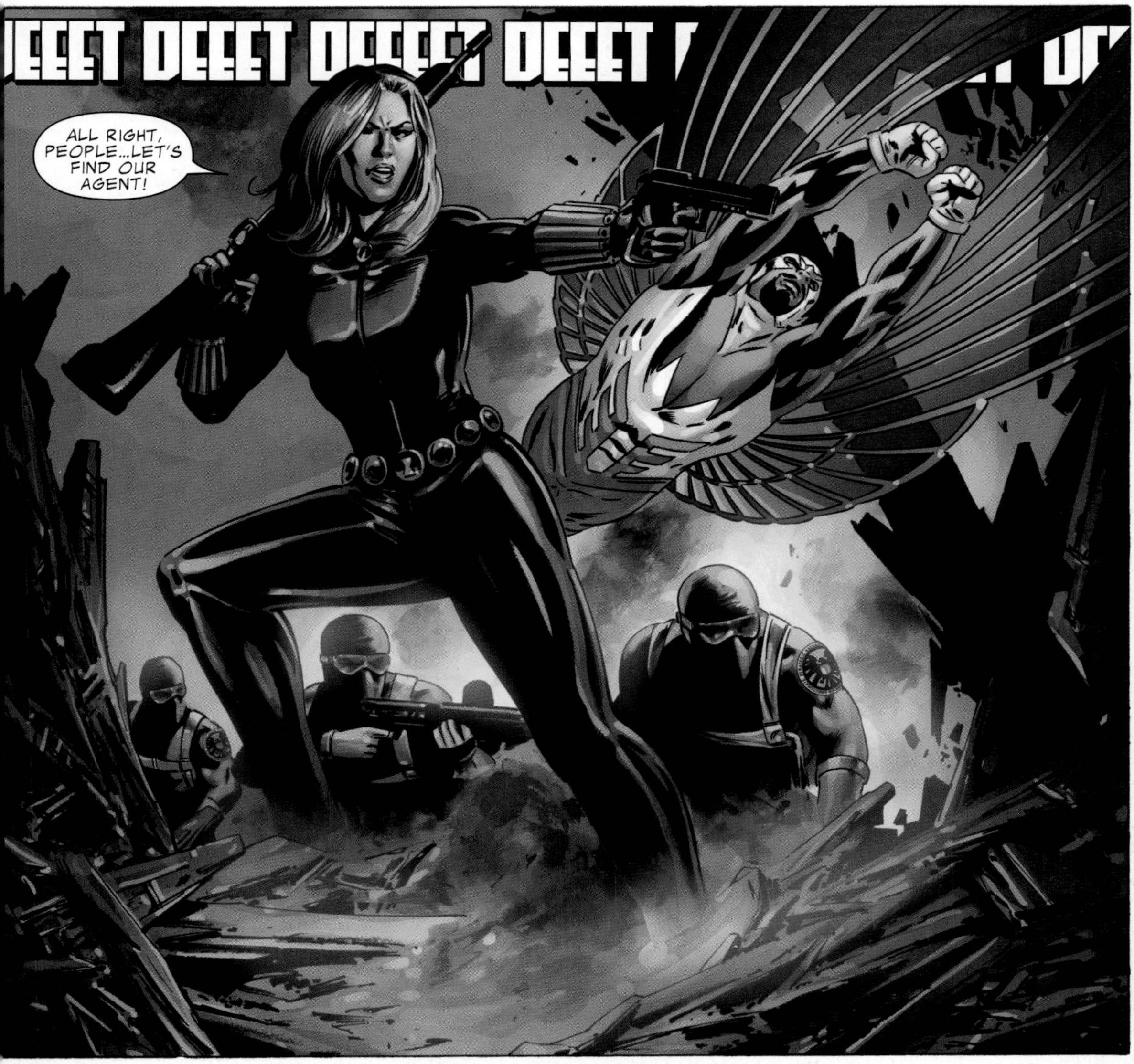
DEEET DEEET
ALL RIGHT, PEOPLE...LET'S FIND OUR AGENT!

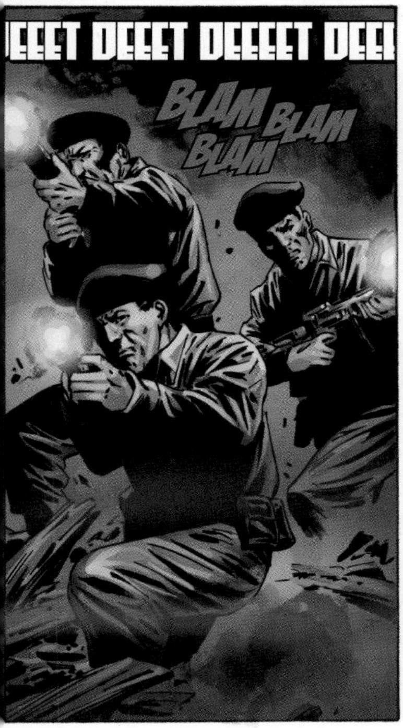
DEEET DEEEET
BLAM BLAM BLAM

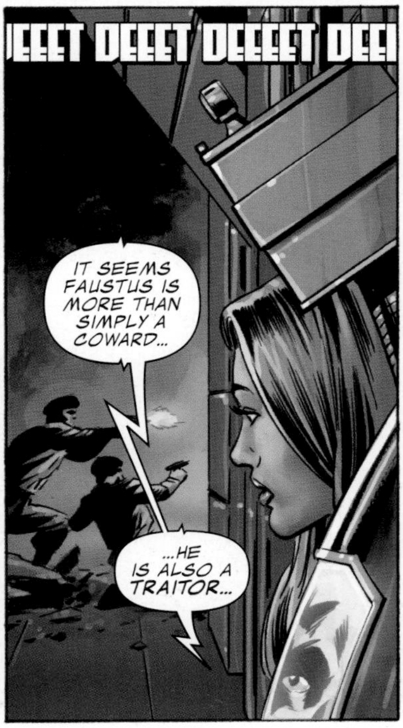
DEEET DEEEET
IT SEEMS FAUSTUS IS MORE THAN SIMPLY A COWARD...
...HE IS ALSO A TRAITOR...

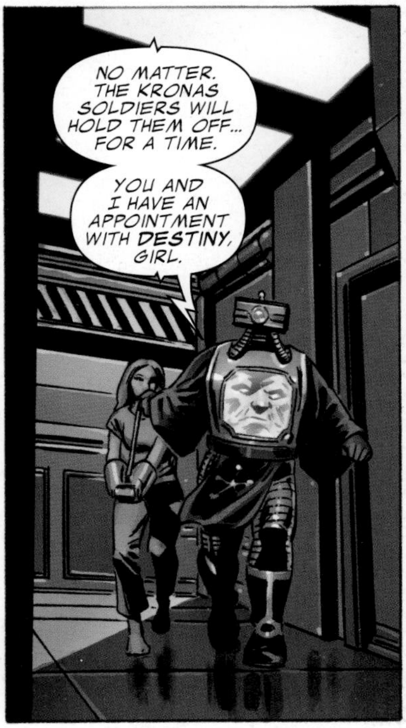
NO MATTER. THE KRONAS SOLDIERS WILL HOLD THEM OFF... FOR A TIME.
YOU AND I HAVE AN APPOINTMENT WITH DESTINY, GIRL.

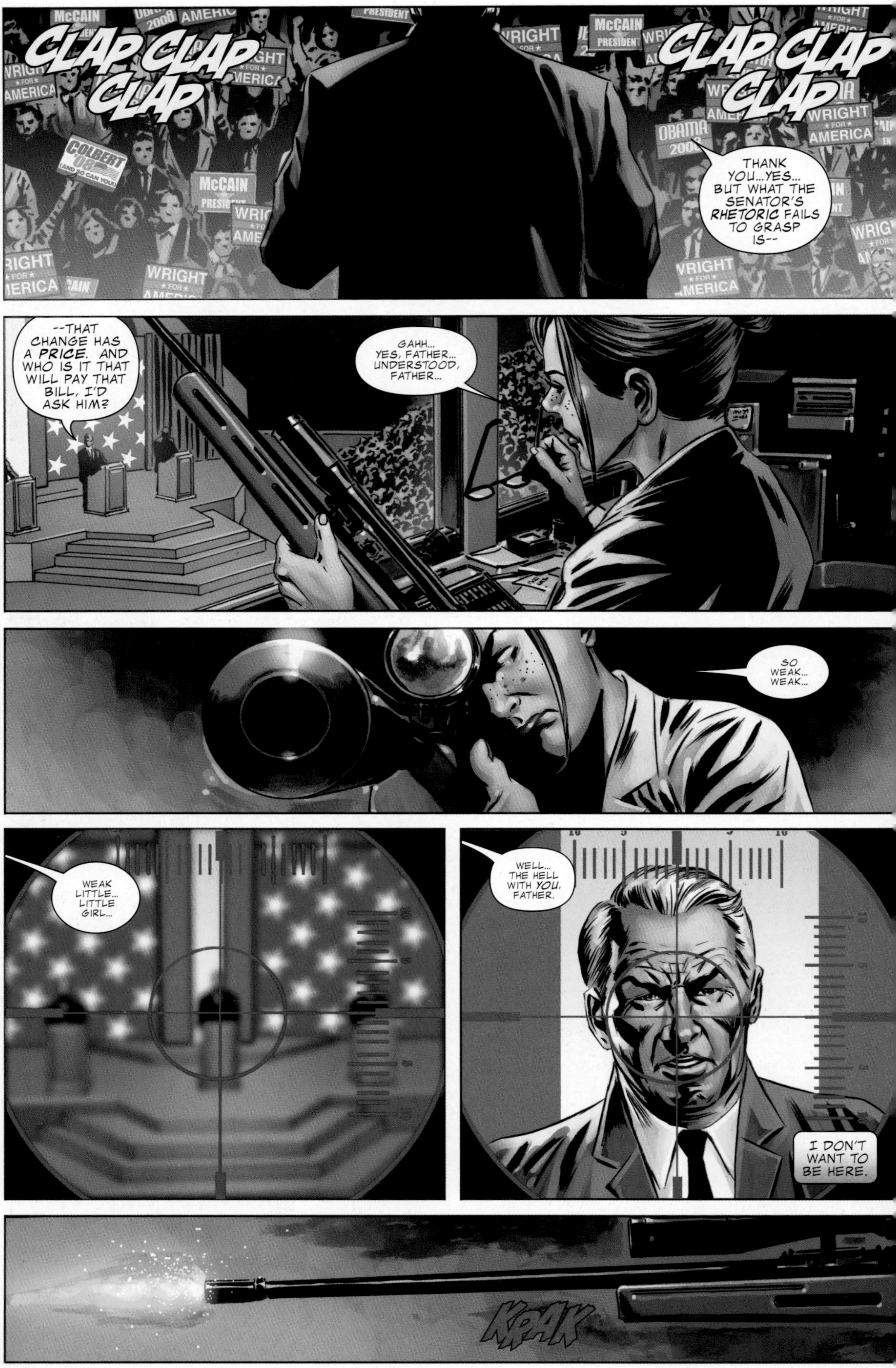
CLAP CLAP CLAP
CLAP CLAP CLAP
McCAIN
OBAMA 2008
COLBERT '08 (AND SO CAN YOU!)
WRIGHT FOR AMERICA
McCAIN PRESIDENT
THANK YOU...YES... BUT WHAT THE SENATOR'S RHETORIC FAILS TO GRASP IS--
--THAT CHANGE HAS A PRICE. AND WHO IS IT THAT WILL PAY THAT BILL, I'D ASK HIM?
GAHH... YES, FATHER... UNDERSTOOD, FATHER...
SO WEAK... WEAK...
WEAK LITTLE... LITTLE GIRL...
WELL... THE HELL WITH YOU, FATHER.
I DON'T WANT TO BE HERE.
KRAK

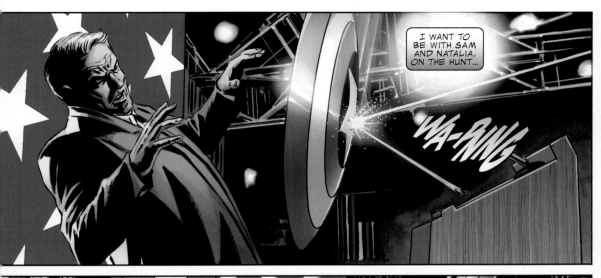

I WANT TO BE WITH SAM AND NATALIA, ON THE HUNT...

WA-RING

I WANT TO BE BASHING THE RED SKULL'S TEETH IN...

NO! NO WAY!

...AND SAVING STEVE'S GIRL.

GET THE CANDIDATES CLEAR!

I CAN HANDLE THIS!

BUT DAMN IT, NATALIA WAS RIGHT...

WHO THE HELL ARE YOU?!

WHAT DOES IT LOOK LIKE?

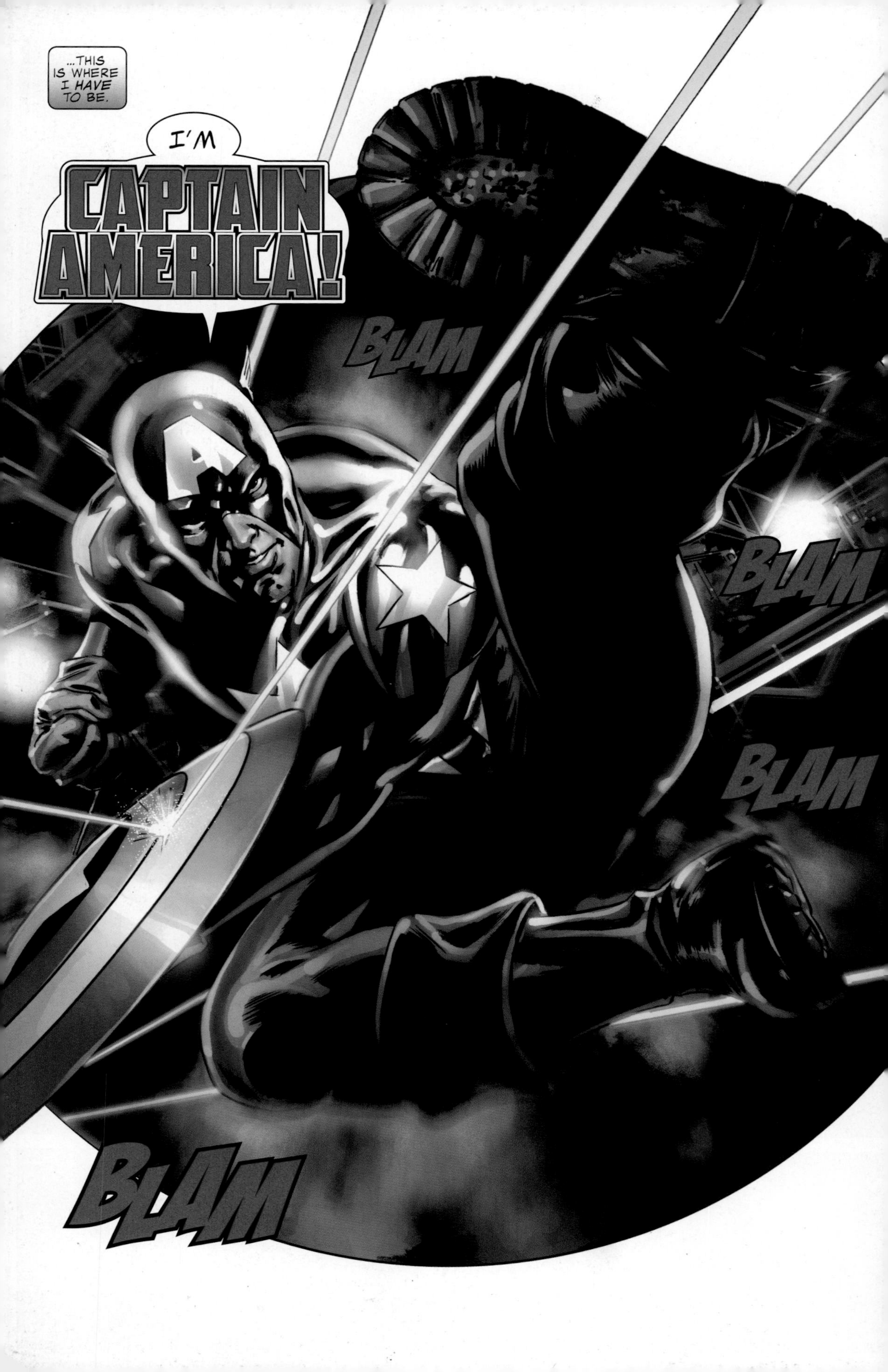
...THIS IS WHERE I HAVE TO BE.
I'M CAPTAIN AMERICA!
BLAM
BLAM
BLAM
BLAM

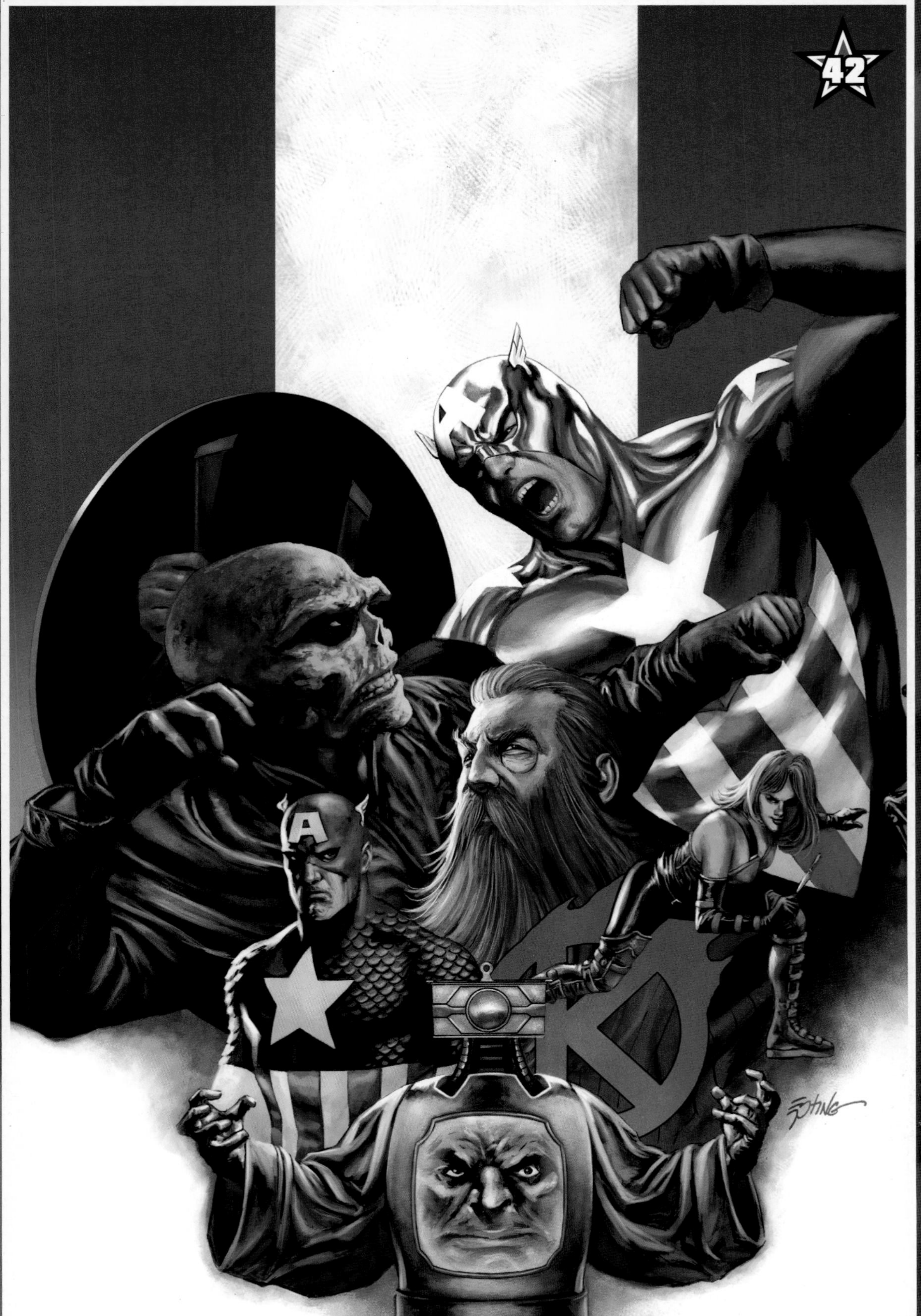
42

PART SIX

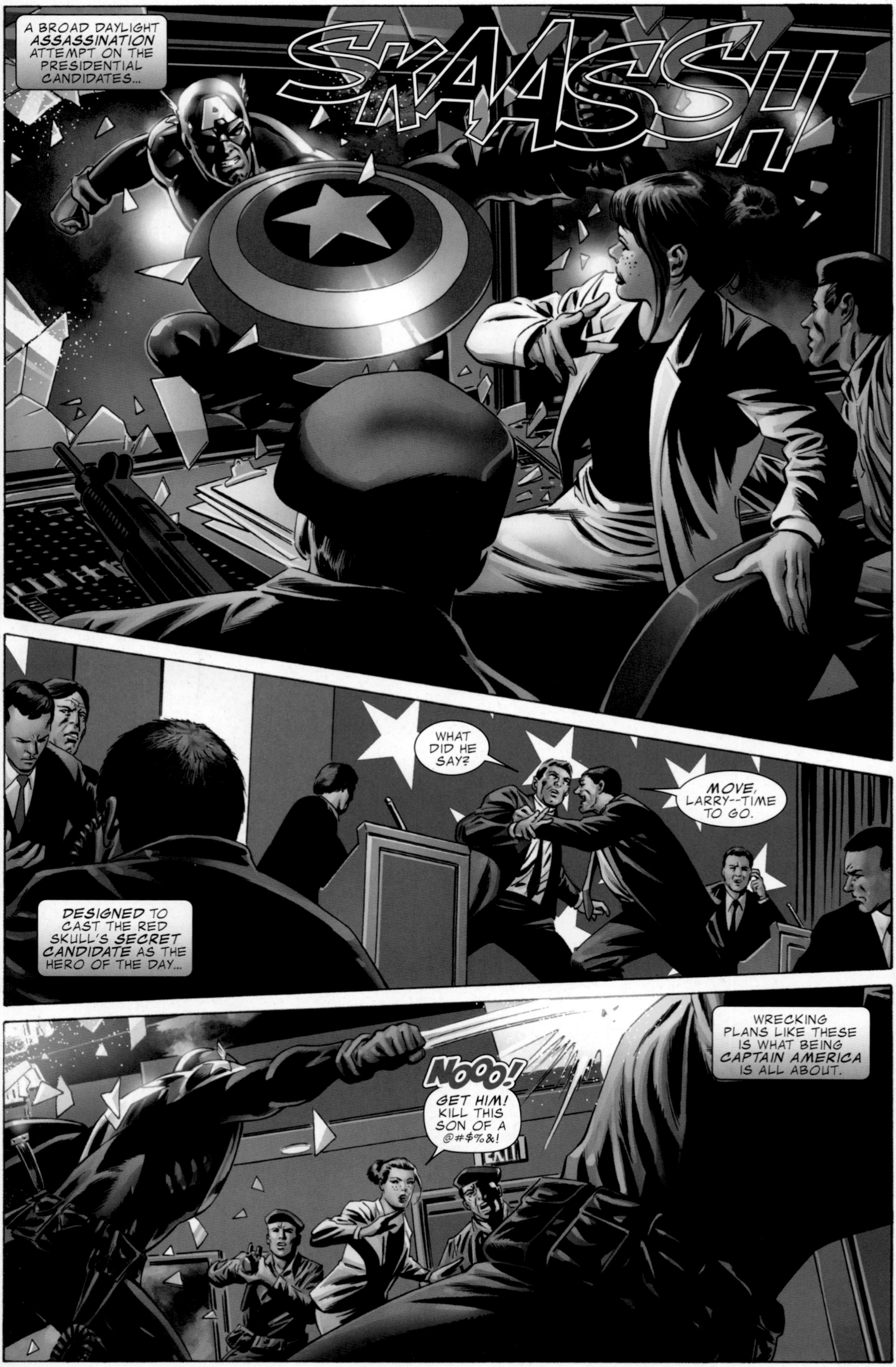
A BROAD DAYLIGHT ASSASSINATION ATTEMPT ON THE PRESIDENTIAL CANDIDATES...
SKAASSH
WHAT DID HE SAY?
MOVE, LARRY--TIME TO GO.
DESIGNED TO CAST THE RED SKULL'S SECRET CANDIDATE AS THE HERO OF THE DAY...
WRECKING PLANS LIKE THESE IS WHAT BEING CAPTAIN AMERICA IS ALL ABOUT.
NOOO! GET HIM! KILL THIS SON OF A @#$%&!
EXIT

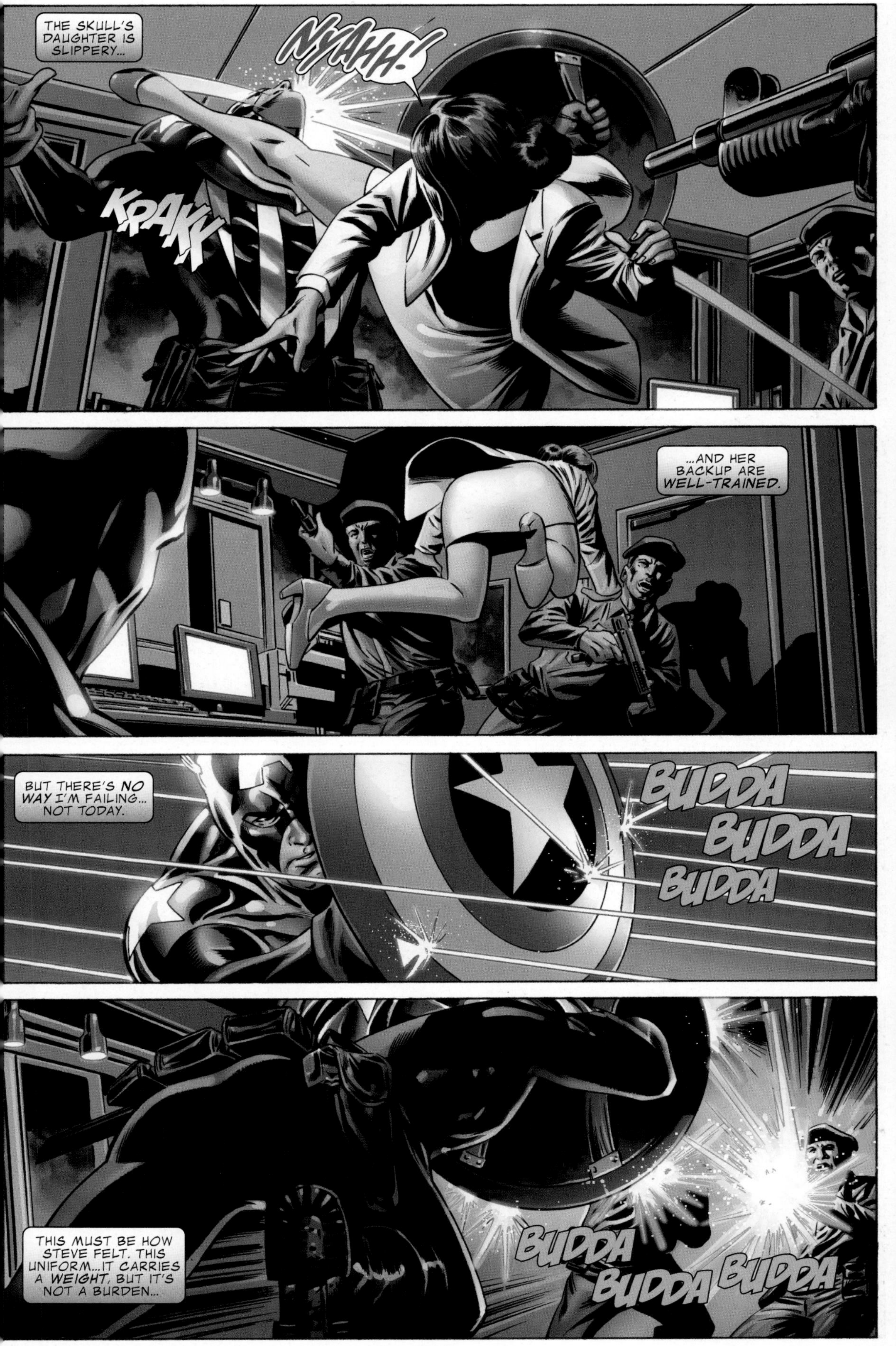
THE SKULL'S DAUGHTER IS SLIPPERY...
NYAHH!
KRAKK
...AND HER BACKUP ARE WELL-TRAINED.
BUT THERE'S NO WAY I'M FAILING... NOT TODAY.
BUDDA BUDDA BUDDA
THIS MUST BE HOW STEVE FELT. THIS UNIFORM...IT CARRIES A WEIGHT, BUT IT'S NOT A BURDEN...
BUDDA BUDDA BUDDA BUDDA

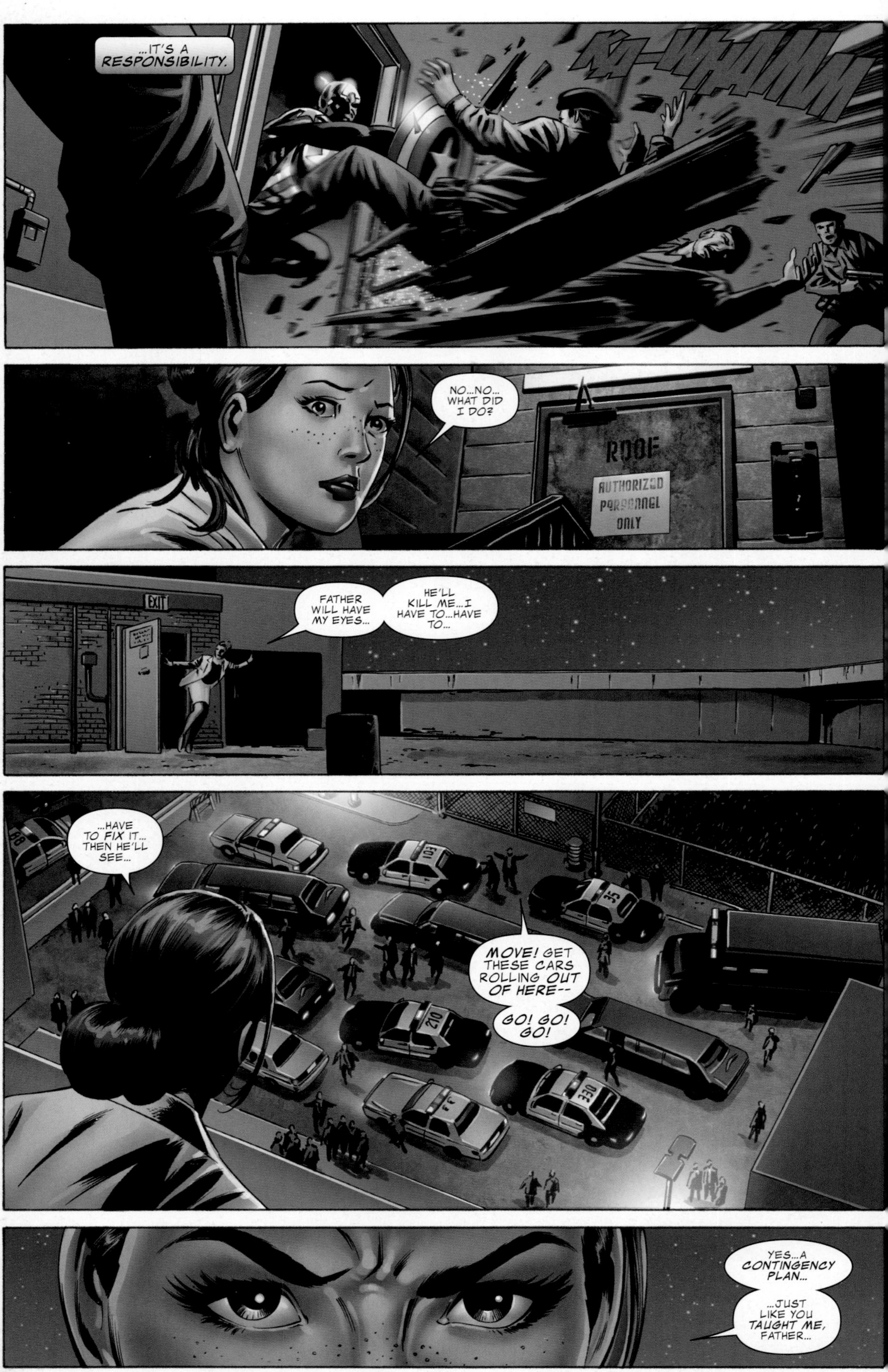

...IT'S A RESPONSIBILITY.
KA-WHAMM
NO...NO... WHAT DID I DO?
ROOF
AUTHORIZED PERSONNEL ONLY
EXIT
FATHER WILL HAVE MY EYES...
HE'LL KILL ME...I HAVE TO...HAVE TO...
...HAVE TO FIX IT... THEN HE'LL SEE...
MOVE! GET THESE CARS ROLLING OUT OF HERE--
GO! GO! GO!
YES...A CONTINGENCY PLAN...
...JUST LIKE YOU TAUGHT ME, FATHER...

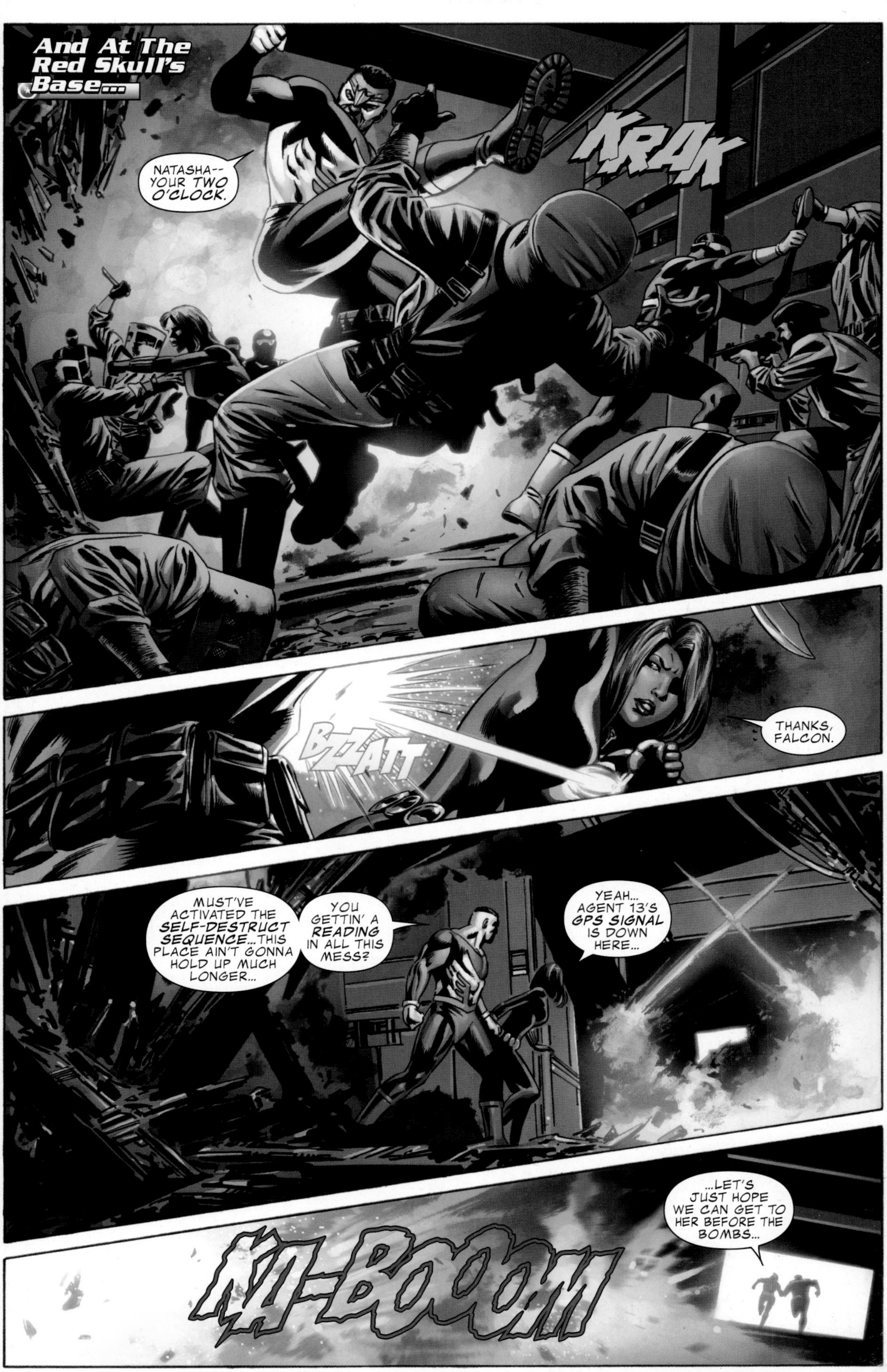
And At The Red Skull's Base...
NATASHA-- YOUR TWO O'CLOCK.
KRAK
BZZATT
THANKS, FALCON.
MUST'VE ACTIVATED THE SELF-DESTRUCT SEQUENCE...THIS PLACE AIN'T GONNA HOLD UP MUCH LONGER...
YOU GETTIN' A READING IN ALL THIS MESS?
YEAH... AGENT 13'S GPS SIGNAL IS DOWN HERE...
...LET'S JUST HOPE WE CAN GET TO HER BEFORE THE BOMBS...
KA-BOOOM

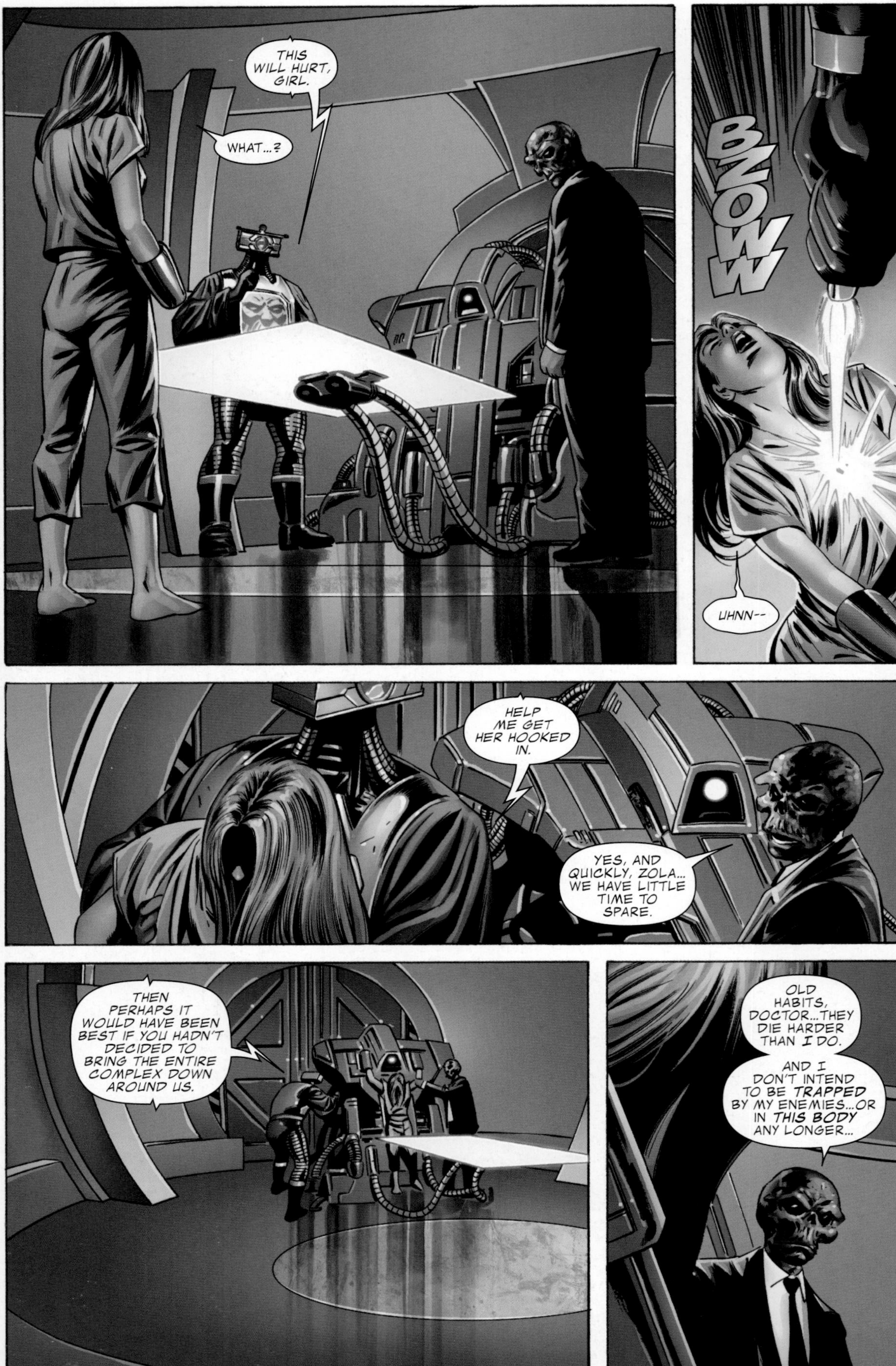
THIS WILL HURT, GIRL.
WHAT...?
BZOWW
UHNN--
HELP ME GET HER HOOKED IN.
YES, AND QUICKLY, ZOLA... WE HAVE LITTLE TIME TO SPARE.
THEN PERHAPS IT WOULD HAVE BEEN BEST IF YOU HADN'T DECIDED TO BRING THE ENTIRE COMPLEX DOWN AROUND US.
OLD HABITS, DOCTOR...THEY DIE HARDER THAN I DO.
AND I DON'T INTEND TO BE TRAPPED BY MY ENEMIES...OR IN THIS BODY ANY LONGER...

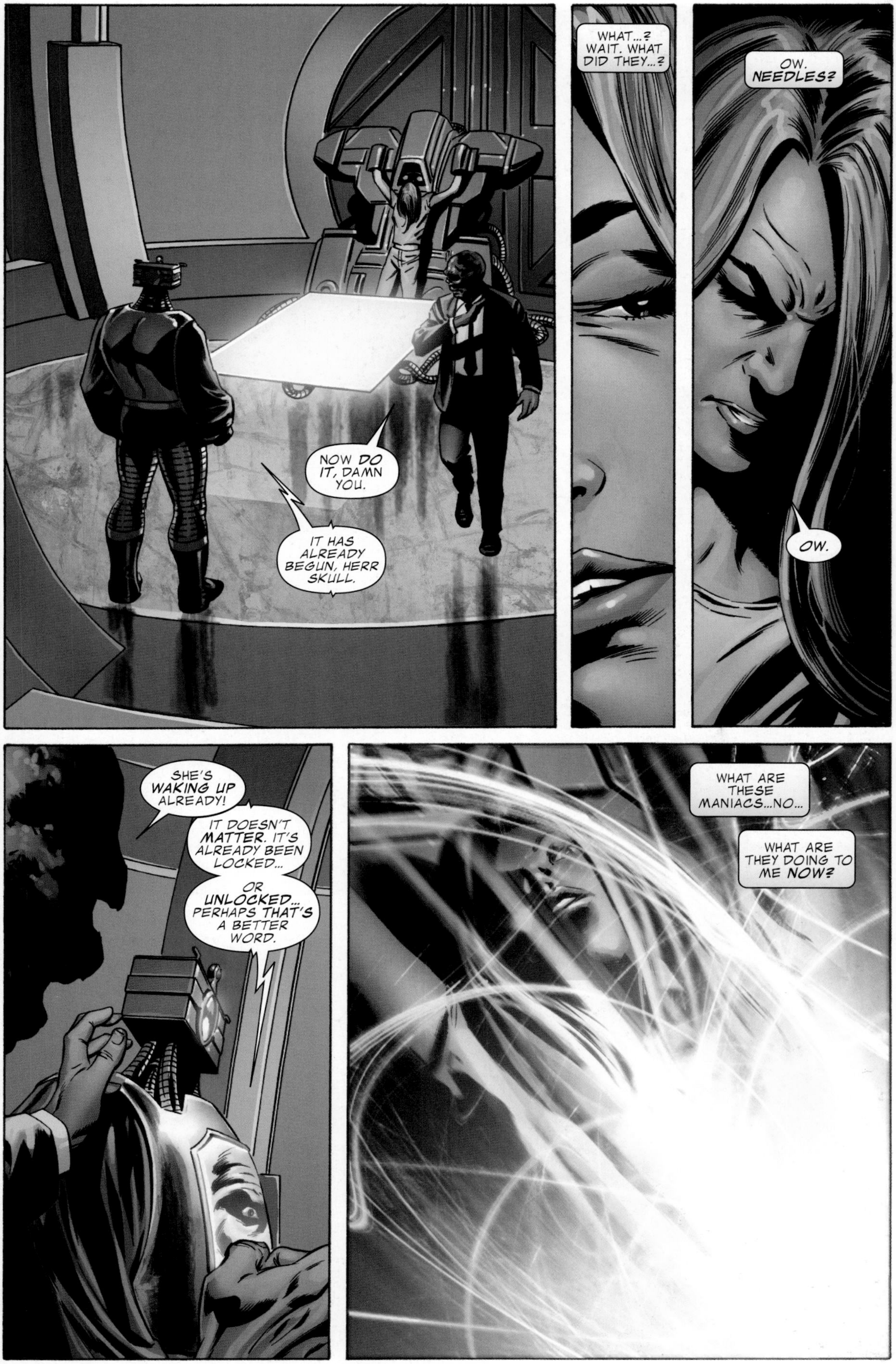
NOW DO IT, DAMN YOU.
IT HAS ALREADY BEGUN, HERR SKULL.
WHAT...? WAIT. WHAT DID THEY...?
OW. NEEDLES?
OW.
SHE'S WAKING UP ALREADY!
IT DOESN'T MATTER. IT'S ALREADY BEEN LOCKED...
OR UNLOCKED... PERHAPS THAT'S A BETTER WORD.
WHAT ARE THESE MANIACS...NO...
WHAT ARE THEY DOING TO ME NOW?

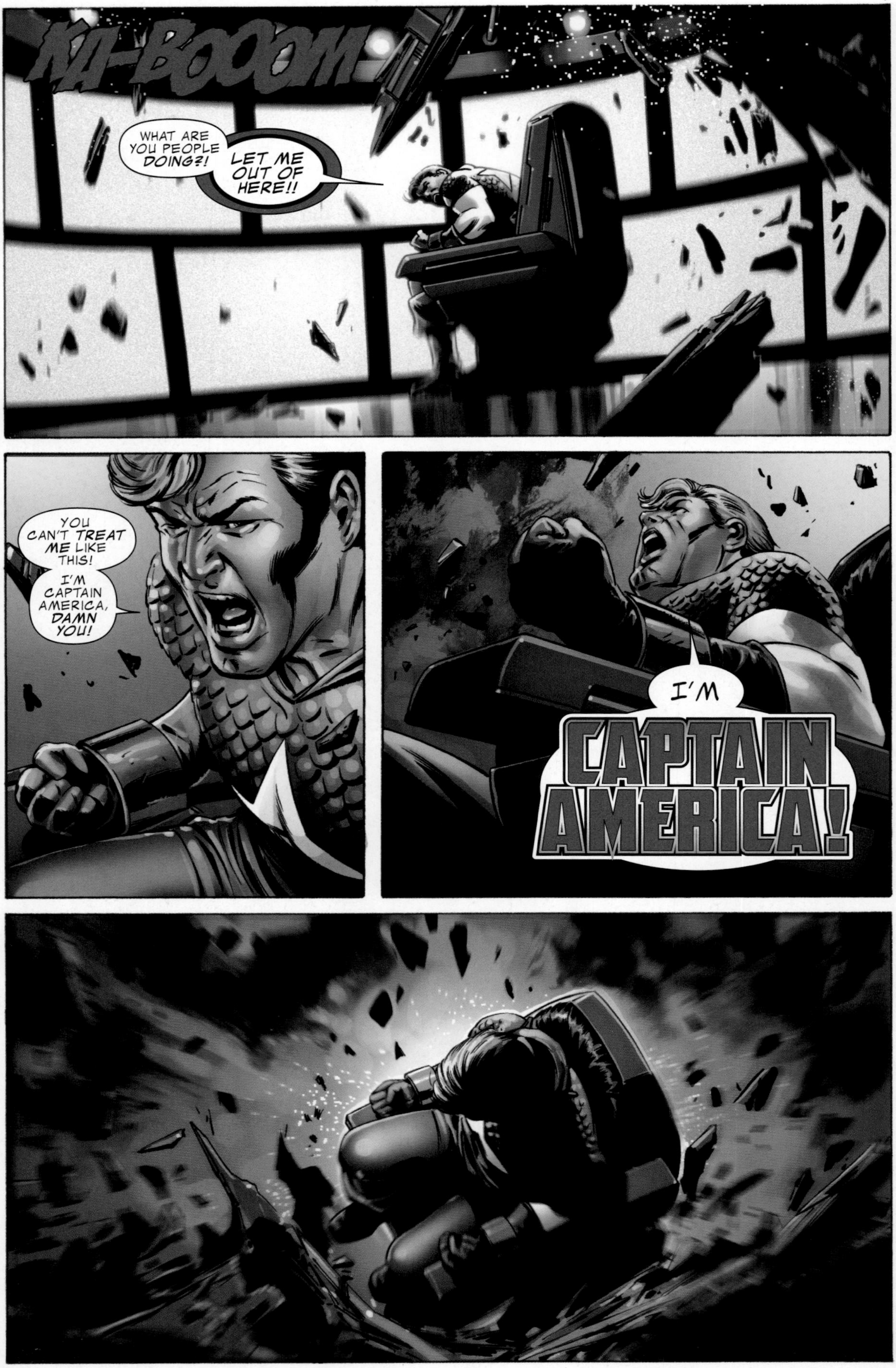
KA-BOOOM
WHAT ARE YOU PEOPLE DOING?!
LET ME OUT OF HERE!!
YOU CAN'T TREAT ME LIKE THIS!
I'M CAPTAIN AMERICA, DAMN YOU!
I'M
CAPTAIN AMERICA!

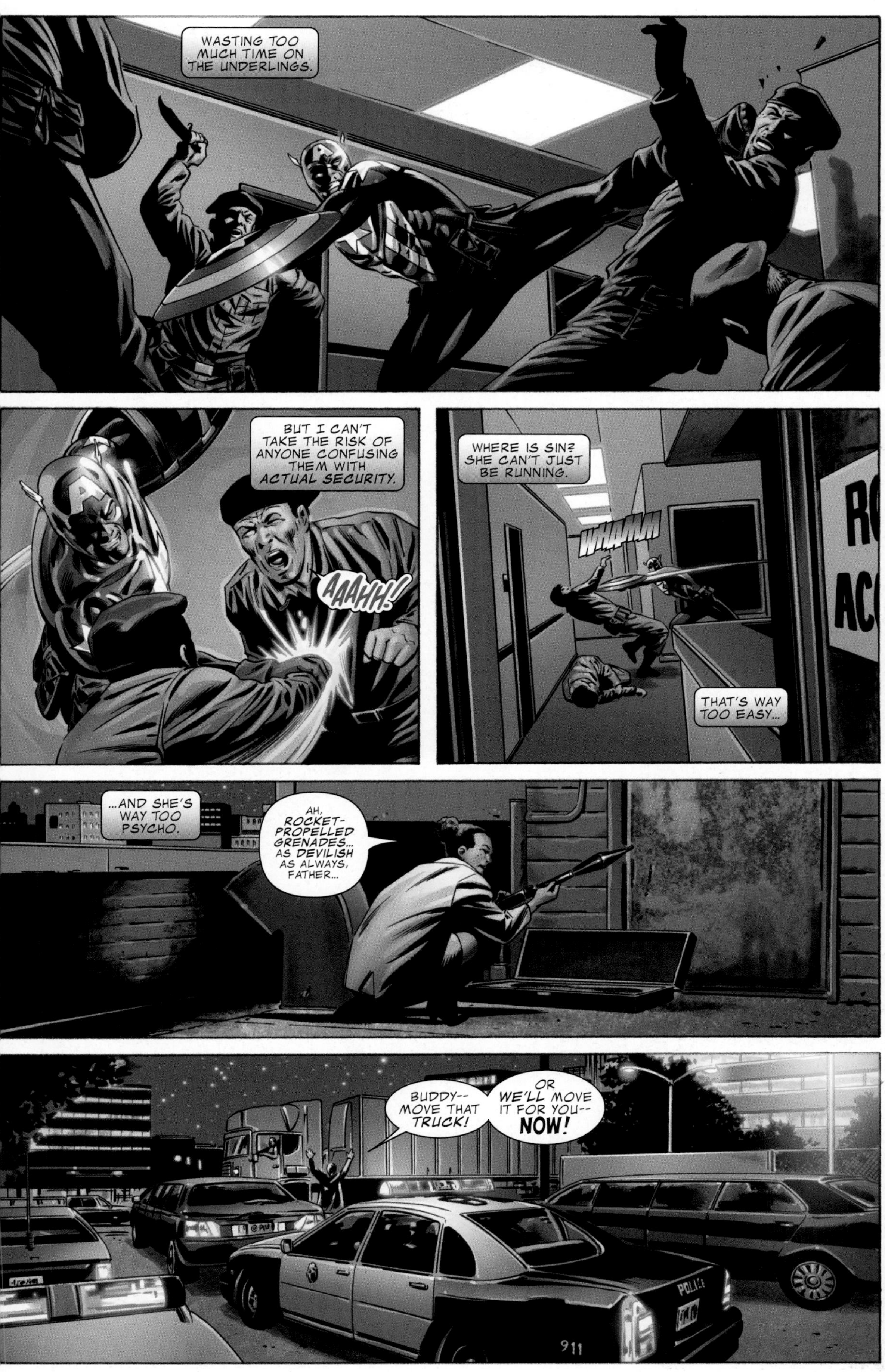
WASTING TOO MUCH TIME ON THE UNDERLINGS.
BUT I CAN'T TAKE THE RISK OF ANYONE CONFUSING THEM WITH ACTUAL SECURITY.
AAAHH!
WHERE IS SIN? SHE CAN'T JUST BE RUNNING.
WHAMM
THAT'S WAY TOO EASY...
...AND SHE'S WAY TOO PSYCHO.
AH, ROCKET-PROPELLED GRENADES... AS DEVILISH AS ALWAYS, FATHER...
BUDDY-- MOVE THAT TRUCK!
OR WE'LL MOVE IT FOR YOU-- NOW!
POLICE
911

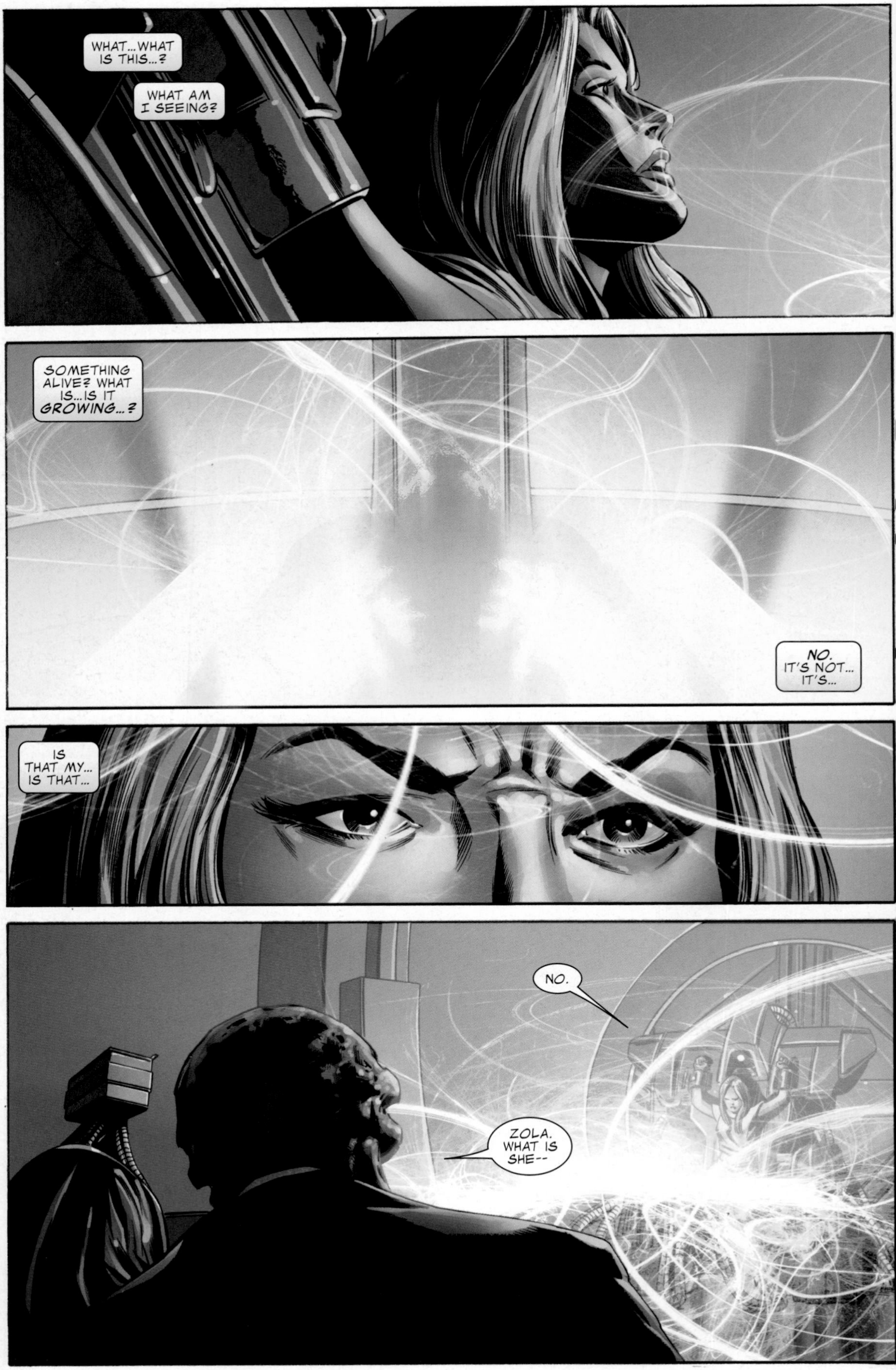
WHAT...WHAT IS THIS...?
WHAT AM I SEEING?
SOMETHING ALIVE? WHAT IS...IS IT GROWING...?
NO. IT'S NOT... IT'S...
IS THAT MY... IS THAT...
NO.
ZOLA. WHAT IS SHE--

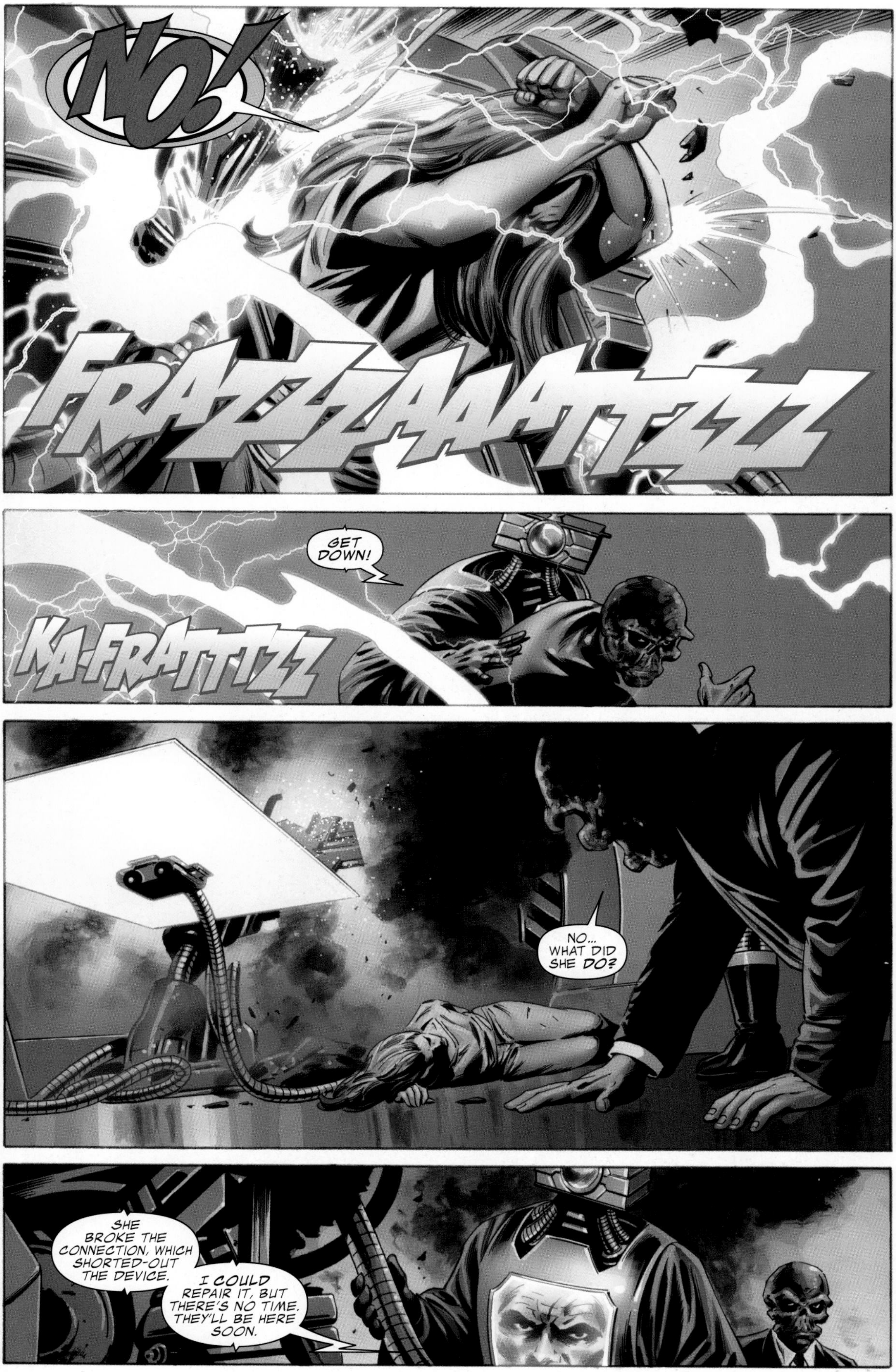
NO!
FRAZZZAAAATTZZ
GET DOWN!
KA-FRATTTZZ
NO... WHAT DID SHE DO?
SHE BROKE THE CONNECTION, WHICH SHORTED-OUT THE DEVICE.
I COULD REPAIR IT, BUT THERE'S NO TIME. THEY'LL BE HERE SOON.

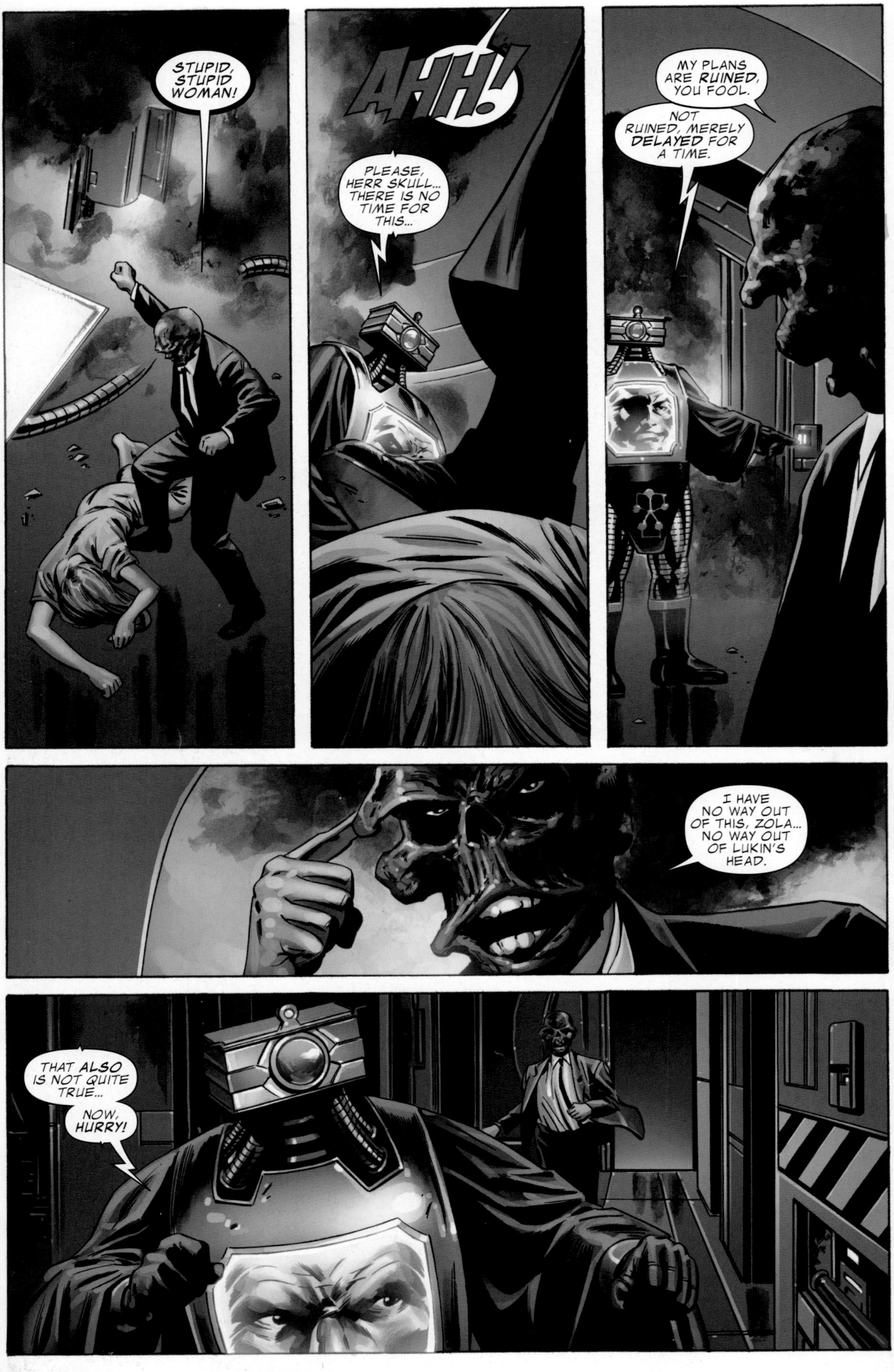
STUPID, STUPID WOMAN!
AHH!
PLEASE, HERR SKULL... THERE IS NO TIME FOR THIS...
MY PLANS ARE RUINED, YOU FOOL.
NOT RUINED, MERELY DELAYED FOR A TIME.
I HAVE NO WAY OUT OF THIS, ZOLA... NO WAY OUT OF LUKIN'S HEAD.
THAT ALSO IS NOT QUITE TRUE...
NOW, HURRY!

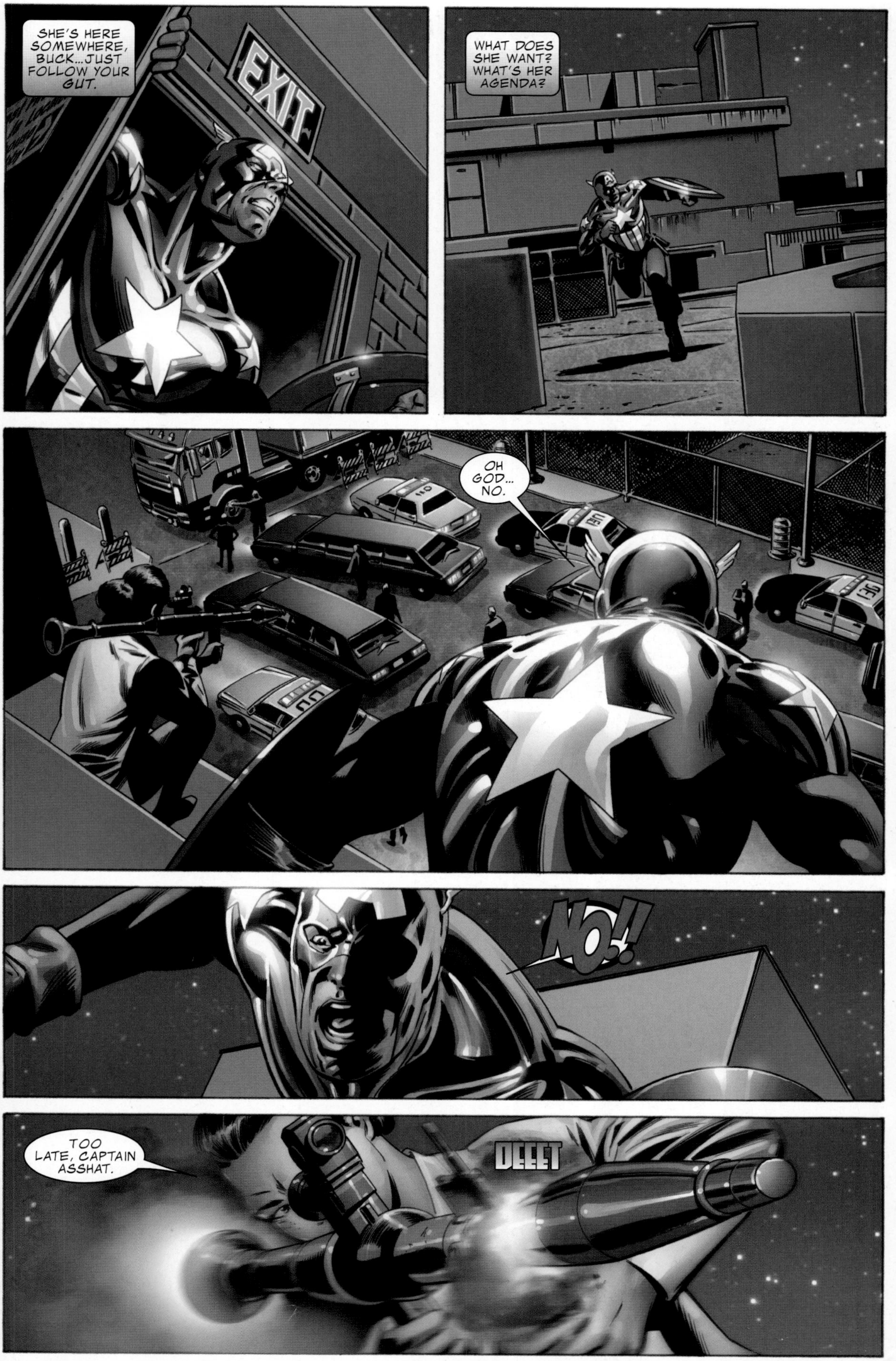

SHE'S HERE SOMEWHERE, BUCK...JUST FOLLOW YOUR GUT.
EXIT
WHAT DOES SHE WANT? WHAT'S HER AGENDA?
OH GOD... NO.
NO!!
TOO LATE, CAPTAIN ASSHAT.
DEEET

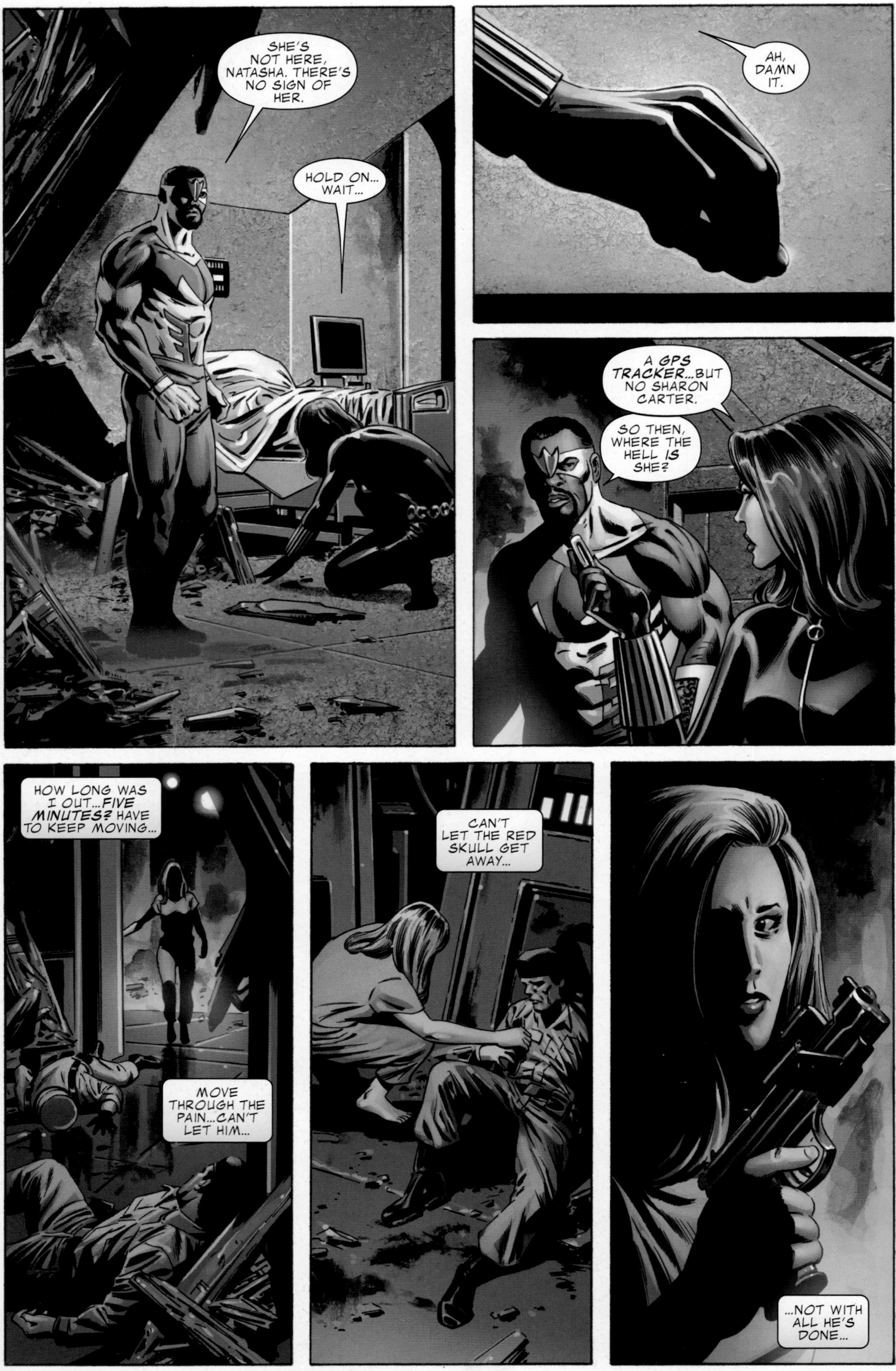
SHE'S NOT HERE, NATASHA. THERE'S NO SIGN OF HER.
HOLD ON... WAIT...
AH, DAMN IT.
A GPS TRACKER...BUT NO SHARON CARTER.
SO THEN, WHERE THE HELL IS SHE?
HOW LONG WAS I OUT...FIVE MINUTES? HAVE TO KEEP MOVING...
MOVE THROUGH THE PAIN...CAN'T LET HIM...
CAN'T LET THE RED SKULL GET AWAY...
...NOT WITH ALL HE'S DONE...

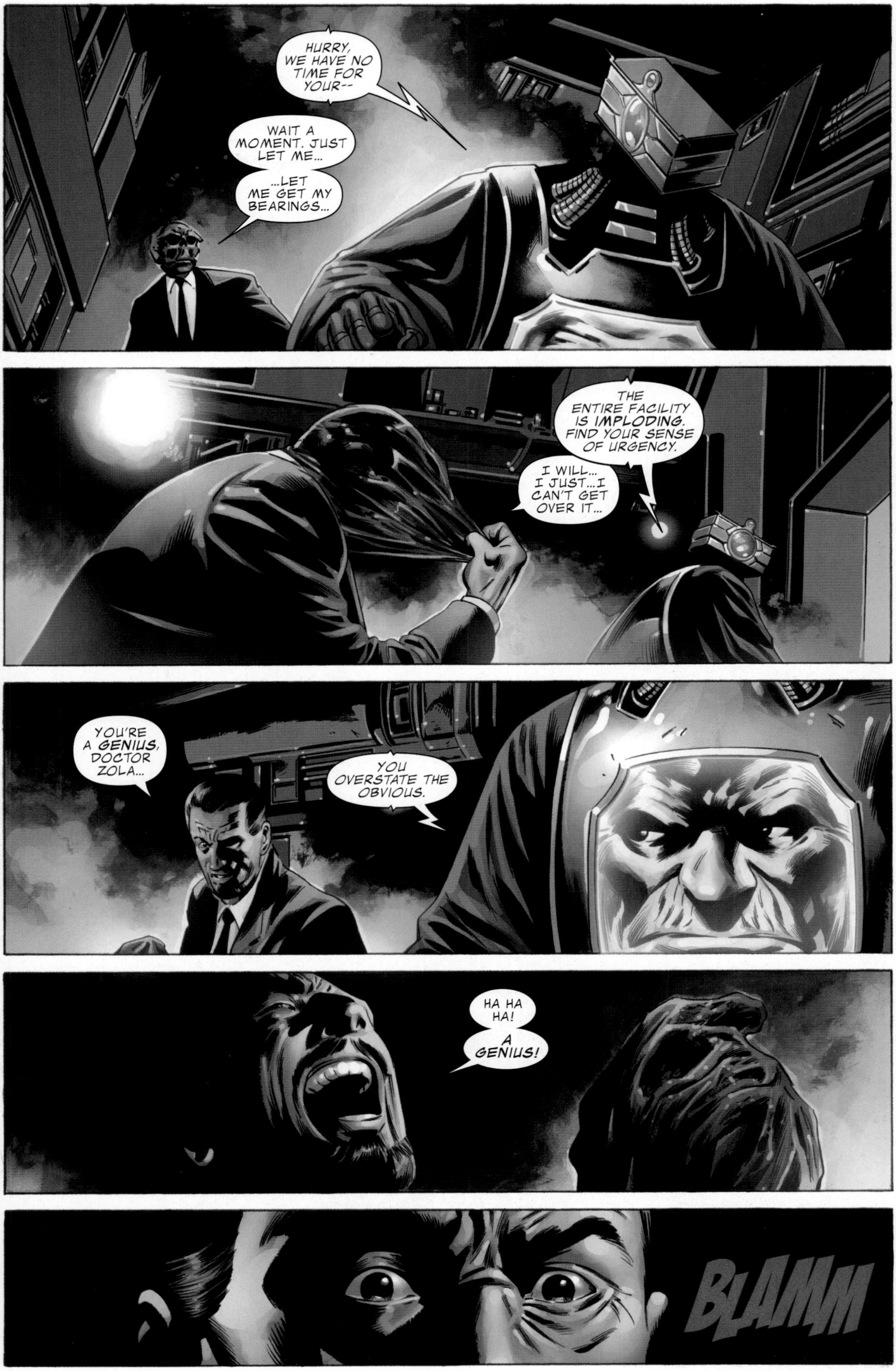
HURRY, WE HAVE NO TIME FOR YOUR--
WAIT A MOMENT. JUST LET ME...
...LET ME GET MY BEARINGS...
THE ENTIRE FACILITY IS IMPLODING. FIND YOUR SENSE OF URGENCY.
I WILL... I JUST...I CAN'T GET OVER IT...
YOU'RE A GENIUS, DOCTOR ZOLA...
YOU OVERSTATE THE OBVIOUS.
HA HA HA!
A GENIUS!
BLAMM

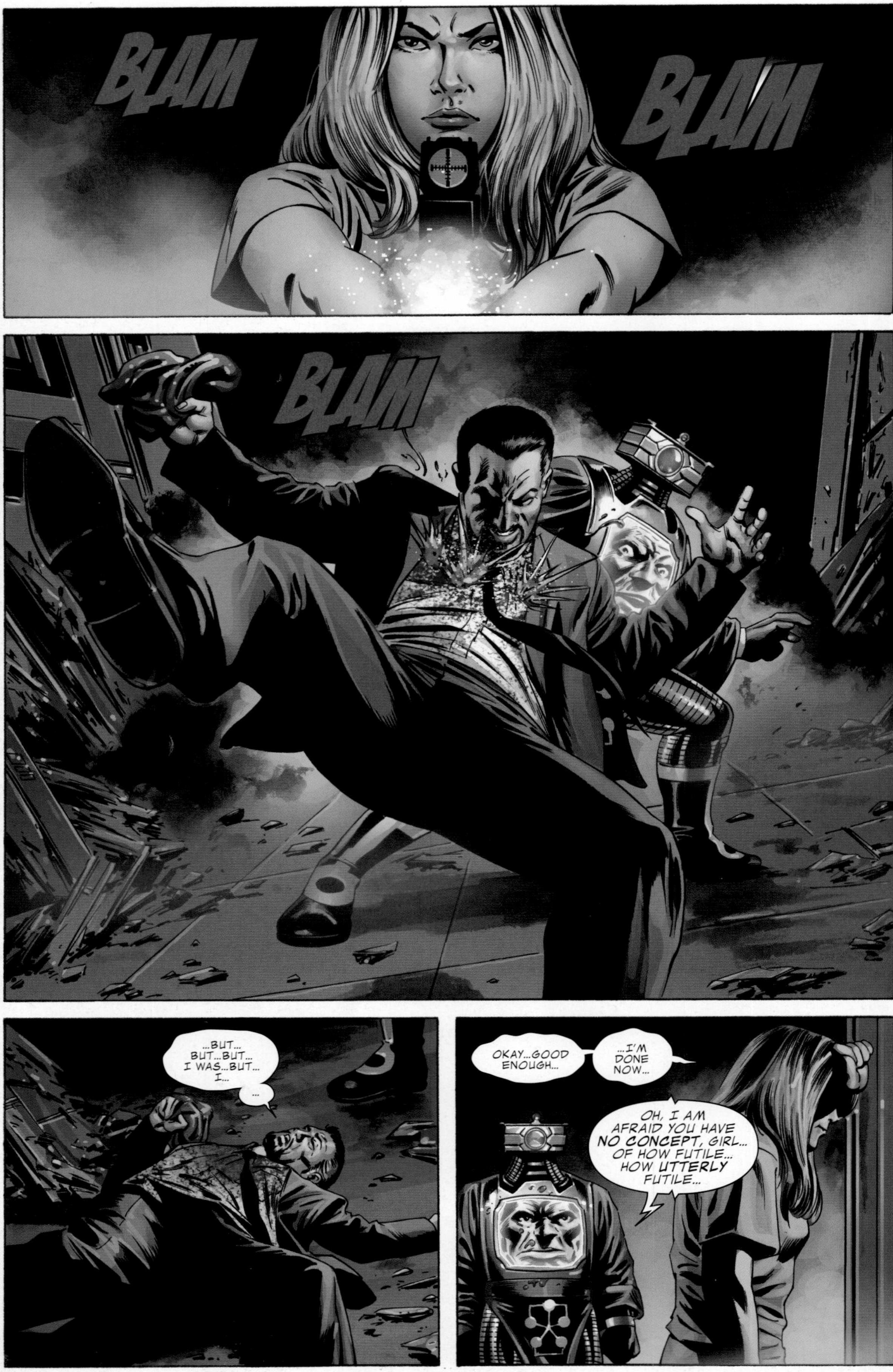
BLAM
BLAM
BLAM
...BUT... BUT...BUT... I WAS...BUT... I...
...
OKAY...GOOD ENOUGH...
...I'M DONE NOW...
OH, I AM AFRAID YOU HAVE NO CONCEPT, GIRL... OF HOW FUTILE... HOW UTTERLY FUTILE...

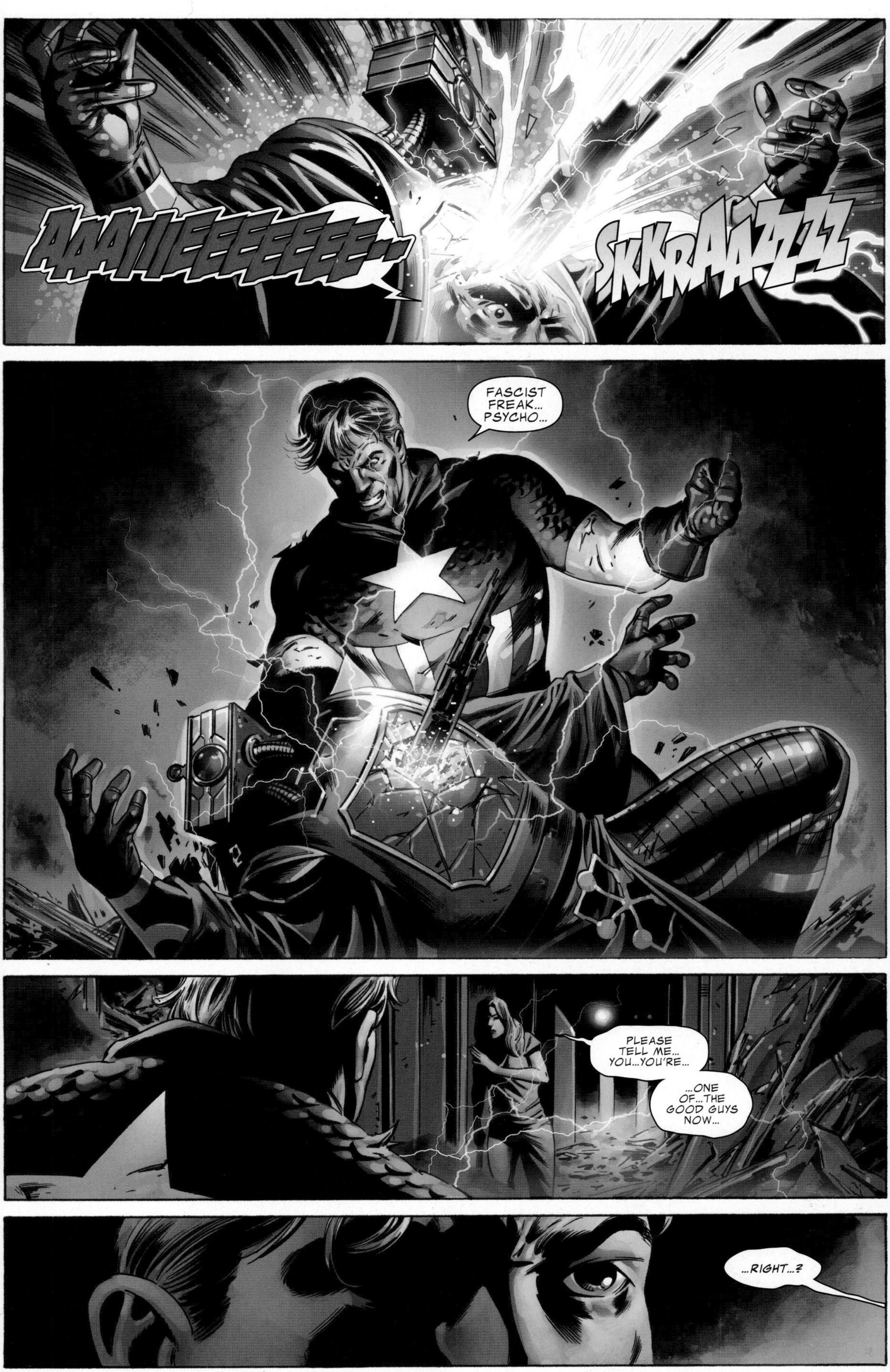
AAAIIIEEEEEEEE..
SKKRAAZZZZ
FASCIST FREAK... PSYCHO...
PLEASE TELL ME... YOU...YOU'RE...
...ONE OF...THE GOOD GUYS NOW...
...RIGHT...?

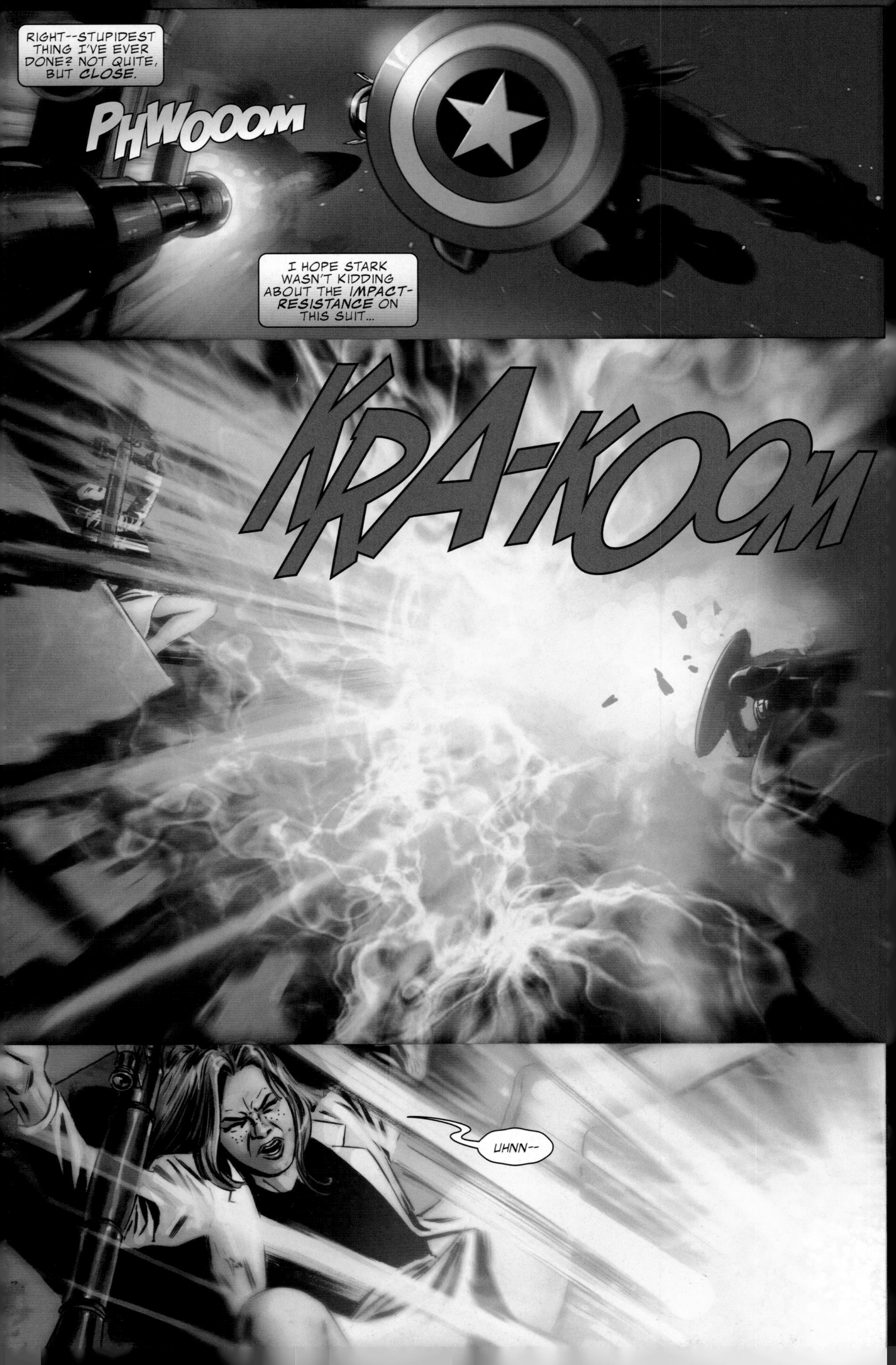
RIGHT--STUPIDEST THING I'VE EVER DONE? NOT QUITE, BUT CLOSE.
PHWOOOM
I HOPE STARK WASN'T KIDDING ABOUT THE IMPACT-RESISTANCE ON THIS SUIT...
KRA-KOOM
UHNN--

SKAASHH

OKAY... AT LEAST I SURVIVED...

...OW...

...EXACTLY ACCORDING TO MY HALF-ASSED PLAN...

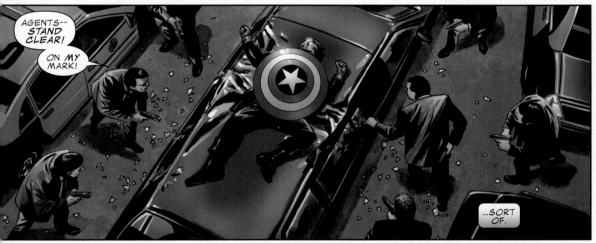

AGENTS-- STAND CLEAR!

ON MY MARK!

...SORT OF.

UH...JUST HOLD ON A...A SECOND...

YELLOW DOG 2, REPORT?

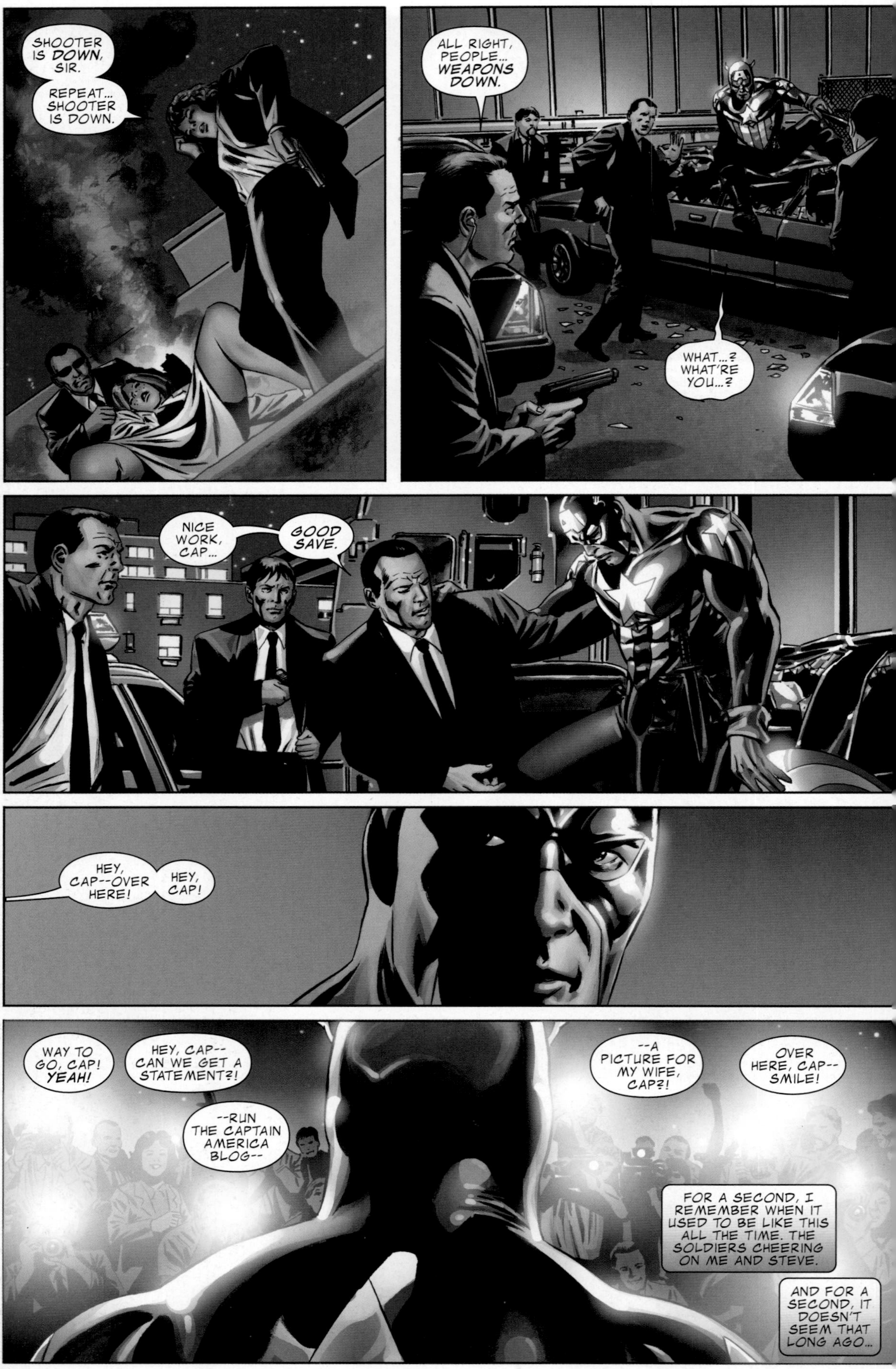
SHOOTER IS DOWN, SIR.
REPEAT... SHOOTER IS DOWN.
ALL RIGHT, PEOPLE... WEAPONS DOWN.
WHAT...? WHAT'RE YOU...?
NICE WORK, CAP...
GOOD SAVE.
HEY, CAP--OVER HERE!
HEY, CAP!
WAY TO GO, CAP! YEAH!
HEY, CAP--CAN WE GET A STATEMENT?!
--RUN THE CAPTAIN AMERICA BLOG--
--A PICTURE FOR MY WIFE, CAP?!
OVER HERE, CAP--SMILE!
FOR A SECOND, I REMEMBER WHEN IT USED TO BE LIKE THIS ALL THE TIME. THE SOLDIERS CHEERING ON ME AND STEVE.
AND FOR A SECOND, IT DOESN'T SEEM THAT LONG AGO...

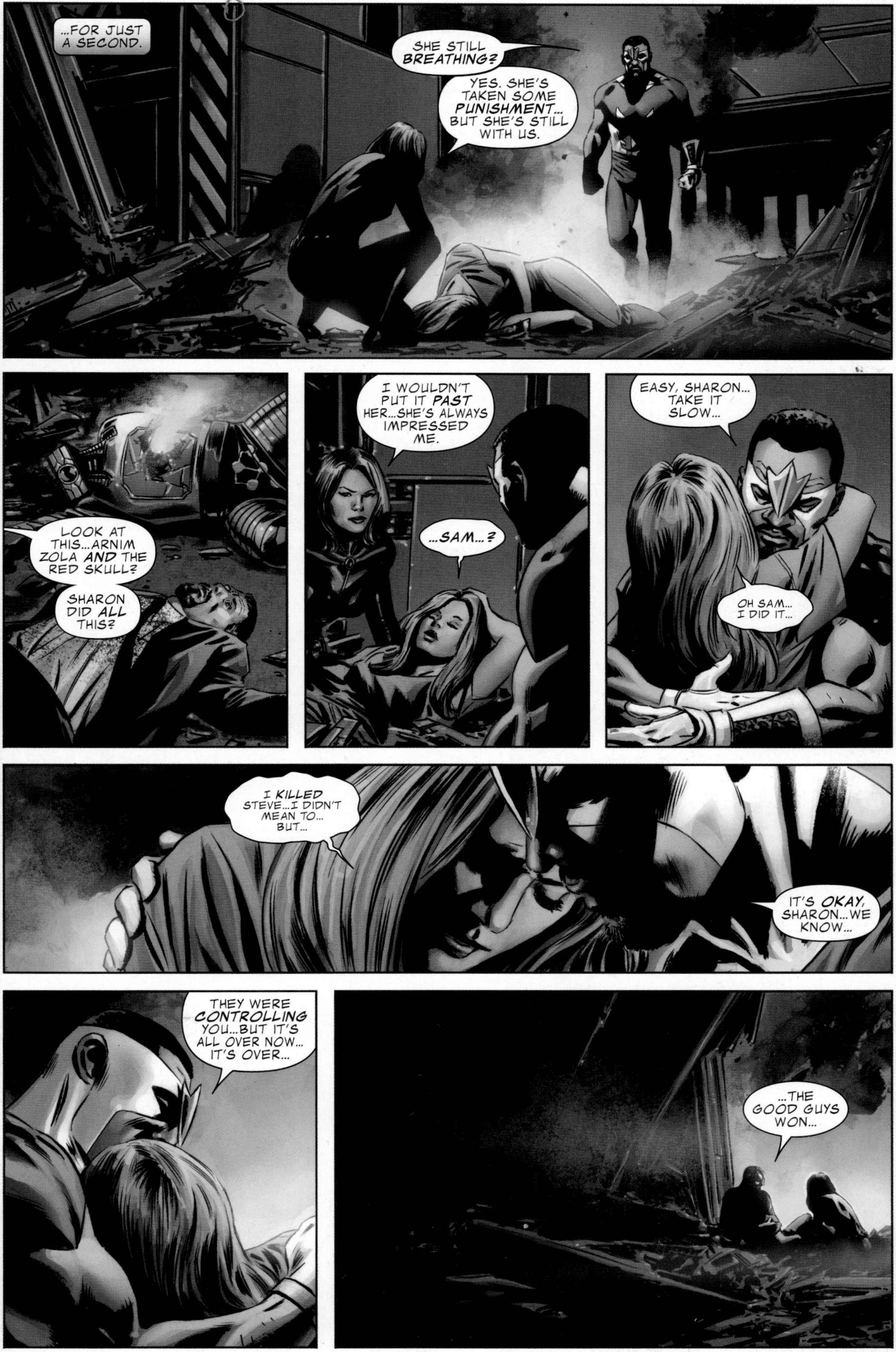
...FOR JUST A SECOND.
SHE STILL BREATHING?
YES. SHE'S TAKEN SOME PUNISHMENT... BUT SHE'S STILL WITH US.
LOOK AT THIS...ARNIM ZOLA AND THE RED SKULL?
SHARON DID ALL THIS?
I WOULDN'T PUT IT PAST HER...SHE'S ALWAYS IMPRESSED ME.
...SAM...?
EASY, SHARON... TAKE IT SLOW...
OH SAM... I DID IT...
I KILLED STEVE...I DIDN'T MEAN TO... BUT...
IT'S OKAY, SHARON...WE KNOW...
THEY WERE CONTROLLING YOU...BUT IT'S ALL OVER NOW... IT'S OVER...
...THE GOOD GUYS WON...

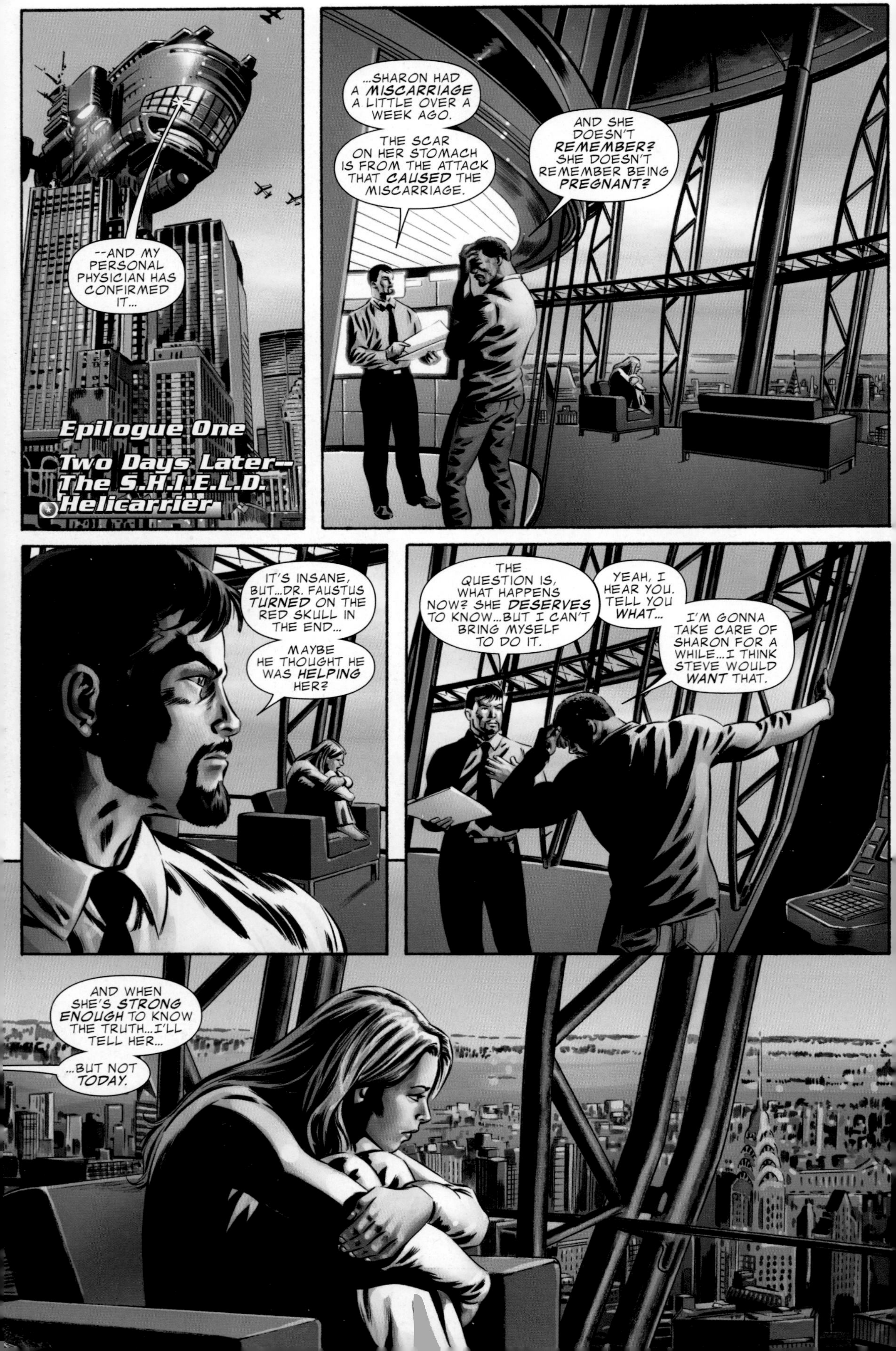
--AND MY PERSONAL PHYSICIAN HAS CONFIRMED IT...
Epilogue One
Two Days Later-- The S.H.I.E.L.D. Helicarrier
...SHARON HAD A MISCARRIAGE A LITTLE OVER A WEEK AGO.
THE SCAR ON HER STOMACH IS FROM THE ATTACK THAT CAUSED THE MISCARRIAGE.
AND SHE DOESN'T REMEMBER? SHE DOESN'T REMEMBER BEING PREGNANT?
IT'S INSANE, BUT...DR. FAUSTUS TURNED ON THE RED SKULL IN THE END...
MAYBE HE THOUGHT HE WAS HELPING HER?
THE QUESTION IS, WHAT HAPPENS NOW? SHE DESERVES TO KNOW...BUT I CAN'T BRING MYSELF TO DO IT.
YEAH, I HEAR YOU. TELL YOU WHAT...
I'M GONNA TAKE CARE OF SHARON FOR A WHILE...I THINK STEVE WOULD WANT THAT.
AND WHEN SHE'S STRONG ENOUGH TO KNOW THE TRUTH...I'LL TELL HER...
...BUT NOT TODAY.

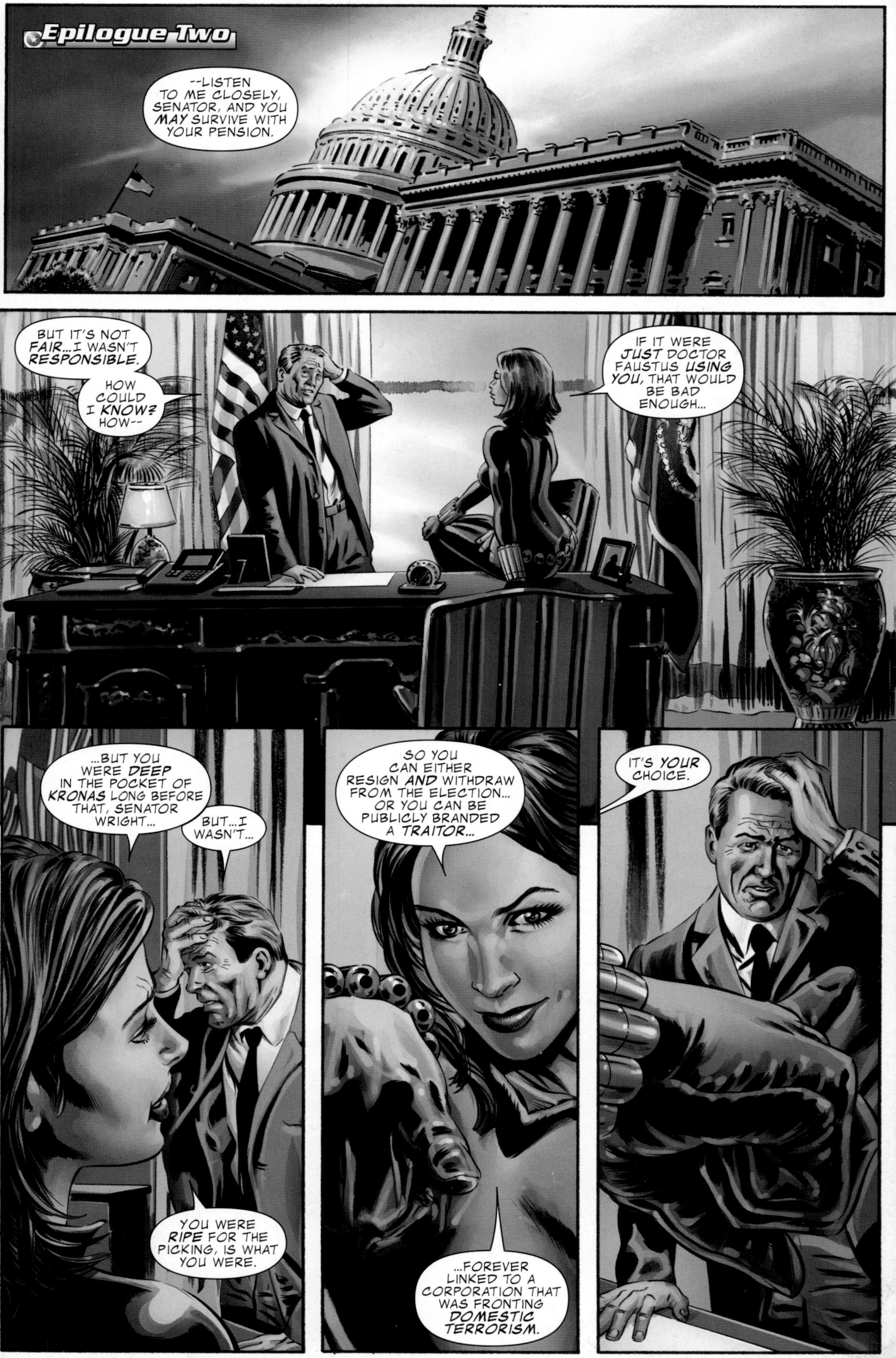
Epilogue Two
--LISTEN TO ME CLOSELY, SENATOR, AND YOU MAY SURVIVE WITH YOUR PENSION.
BUT IT'S NOT FAIR...I WASN'T RESPONSIBLE.
HOW COULD I KNOW? HOW--
IF IT WERE JUST DOCTOR FAUSTUS USING YOU, THAT WOULD BE BAD ENOUGH...
...BUT YOU WERE DEEP IN THE POCKET OF KRONAS LONG BEFORE THAT, SENATOR WRIGHT...
BUT...I WASN'T...
YOU WERE RIPE FOR THE PICKING, IS WHAT YOU WERE.
SO YOU CAN EITHER RESIGN AND WITHDRAW FROM THE ELECTION... OR YOU CAN BE PUBLICLY BRANDED A TRAITOR...
...FOREVER LINKED TO A CORPORATION THAT WAS FRONTING DOMESTIC TERRORISM.
IT'S YOUR CHOICE.

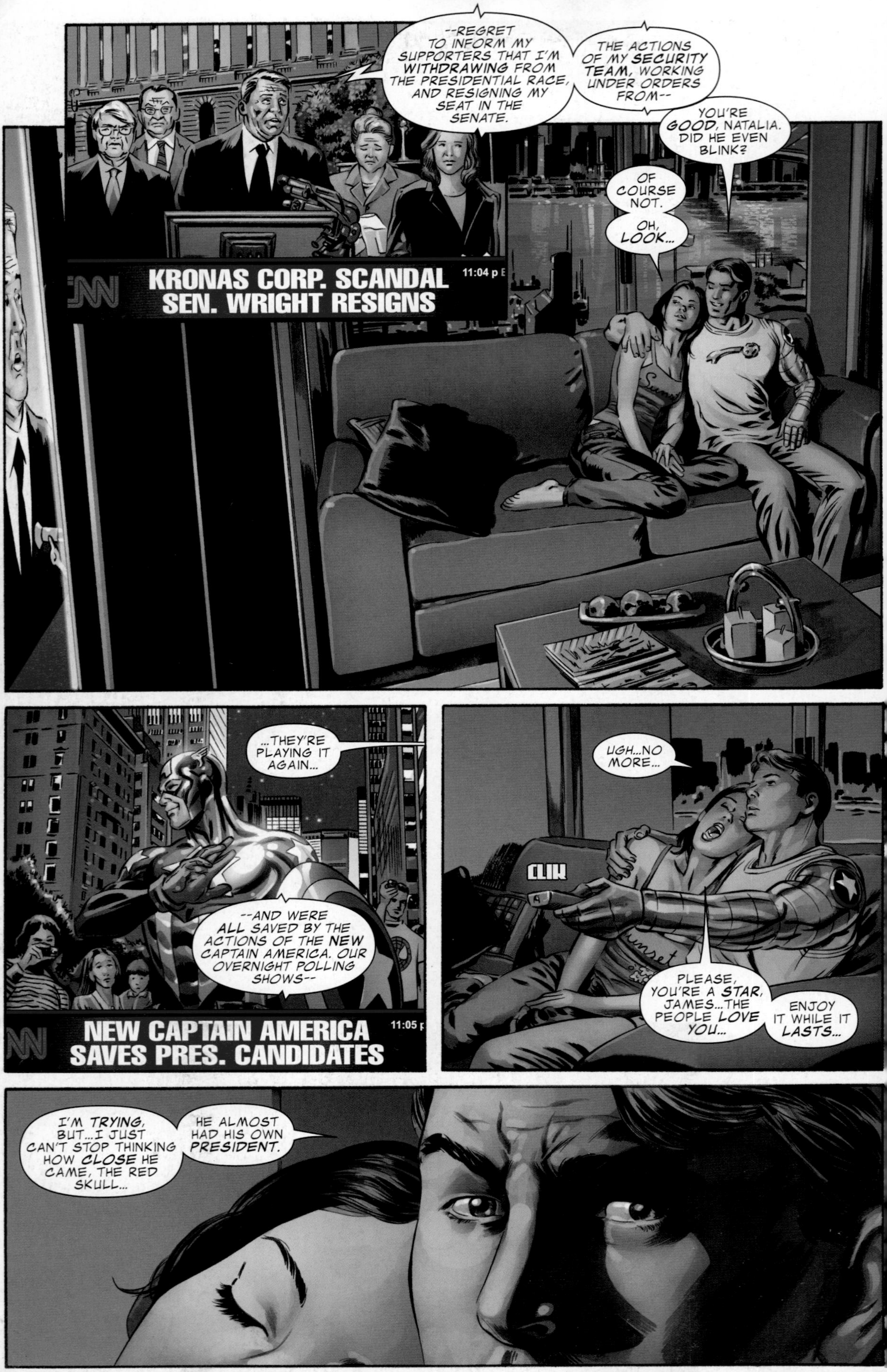
--REGRET TO INFORM MY SUPPORTERS THAT I'M WITHDRAWING FROM THE PRESIDENTIAL RACE, AND RESIGNING MY SEAT IN THE SENATE.
THE ACTIONS OF MY SECURITY TEAM, WORKING UNDER ORDERS FROM--
YOU'RE GOOD, NATALIA. DID HE EVEN BLINK?
OF COURSE NOT.
OH, LOOK...
KRONAS CORP. SCANDAL
SEN. WRIGHT RESIGNS
11:04 p
...THEY'RE PLAYING IT AGAIN...
--AND WERE ALL SAVED BY THE ACTIONS OF THE NEW CAPTAIN AMERICA. OUR OVERNIGHT POLLING SHOWS--
NEW CAPTAIN AMERICA
SAVES PRES. CANDIDATES
11:05 p
UGH...NO MORE...
CLIK
PLEASE, YOU'RE A STAR, JAMES...THE PEOPLE LOVE YOU...
ENJOY IT WHILE IT LASTS...
I'M TRYING, BUT...I JUST CAN'T STOP THINKING HOW CLOSE HE CAME, THE RED SKULL...
HE ALMOST HAD HIS OWN PRESIDENT.

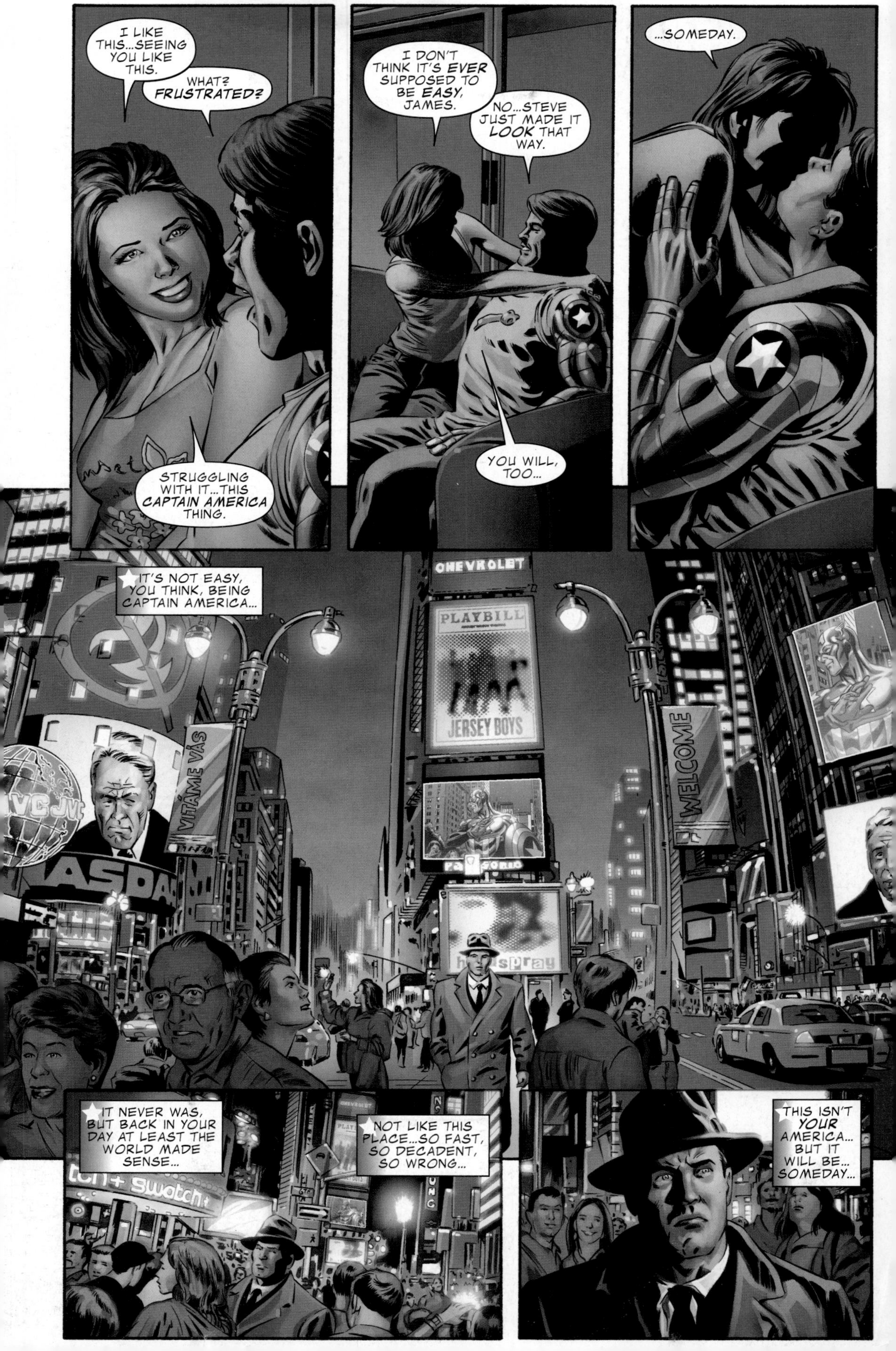
I LIKE THIS...SEEING YOU LIKE THIS.
WHAT? FRUSTRATED?
STRUGGLING WITH IT...THIS CAPTAIN AMERICA THING.
I DON'T THINK IT'S EVER SUPPOSED TO BE EASY, JAMES.
NO...STEVE JUST MADE IT LOOK THAT WAY.
YOU WILL, TOO...
...SOMEDAY.
IT'S NOT EASY, YOU THINK, BEING CAPTAIN AMERICA...
CHEVROLET
PLAYBILL
JERSEY BOYS
WELCOME
VITÁME VÁS
JVC JVC
IT NEVER WAS, BUT BACK IN YOUR DAY AT LEAST THE WORLD MADE SENSE...
NOT LIKE THIS PLACE...SO FAST, SO DECADENT, SO WRONG...
THIS ISN'T YOUR AMERICA... BUT IT WILL BE... SOMEDAY...

Epilogue Three

--SOMEDAY YOU WILL *SEE,* AND THEN YOU WILL FORGIVE ME, MASTER... I AM CERTAIN OF THAT.

THERE WAS SIMPLY NO OTHER CHOICE... NO TIME FOR OPTIONS.

BUT I PROMISE YOU IT IS ONLY TEMPORARY.

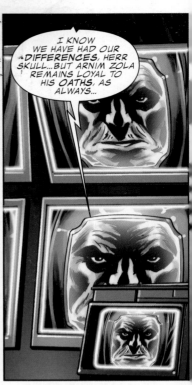

I KNOW WE HAVE HAD OUR *DIFFERENCES,* HERR SKULL...BUT ARNIM ZOLA REMAINS LOYAL TO HIS *OATHS,* AS ALWAYS...

...AND I SWEAR I WILL BE BACK FOR YOU SOON...AND I WILL FIX THIS.

NO...NO... NO...